D0947277

The Kaiser's
Pirates

Dedication
To Commander Richard Townsend
HMS *Invincible*
Born 25 July 1879
Killed in Action 31 May 1916

The Kaiser's Pirates

Hunting Germany's Raiding Cruisers 1914–1915

Nick Hewitt

Pen & Sword
MARITIME

In association with Imperial War Museums

First published in Great Britain in 2013 by
PEN & SWORD MARITIME
An imprint of
Pen & Sword Books Ltd
47 Church Street
Barnsley
South Yorkshire
S70 2AS

ISBN 978-1-84884-773-6

Typeset by Concept, Huddersfield, West Yorkshire, HD4 5JL.
Printed and bound in England by CPI Group (UK) Ltd, Croydon CR0 4YY.

Pen & Sword Books Ltd incorporates the imprints of Pen & Sword Aviation,
Pen & Sword Family History, Pen & Sword Maritime, Pen & Sword Military,
Pen & Sword Discovery, Wharncliffe Local History, Wharncliffe True Crime,
Wharncliffe Transport, Pen & Sword Select, Pen & Sword Military Classics,
Leo Cooper, The Praetorian Press, Remember When, Seaforth Publishing and
Frontline Publishing.

For a complete list of Pen & Sword titles please contact
PEN & SWORD BOOKS LIMITED
47 Church Street, Barnsley, South Yorkshire, S70 2AS, England
E-mail: enquiries@pen-and-sword.co.uk
Website: www.pen-and-sword.co.uk

Contents

List of Maps

List of Plates

Goeben and *Breslau* at anchor near Constantinople, 1914.

Vizeadmiral Maximilian Graf von Spee, commanding officer of Germany's *Kreuzergeschwader Ostasien*.

Korvettenkapitän Karl Friedrich Max von Müller, SMS *Emden*.

Fregattenkapitän Max Looff, SMS *Königsberg*.

Fregattenkapitän Erich Köhler, SMS *Karlsruhe*.

Fregattenkapitän Fritz Lüdecke, SMS *Dresden*.

Rear Admiral Sir Christopher 'Kit' Cradock.

Commander Richard Denny Townsend, HMS *Invincible*.

The dapper, determined Captain Sidney Drury-Lowe of HMS *Chatham*.

Dogged, resourceful and inspiring: Captain John Allen of HMS *Kent*.

Konteradmiral Wilhelm Souchon, with Colonel Holland, the British Chief of Staff of the Turkish Naval College in Istanbul, Kemal Pasha, the Turkish Navy Minister, and Turkish officers, 1910.

Vice Admiral Sir Frederick Doveton Sturdee and his staff take a relaxed stroll on East Falkland, 7 December 1914.

SMS *Karlsruhe* in 1914.

Raider at work. Photographed from *Kabinga*, her first 'rubbish dump', *Emden* approaches the collier *Killin*, 12 September 1914.

Shocked, half-naked *Zhemchug* survivors help a badly wounded comrade on the waterfront at Penang, 28 October 1914.

An Eastern Telegraph Company employee and members of von Mücke's landing party watch *Emden*'s last battle from the roof of the cable relay station, 9 November 1914.

Emden after the battle.

HMS *Glasgow*, veteran of Coronel, the Falklands, and the *Dresden* action. *Gloucester*, *Bristol*, *Chatham* and other Town Class light cruisers were similar ships.

Captain John Luce and his officers aboard HMS *Glasgow*.

Glasgow sights the *Kreuzergeschwader*, 1 November 1914.

Officers of HMS *Good Hope* at Port Stanley, October 1914.

Barely visible in the centre of the crowd, von Spee arrives in Valparaiso, 2 November 1914.

The massive armoured bulk of *Scharnhorst*, taking on coal and supplies at Valparaiso after Coronel. *Gneisenau* was an identical ship.

Scharnhorst, *Gneisenau*, and *Nürnberg* leave Valparaiso after Coronel, November 1914. The Chilean warships are the cruisers *Esmeralda*, *O'Higgins* and *Blanco Encalda* and the battleship *Capitan Prat*.

HMS *Invincible* in pursuit of the *Kreuzergeschwader*, photographed from *Carnarvon*, 8 December 1914.

Curious crowds gather on *Invincible*'s upper deck at the end of the battlecruiser action, 8 December 1914.

Inflexible sends out her cutters to rescue *Gneisenau*'s survivors, photographed by Arthur Duckworth, 8 December 1914.

The sinister hole next to HMS *Kent*'s starboard 6-inch casemate which nearly spelled disaster.

Royal Marine Sergeant Charles Mayes, who turned a hose on burning charges and probably saved his ship, on *Kent*'s battered upper deck after the battle. He was later awarded the Conspicuous Gallantry Medal.

HMS *Kent*'s crew get stuck in with their shovels. Note the filthy decks, littered with coal dust and sacks, and the men's tatty coaling rig.

Breaking up HMS *Kent*'s decks for fuel during the pursuit of *Dresden*, 8 March 1915.

White flags fluttering at her foremast, *Dresden* lies anchored in Cumberland Bay under the towering peak of El Yunque, Isla Más a Tierra.

Nearly a hundred years later: an unexploded British 6-inch shell embedded in the cliff face at Más a Tierra.

Dresden after the so-called 'Battle of Más a Tierra', almost deserted with smoke rising from her decks, photographed from the boat carrying across Lieutenant Commander Wilfred Thompson and Surgeon Robert Gilmour.

Oberleutnant zur See Wilhelm Canaris clambers from *Dresden*'s steam pinnace to negotiate in vain with the implacable Captain John Luce.

Tirpitz the Pig and an admirer.

HMS *Carmania*'s wrecked bridge after the action with *Cap Trafalgar*.

Preface

My first book, *Coastal Convoys 1939–1945: The Indestructible Highway*, came about as a result of that thrilling moment for any historian: the discovery of a subject which, if not entirely unexplored, had at least rarely been the subject of recent literary attention. In following Germany's raiding cruisers, and those who hunted them across the world's oceans during the first year of what used to be called the Great War, I chose a different and to an extent well-trodden path. It is, however, one which has fascinated me for years, ever since my parents slipped a copy of Dan van der Vat's *The Last Corsair* under the Christmas tree when I was a teenager. One can never really 'know' any historical figure, of course, and I have no intention of falling for such a conceit here, but nevertheless at least part of the attraction derives from the pirates' personalities, aspects of which are apparent from their exploits: von Müller's buccaneering spirit; Lüdecke's sense of duty; Souchon's impudence; Looff's patience. And there is tragedy, on all sides: von Spee and Cradock are haunting figures, men who went into battle perfectly aware that they would probably not survive it.

Of all those who appear in the book, I was particularly touched by Commander Richard Townsend of HMS *Invincible*, not just for his insights into the Battle of the Falklands, but also for the self-deprecating humour, compassion and love which shine from each letter he wrote to Phyllis, his wife of two years, and their baby daughter Barbara. On 31 May 1916 *Invincible* blew up and sank at the Battle of Jutland and, in common with almost everyone else on board, this devoted husband and father went down with his ship. He was 37 years old. My dedication is a small tribute to a life lost, and a family destroyed.

In writing the book, I have at all times tried to do justice to the extraordinary stories of these real people from a hundred years ago, as much as I have to the rigours of good scholarship. Above all else, I hope that I have got this balance right.

Nick Hewitt
December 2012

Acknowledgements

It is no exaggeration to say that I have been standing on the shoulders of giants throughout this process. There are too many books to acknowledge here, including one, by John Walter, with the same title, for which I hope I can be excused, as he was not the first to use the sobriquet, and this is a very different book. They all appear in the bibliography, and I am grateful to every one for the illumination and inspiration they have given me.

Special thanks are due to Roger Welby-Everard and his colleagues at *The Naval Review*, for so kindly and quickly giving permission to quote extensively from that journal's excellent online archive, a remarkable and readily accessible treasure trove of contemporary accounts. I am also profoundly grateful to the copyright holders who have given permission to quote from unpublished material held at the Imperial War Museum. Every effort has been made to contact copyright holders, but if any permissions have been inadvertently overlooked, I will be pleased to make the necessary and reasonable arrangements at the first opportunity. Any mistakes are of course entirely my own.

As ever, there are many individuals to thank, notably my former IWM colleagues. It has been a privilege to write an IWM 'in association' book and I am very grateful to Liz Bowers and Peter Taylor for giving me the opportunity. Further thanks are due to Tony Richards, Richard McDonagh, and their colleagues, for helping me to mine the extraordinary riches of the Document and Sound Archive collections, and the incomparable Rod Suddaby, former Keeper of Documents at the IWM and a fine naval historian, for all his advice and for patiently proof reading the final manuscript in such minute detail. I was devastated to learn that Rod passed away as this book was going to print. His wisdom, expertise and generosity with his knowledge will be sorely missed by all who work in this field.

Thanks are also due to Ian Proctor, for his help finding at least some photographs of the 'Pirates' which have not appeared in several hundred books over the years; 'Team Digital' for their efficient production of the same; and lastly Terry Charman, James Taylor and everyone in the Research and Information Office, for their guidance, support, and for tolerating my spending my final month researching this book.

Once again I am indebted to Karen Balme for another fabulous set of maps, and notably for rising to the challenge of reproducing the Rufiji Delta! And finally, thanks to Andrew Lambert, Laughton Professor of Naval History at the Department of War Studies, King's College London, for his advice and encouragement, and for inspiring me to take up naval history in the first place nearly twenty years ago, and to Rupert Harding and all at Pen & Sword Books Ltd for their continued faith.

Closer to home, I want to thank Ngaire, who did me the very great honour of becoming my wife on 5 May 2012, and then spent her first year of married life living with a houseful of disreputable German cruiser captains. I cannot adequately express how grateful I am for her patient proof reading, welcome suggestions and for picking up far, far more than her share of home-building. This book would quite literally never have happened without her, and I promise I'll cook dinner again now it's done. And I cannot close without thanking my children, Cerys and Dan, for hiding their disappointment at their father producing a book about 'pirates' which entirely lacks buried treasure, eye patches and Jolly Rogers. I hope that if they read it, they may find consolation in the occasional sailing ship, a shower of gold sovereigns, several desert islands, notably South Keeling (a pirates' lair if ever I saw one), and the swashbuckling, one-handed, red-bearded Albert Pagels who swaggers through Chapter 8. There are even two parrots, not to mention a pig and twenty sheep. It was a very old-fashioned war in so many ways.

Notes on Sources

Times
Although the 24-hour clock was not in general use during the First World War, this book conforms to subsequent naval custom and avoids any confusion between a.m. and p.m. by using it throughout, except where eyewitness testimony is quoted verbatim.

Technical Data
In accordance with respective national customs, German and other European gun calibres and technical data have been expressed in metric measurements and British in imperial measurements. Speeds are in knots (nautical miles per hour) throughout. For interested readers, technical data for the principal ships can be found in the appendices.

Use of German
German units, shipping lines and ranks have been rendered in the original German. A comparative table of German, British and US naval ranks can be found in the appendices.

Spelling and Grammar
Because many of the personal accounts quoted in this book were not written or recorded for publication, words and punctuation necessary to make them comprehensible and easy to read have sometimes been omitted by their authors. Alternatively, the spelling or grammar can be faulty. I have therefore occasionally taken the liberty of making small changes to assist with the narrative flow. When I have added words to help the sense I have placed them in [square] brackets and when words have been omitted I have marked the omission by inserting ellipses (...) Such intrusions have been kept to an absolute minimum.

Penang, Straits Settlement, 28 October 1914

Penang was a vital staging post on the trade routes connecting Europe, China and Japan, a melting pot of different cultures that had been a British colony since 1867. An island on the west coast of the Malayan Peninsula, its eastern side ended in a cape at the northern extremity, pointing like an arrow at the mainland. The colonial capital, Georgetown, huddled at the end of this cape, separated from the mainland by two miles of water known as the Penang Roads. In 1914 Georgetown had just one deep water wharf, and most visiting freighters anchored out in the Roads, discharging their cargo by lighter.

In October 1914 the British Empire was committed to a desperate struggle on the other side of the world, but for sleepy Georgetown the war seemed far away; so far, in fact, that no British warships were present on the morning of 28 October, the day war came to Penang. The settlement and the merchant ships at anchor in the harbour were instead guarded by a scattering of elderly French torpedo boat destroyers (TBDs) and the Russian light cruiser *Zhemchug*. Defensive precautions were almost non-existent, with the harbour lights on and many of the ships brightly lit.

At around 02:00 a weather-beaten warship approached the harbour from the north-west. Barely visible in the moonlight, White Ensign flying as she steamed confidently down the Straits of Malacca at a steady 11 knots, she was apparently a four-funnelled Royal Navy cruiser, although the mystery captain's decision to steam his ship in circles outside the harbour until the bright tropical moon had set might perhaps have aroused suspicion had anyone been awake to see it. But no one saw her arrive. Finally, in the grey dawn the warship turned again and entered the Roads. To starboard, the lights of Georgetown sparkled, with the bulk of the old citadel, Fort Cornwallis, looming at the end of the cape. Fishing boats slid past without incident, as did an anchored cargo ship, waiting for dawn before entering the harbour. Just before 04:00 the Georgetown pilot boat appeared unexpectedly alongside, but nobody on board it noticed anything suspicious. At 04:50 the mystery warship glided into the narrow bottleneck of Penang Harbour, but she was not British; rather than preparing for a relaxed entry into a friendly harbour, her crew were rushing to action stations, at the same time hauling down the White Ensign. In its place they hoisted the iron cross and eagle of Imperial Germany.

The mystery ship, her disguise enhanced by an extra, false, funnel as well as by the British flag, was the German cruiser *Emden*. Her captain was the redoubtable 39-year-old *Korvettenkapitän* Karl Friedrich Max von Müller, the man destined to become the most notorious of the 'Kaiser's Pirates', the cruiser skippers who marauded across the world's oceans during the First World War's opening months. The son of an army officer, von Müller had made an unfashionable choice to join the fledgeling *Kaiserliche Marine* (Imperial Navy) in 1891; *Emden* was his first command. No self-publicist, von Müller was a reserved but popular commanding officer, for whom the monotony of peacetime naval routine had offered little opportunity to shine; only the outbreak of war had allowed him to really demonstrate his qualities. By October 1914 little *Emden*, nicknamed *'der Schwan von Osten'* (the Swan of the East) in the balmy days of peace thanks to her snow-white tropical paint, had sunk or captured twenty-seven (mostly British) merchant ships and bombarded the Indian port of Madras. This attack on the 'jewel in the crown' of the British Empire prompted a furious Winston Churchill, Britain's First Lord of the Admiralty, to set ten British and allied warships searching for her.

One of *Emden*'s junior officers was a distant relative of the Kaiser, 23-year-old *Leutnant zur See* Franz Joseph, Prince of Hohenzollern. Stationed in the torpedo flat deep inside the ship as *Emden* swept into the peaceful harbour, Franz Joseph and his men could see nothing; with the tubes loaded and the electrical release gear already connected, all they could do was wait. At 05:05 the order came down the voice-pipe from the bridge to 'clear away the starboard tube'; in other words, to prepare for firing. Three minutes later Franz Joseph was told to fire: 'The fish was out and away. We waited in suspense, holding our breath. There was a dull bang.'[1] As the torpedo exploded, *Emden*'s 105mm guns opened fire at point-blank range. Deep in his steel burrow, Franz Joseph had no way of knowing that his target was the Russian cruiser *Zhemchug*.

William Meager, an eyewitness aboard the British merchant ship *Nigaristan*, was asleep when the torpedo exploded against *Zhemchug*'s side with what he later recalled as a 'dull, metallic rattle'. Startled awake, Meager raced on deck in time to see the flashes and hear the retort of *Emden*'s guns. To his horror, the cruiser was steaming slowly between his own ship and the hapless *Zhemchug*, firing steadily. Later that day Meager wrote down his impressions of the action in an extraordinarily vivid account: 'Dawn was just breaking and the dim and uncertain light helped the impression one received that two ghastly visitants from some other world were present. For the next fifteen minutes we saw an actual Hell upon Earth, in which were embodied the extremes of many emotions – desperate bravery, exultation, hate, despair and terror.'[2]

It was chaos aboard *Zhemchug*. Although the Russian cruiser was of a similar age and size to *Emden*, the odds were stacked against her. The commanding officer, Baron Cherkassov, was ashore, visiting a 'lady friend'.[3] No extra look-outs had been posted, *Zhemchug*'s torpedoes and much of her ready-use ammunition had been stowed away, and the fires were out in all but one of her boilers, leaving the ship immobile. Some Russian gunners managed to bring their weapons into action, but their firing was wild; several over-shoots came dangerously close to smashing into *Nigaristan*'s thin plating, much to William Meager's consternation: 'Several of her shells shrieked over us, just above our after well-deck, and two hit a ship (the *Cranleigh*) just at the other side of us, seriously wounding their Second Engineer. Each flash of the *Zhemchug*'s guns gave us an expectant thrill for a second, until we knew they hadn't hit us.'[4]

The French gunboat *D'Iberville* was also firing at *Emden* from her mooring among the merchant ships anchored further inside the harbour, but it was too late; by now, the battered *Zhemchug* was sinking slowly by the stern. Amidships a great hole had been ripped in her hull, behind which fires burned fiercely, and the rest of her side was riddled with shot holes. All the while *Emden* poured shell after shell into the wreckage.

Von Müller could see that *Zhemchug* was mortally wounded but not yet finished. He also knew that a sand bar blocked the far end of Penang Harbour, leaving him no choice but to take *Emden* out of the narrow anchorage by the same route he had entered. Ordering the helmsman to turn the wheel hard to port, he turned and passed *Zhemchug* once again, ordering Franz Joseph to fire the port tube: 'The torpedo hissed out,' the young officer recalled. 'At once there was a fearful crash, which also gave the *Emden* a considerable shock.'[5] Franz Joseph's second torpedo impacted directly in *Zhemchug*'s forward magazine. A column of light shot skywards, accompanied by a strangely muffled explosion. Immediately afterwards a dense cloud of filthy yellow smoke obscured the scene as the Russian cruiser slipped under the water. For an instant there was silence, followed by wild cheering aboard *Emden*.

Emden's *Oberleutnant zur See* Ernst von Levetzow watched as *Zhemchug* was 'literally torn into two parts', enormous pieces of wreckage flying through the air before crashing into the harbour. As the smoke cleared, nothing could be seen of the Russian cruiser except for the tops of her masts, rising pitifully from the water, surrounded by floating wreckage and desperately thrashing survivors. The entire action had taken just fifteen minutes. Nearly a hundred

Russian sailors died, almost a third of *Zhemchug*'s crew. The remainder were rescued in dreadful condition, according to one eyewitness, a French officer, who was interviewed immediately afterwards by a local *New York Times* correspondent. The shaken officer related how most of the survivors were naked and bleeding from multiple wounds, while others had lost limbs: 'it was like living a frightful nightmare,' he recalled; 'everywhere you turned there was a groaning, greasy mass of humanity.'[6] Another eyewitness remembered the 'wonderful courage' of the suffering Russians: 'although they must have been in fearful agony [they] never whimpered.'[7] For his negligence, the absent Cherkassov was later court-martialled and imprisoned.

As the survivors struggled in the water, von Müller prepared to turn again and sink the French gunboat *D'Iberville*. But as he began the manoeuvre, look-outs sighted a small vessel approaching from the north at speed, belching clouds of black smoke. Fearing a torpedo attack, von Müller turned *Emden* to face the new opponent, opening fire at around 6,000 metres range. The target turned away, revealing itself to be another unarmed pilot cutter, and *Emden* ceased fire immediately, but with the sun coming up, von Müller decided to make for the safety of open water.

As *Emden* ploughed steadily out into the sheltering vastness of the Indian Ocean, von Müller stood his crew down from action stations. In the galley the cruiser's cooks were preparing a belated but welcome breakfast when look-outs sighted another ship approaching from the north. While von Müller turned *Emden* to bring all her guns to bear on the stranger, his weary sailors rushed to action stations once again, relaxing only after they discovered that the approaching ship was the British freighter *Glenturret*, flying the yellow flag that indicated she was full of explosives. The lumbering merchant-man stopped, wallowing in the water, while a boarding party rowed slowly across, commanded by 37-year-old *Oberleutnant zur See* Julius Lauterbach. Lauterbach's 18-stone bulk and jolly persona belied his worth; a reservist, he was an experienced merchant mariner who had been at sea since he was 17. Before joining *Emden* he had been Master of the Hamburg–Amerika Line steamer *Staatsekretär Kraetke*.[8]

Von Müller ordered Lauterbach to destroy *Glenturret*, as a ship carrying explosives was a legitimate military target, but he also instructed Lauterbach to ensure that the crew abandoned ship safely, and asked them to pass a message to the authorities in Penang apologising for firing on the unarmed pilot cutter. Without over-sentimentalising a ruthless and effective officer, von Müller's chivalrous humanitarianism stood out like a beacon at a time when the war in Europe was rapidly becoming characterised by unprecedented levels of hate propaganda.

Lauterbach had set his charges when he was urgently ordered back to *Emden;* a warship had been sighted, closing rapidly on the cruiser's starboard beam. *Emden* cleared for action for a third time, and steamed at high speed towards the approaching enemy ship, the 298-ton French TBD *Mousquet,* launched in 1903 and commanded by 43-year-old *Lieutenant de Vaisseau* Felix Théroinne. Poorly armed and completely unarmoured, she was no match for *Emden* unless she could close to torpedo range, but Théroinne was not planning to avoid action; aware that just one lucky shot might leave the lone German raider crippled many miles from home, he desperately tried to bring his tiny warship closer.

Von Müller opened fire at about 4,500 metres range. *Emden*'s first salvo fell beyond *Mousquet,* her second slightly short – a perfect straddle. With dreadful inevitability, the third crashed down on target, smashing the TBD's boiler room and reducing her upper decks to scrap. Théroinne's legs were shot off, but the gallant French officer ordered his men to tie him to the bridge rails so that he could continue the fight.[9] With her speed drastically reduced, *Mousquet* was a sitting target, but as salvo after salvo from *Emden* smashed into her flimsy plating, Théroinne's men managed to get at least one torpedo away, as well as enthusiastically but ineffectively peppering the German cruiser with shots from her 9-pounder quick-firers.

Emden's second one-sided action of the morning took just seven minutes, at the end of which *Mousquet* sank in a cloud of filthy yellow smoke. She plunged bow first below the calm water like a primitive submarine, although her stern remained above the surface for a while like a macabre memorial to her forty-two dead. Despite the danger to his own ship, von Müller stopped near the wreck and ordered away his boats to pick up survivors. Théroinne had gone down with his ship, still lashed to the bridge rails, but the Germans managed to pick up *Mousquet*'s executive officer, *Ensigne de Vaisseau* Carrissan, and thirty-six men, many of them wounded. 'I can always picture one of the men,' Franz Joseph recalled years later. 'He had been hit so badly in the stomach that his entrails were hanging out ... two of the wounded men had had their legs shattered and, as the wounds had already begun to fester, required immediate amputation.'[10]

As *Emden*'s crew made the survivors as comfortable as possible, given the heat, humidity and cramped conditions, look-outs spied another French TBD, *Fronde,* emerging from the harbour. Von Müller, deciding that *Emden* had lingered in this potentially dangerous area for long enough, made off to the north-west. *Fronde* set off in pursuit, broadcasting *Emden*'s depredations to the world on her wireless, 'mouthing incessantly like an old slut', as *Emden*'s dashing, 33-year-old executive officer, the outspoken and cheerfully anglophobic *Kapitänleutnant* Hellmuth von Mücke, colourfully recalled later. But she was unable to overhaul the German cruiser and after less than an hour von Müller lost his pursuer in a rain squall. The most daring and effective of the 'Kaiser's Pirates' had carried out the most audacious operation of his short but lively career, leaving the shocked inhabitants of Penang to pick up the pieces.

Chapter 1

Kreuzerkrieg

'Our future is on the water'

Kaiser Wilhelm II, Stettin, 1891

When is a navy 'born'? Sometimes this can be hard to determine. Did the spiritual birth of Great Britain's Royal Navy take place in the time of Alfred the Great, or with the defeat of the Spanish Armada in 1588? Were the US Navy's first ancestors the Revolutionary War privateers, or their British predecessors? In other cases it can be easier to apply the specific markers beloved of historians, and Germany's navy is arguably one such. This book is not a history of the Imperial German Navy, nor of the arms race between Great Britain and Germany and its contribution to the outbreak of the First World War. However, some background is essential to understand the circumstances which created the tiny, scattered band of pirates in 1914.[1]

Prussia entered the Franco–Prussian War in 1870 with just four modern warships, built as a concession to Kaiser Friedrich Wilhelm IV's 'navalist' cousin, Prince Adalbert, and they spent the conflict languishing impotently in port, blockaded by the superior French Navy. Although Prussia won the war comprehensively, seizing the disputed provinces of Alsace and Lorraine and destroying Napoleon III's Second Empire in the process, for the navy the experience was humiliating, and did nothing to endear the fledgeling service to the militarist ruling classes of the new, united Germany. Prince Adalbert retired in 1872 and his small fleet was placed under the command of a succession of generals and condemned to a coast defence role.

Seventeen years later German navalism revived with the accession to the throne in June 1888 of the 29-year-old Kaiser Wilhelm II. Wilhelm was distinguished by a peculiarly contradictory ability simultaneously to admire and despise his relatives on the other side of the North Sea, his grandmother Victoria, Queen of Great Britain and Ireland and Empress of India, and her son, the Prince of Wales and future King Edward VII. At times Wilhelm's insecurities about these more powerful and influential members of his extended family bordered on the paranoid; today we would certainly call him 'chippy'. But he also made no secret of his desire to imitate the most notable outward features of British dynastic power: the greatest global trading empire and, in particular, the largest and most sophisticated fleet the world had ever seen.

Arriving late to the largely western European party which was nineteenth-century imperialism, Wilhelm nonetheless dived enthusiastically into what became known as the 'Scramble for Africa'. In swift succession Germany acquired extensive territories across the continent, as well as a scattering of Pacific islands, a generous helping of New Guinea, and the important trading outpost of Tsingtao (modern Qingdao) on the east coast of China. In 1901 Wilhelm famously announced to the North German Regatta Association that 'We have conquered for ourselves a place in the sun. It will now be my task to see to it that this place in the sun shall remain our undisputed possession, in order that the sun's rays may fall fruitfully upon our activity and trade in foreign parts.'[2]

Germany had annexed approximately a million square miles of territory and some 13 million people by the start of the First World War. This belated but exuberant land-grabbing was accompanied by an ambitious policy of naval expansion. In the same speech Wilhelm went on to reiterate the point he had first made at Stettin ten years earlier: 'Our future lies upon the water. The more Germans go out upon the waters, whether it be in races or regattas, whether it be in journeys across the ocean, or in the service of the battle flag, so much the better it will be for us.'[3]

But Wilhelm had missed the point. The British acquired their 'informal empire' almost by accident, first building up influence and cultivating relationships with local rulers, then facilitating an influx of entrepreneurs of sometimes dubious moral repute, but possessed of an extraordinary ability to extract resources of every kind from the furthest-flung corners of the world. The fleet and its attendant bases spread across the globe almost organically, to protect the interests of these entrepreneurs and the revenue they generated. Britain needed a fleet because she had an empire, on which she depended to maintain her status as the world's only superpower.

Wilhelm, conversely, wanted a fleet above all else, and it seemed sometimes that his colonies were only an excuse to build ships; the naval tail was perhaps wagging the colonial dog. In June 1904 he confessed at a dinner in Kiel that as a small boy, visiting 'the family' at Osborne House on the Isle of Wight and seeing the mighty Royal Navy spread across the Solent, 'there awoke in me the wish to build ships of my own like these someday, and when I was grown up to possess as fine a navy as the English'.[4]

Wilhelm's ambitions did not lack support in Germany's corridors of power. The ageing creator of modern Germany, Prince Otto von Bismarck, was a late convert to colonialism, and one of his most prominent successors, the vain, ambitious Bernhard von Bülow, could legitimately be described as an enthusiast. But there was no more passionate advocate for naval expansion than Alfred von Tirpitz. In 1890 this relatively young and junior naval officer had at a formal dinner so impressed the new monarch with his ambitions for a German fleet that nine months later Wilhelm tasked him with developing the strategy.[5] Tirpitz presented his ideas to the Kaiser on 1 December 1892. An informed naval thinker, he believed that true world power – *Weltmacht* – could only derive from a strong battle fleet capable of challenging the British for strategic control of the oceans. A battle fleet meant battleships: the large, heavily armed and armoured warships that were the currency by which a nation's naval power was measured.

The Kaiser was suitably impressed, but Tirpitz's growing influence brought him into open conflict with powerful figures at court and in the government, notably the State Secretary for the Navy, Admiral Friedrich von Hollmann, a man whose decisions Tirpitz later described in his memoirs as 'absolutely devoid of principle'.[6] This was perhaps unfair; von Hollmann was more concerned with the day-to-day, practical challenges of securing sufficient funds to build a navy – any navy – in the face of conflicting demands from the Army and other influential government departments, and was happy to settle for smaller, cheaper, coastal defence craft and commerce-raiding cruisers. It was the classic conflict between a single-minded visionary, lacking real authority or responsibility and thus able to think 'outside the box', and a politician consumed by the 'art of the possible', fighting for the very existence of his small, unfashionable department.

In the middle sat the Kaiser, driven by his desire to replicate the most visible elements of British power and anxious to claim his place at the 'top table' of global influence as soon as possible. Wilhelm wanted everything: Tirpitz's battleships in the North Sea to challenge Great Britain's Royal Navy, accompanied by Hollman's hordes of smaller, more versatile cruisers. However, the Kaiser was instinctively inclined to the cruiser option, which seemed to offer the 'quickest win'. Wilhelm saw cruisers, based in his new colonies, as an immediate way to make the new world power's presence felt. His ambitions were rooted in a misunderstanding of the application of sea power, which would contribute to the ultimate downfall of his pirates in 1914–15. British cruisers could indeed range across the globe enforcing British policy, but only because behind them loomed the world's most powerful battle fleet. The arrival of a British cruiser shaped the fate of nations not because of its own, often lamentable, firepower, but because of what it represented. Wilhelm failed to understand that it was not possible to pick and choose from the elements of a balanced fleet required to secure global sea control.

At first, the naval question was avoided by a series of unhappy compromises, essentially forced upon the protagonists by the trickle of funds made available by the Reichstag and the vacillation of the Kaiser himself, a man who, despite his obsession with sea power, never really understood it. In the course of one of the endless series of conferences, meetings and earnest debates which characterised German naval policy at this time, Tirpitz cornered the Kaiser, again pushing the case for a battle fleet. It is only too easy to picture the inexperienced monarch, trapped by his older, intensely intellectual subordinate, his magnificent domed head gleaming and legendary forked beard bristling as he forcefully made his case yet again. Desperately trying to maintain an argument with Tirpitz but exposing once again his essential ignorance, Wilhelm piped 'Why was Nelson then always calling for frigates?' 'Because', responded the sailor, 'he had a battle fleet.'[7]

Tirpitz's persistence was rewarded when he was asked to submit, at the Kaiser's request, a detailed recommendation for German naval construction. His submission called for sixteen modern battleships. Unfortunately, it coincided with an event on the other side of the world which, from a German perspective, illustrated all too clearly the high-handed arrogance of the British. In 1895 Cecil Rhodes, the Prime Minister of Cape Colony, sponsored the so-called 'Jameson Raid' into the Transvaal, in an attempt to provoke war and the eventual absorption of the independent, gold-rich Boer Republic into the British Empire. The raid, on 29 December, outraged many Germans, including the Kaiser, who sentimentally perceived the Boers as vulnerable kin of the German people, though the redoubtable Afrikaners proved perfectly capable of handling Rhodes' shambolic experiment in freelance warfare on their own. As far as naval policy was concerned, the raid caused Wilhelm to dither again. Cruisers in his African colonies, he naively believed, would have allowed him to help the Boers, and he ordered 'the purchase of armoured cruisers and cruisers wherever we can find them as soon as possible'.[8]

The Kaiser's thinking was deeply flawed. Had Germany sent cruisers to South Africa, the British could simply have sent their vastly superior battle fleet into the Baltic and blockaded Germany into submission. The only way to achieve sea power was to build a battle fleet of equal or larger size. Nevertheless, Wilhelm succeeded in amending naval policy, and Hollmann was charged with delivering a badly compromised shipbuilding programme which pleased no one: one battleship to appease Tirpitz, three cruisers for the Kaiser, and a promise to the generals not to ask for any more money at the expense of the army. Tirpitz was promoted to *Konteradmiral* and in 1896 he was posted out of harm's way to take command of the *Kreuzergeschwader Ostasien*, or East Asiatic Cruiser Squadron. He remained in Asia until the autumn of 1897, and perhaps his most notable achievement was one with long-term implications for the Kaiser's pirates in 1914. Frustrated at his squadron's dependence on British facilities in Hong Kong, he was determined to establish an independent German base. After reconnoitring a series of potential locations, Tirpitz identified Kiaochow Bay (now Jiaozhou Bay) and its principal town, Tsingtao, as the most suitable location.

Tirpitz returned to Berlin in March 1897, but his successor, *Konteradmiral* Otto von Diederichs, concurred with his assessment and set about creating the circumstances to make Tirpitz's ambition a reality. What followed was a textbook example of European penetration. On 1 November 1897 two German missionaries were murdered in the Kiaochow area. The following week German marines stormed ashore, and Tsingtao fell in a few hours. In early 1898 the German Empire legalised this blatant piracy by 'leasing' the territory from the Chinese government for ninety-nine years, mirroring Great Britain's leasing of Hong Kong's 'New Territories' in the same year. Over the next sixteen years Tsingtao was transformed into a model German colony. As well as a modern base for the *Kreuzergeschwader*, by 1914 it boasted paved streets, banks, schools, government buildings, electric power, modern drainage and safe drinking water, as well as the famous brewery.

Of course, when Tirpitz steamed his cruisers out of the bay, all of this lay in the future. Back in Berlin, Hollmann's best efforts to please all of the people, all of the time, had failed. The politicians in the Reichstag, recognising weakness when they saw it, slashed his meagre budget in March 1896. Hollmann resigned and the Kaiser summoned Tirpitz back to Berlin, appointing him Secretary of State of the Imperial Naval Office. It took Tirpitz just nine days to present the Kaiser with his vision for the Imperial Navy, suggesting that he had spent much of his extended journey home preparing it. His concise memorandum pulled no punches. If the Kaiser wished to confront the British in South Africa and elsewhere, enlarge his empire, and win for Germany the international respect to which both men felt she was entitled, he wrote, only a strategic battle fleet capable of taking on the British in home waters would do the job. Tirpitz was a disciple of the American naval theorist Alfred Thayer Mahan. Like Mahan, he believed that 'the vital centre of English commerce is in the waters surrounding the British Isles'.[9] Overseas cruiser warfare was now yesterday's news: 'When [Britain's] wealth is scattered in thousands of coming and going ships, when the roots of the system spread far and wide, it can stand many a cruel shock ... Only by military command of the sea ... can such an attack be fatal; and such control can be wrung from a powerful navy only by fighting and overcoming it.'[10]

He might have won the argument, but tortuous negotiations still awaited Tirpitz, with an endless succession of suspicious princes and politicians. Tirpitz responded by rousing the people. He created a Press Bureau staffed with enthusiastic young naval officers, who wrote tirelessly to the newspapers and toured the country, speaking on behalf of naval enlargement. He promoted the formation of a *Flottenverein*, or Navy League, which had over a million members by 1914. He relentlessly cultivated industrialists and others likely to benefit from naval expansion. On 26 March 1898 his efforts came to fruition with the passing of his first Navy Bill through the Reichstag.[11] The Imperial Navy was to receive seven new battleships, a figure which doubled a year later when Tirpitz exploited public outrage about Britain's prosecution of the second Boer War in South Africa to push through a second Navy Bill.

Between 1898 and 1914 German naval building was all about battleships, as the country plunged into a ruinous arms race with Great Britain. Tirpitz may have been correct in theory, but in practice Germany simply could not afford to outbuild the British at sea whilst simultaneously maintaining the largest army in Europe. Between 1905 and 1914 the Reich's defence budget increased by a staggering 142 per cent. And the British still had more battleships; hindsight tells us that Tirpitz merely succeeded in provoking them. He and the Kaiser failed to understand that the empire, and by extension the Royal Navy, represented Britain's lifeblood; as Sir Walter Raleigh wrote centuries before, 'there are two ways in which England may be inflicted. The one by invasion ... the other by impeachment of our Trades'.[12] Unlike France, Germany and Russia, continental powers with huge standing armies and all of Europe's resources potentially at their disposal, the tiny, windswept North Sea island depended on sea power for survival.

In 1906, under the dynamic leadership of the maverick First Sea Lord, Admiral of the Fleet Sir John 'Jackie' Fisher, the British responded to the challenge. Fisher tore up the rule book and launched the revolutionary battleship HMS *Dreadnought*. Her lighter, more efficient turbine engines meant she could carry heavier armour and more big guns than anything else afloat; she put both sides back to 'Year Zero'. Britain also pragmatically abandoned her commitment to 'splendid isolation', entering into alliances and agreements first with Japan, and later with Russia and France, turning old enemies into what Winston Churchill called 'trustworthy friends'.[13] And these friends had ships. With the Japanese watching Asian waters and the French in the Mediterranean, Britain could concentrate her naval strength in home waters to face the Germans.

Fisher's new 'dreadnoughts' pressed the reset button on the naval arms race just as the demands of the German Army grew more strident, making it a race the Germans could no longer win. When Britain declared war on 4 August 1914, her Grand Fleet had twenty-eight dreadnought battleships and nine of the lighter, faster, battlecruisers. With just sixteen dreadnoughts and five

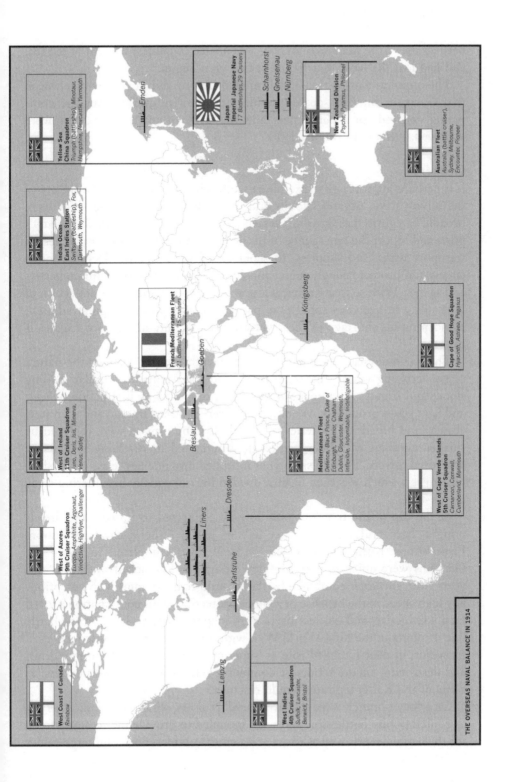

West Coast of Canada
Rainbow

West of Azores
9th Cruiser Squadron
*Europa, Amphitrite, Argonaut,
Vindictive, Highflyer, Challenger*

West of Ireland
11th Cruiser Squadron
*Juno, Doris, Isis, Minerva,
Venus, Sutlej*

Indian Ocean
East Indies Station *Fox,
Swiftsure (battleship),
Dartmouth, Weymouth*

Yellow Sea
China Squadron
*Triumph (battleship), Minotaur,
Hampshire, Newcastle, Yarmouth*

Emden

Japan
Imperial Japanese Navy
17 Battleships, 29 Cruisers

Scharnhorst

Gneisenau

Nürnberg

New Zealand Division
Psyche, Pyramus, Philomel

Australian Fleet
*Australia (battle cruiser),
Sydney, Melbourne,
Encounter, Pioneer*

French Mediterranean Fleet
21 battleships, 15 cruisers

Goeben

Königsberg

Breslau

Mediterranean Fleet
*Defence, Black Prince, Duke of
Edinburgh, Warrior, Chatham,
Dublin, Gloucester, Weymouth,
Inflexible, Indomitable, Indefatigable*

Cape of Good Hope Squadron
Hyacinth, Astraea, Pegasus

Liners

Dresden

Karlsruhe

Leipzig

West Indies
4th Cruiser Squadron
*Suffolk, Lancaster,
Berwick, Bristol*

West of Cape Verde Islands
5th Cruiser Squadron
*Carnarvon, Cornwall,
Cumberland, Monmouth*

THE OVERSEAS NAVAL BALANCE IN 1914

battlecruisers, the *Kaiserliche Marine* was unable to contest control of the sea, and had lost the naval war before it had even begun.

The appointment of the single-minded Tirpitz did not, of course, mean that German shipyards ceased building cruisers altogether. But the competing demands of a battle fleet and the army meant that very few were deployed overseas in August 1914.

Cruisers

It is perhaps appropriate to examine exactly what a 'cruiser' was. In the era of the sailing navy, frigates, sloops and other small, fast, fighting ships were broadly categorised as 'cruising vessels', and were used to watch the enemy's ports and report the emergence of his fleet; to collect mail and despatches; to transport water and supplies; to scout ahead of the battle fleet; to harass enemy and protect friendly merchant ships; and to put ashore landing parties and agents. With so many roles, it is scarcely surprising that one collection of Nelson's writings cites some nine pages of quotes from the great admiral, bemoaning his shortage of these versatile vessels: 'my distress for frigates is extreme!'[14]

The technological advances of the nineteenth century changed the nature of the 'cruising vessel', although its myriad roles remained similar. Sailing sloops and frigates became steam-powered, propelled by first paddle-wheels and later screw propellers. Wooden ships were replaced by iron and then steel vessels, and broadside batteries of muzzle-loading cannon were replaced by smaller numbers of modern rifled guns mounted in revolving mounts or armoured turrets. The old ship types morphed into one new class of warship, the cruiser, which was then in turn divided into an equally bewildering array of sub-types.

At the top of the tree, but only loosely connected to it, were the dreadnought 'battlecruisers', the other half of Jackie Fisher's naval revolution. Fisher's first battlecruiser, HMS *Invincible*, was completed in 1908; the Germans were quick to copy the new design, and launched their own two years later. *Invincible* combined battleship-calibre heavy guns with exceptionally high speed at the expense of armour protection. This combination proved fatally seductive, and battlecruisers were inappropriately placed in the battle line throughout the First World War, with sometimes tragic consequences.[15] However, in their intended role as 'super cruisers', capable of hunting down and destroying enemy scouts or commerce raiders, they proved peerless, as some of the Kaiser's pirates would discover.

On a lower branch were the 'armoured' cruisers, which were almost as big as contemporary battleships and were intended to provide the scouting force for the battle fleet, as well as to act as commerce-raiders and commerce-raider destroyers. Although they had a belt of armour plating along their sides, protecting their vulnerable engines, boilers and ammunition magazines, they tended to sacrifice both armament and armour for a marginal advantage in speed. Battlecruisers rendered even the most modern armoured cruiser obsolete. Too weak to fight and too slow to run away, the type suffered grievously during the First World War.

Older and still more vulnerable were the somewhat misnamed 'protected' cruisers, their vulnerable compartments shielded only by carefully placed coal bunkers and marginally strengthened decks. In the Royal Navy trade protection and colonial policing were the principal roles of these tired old ships, 154 of which Fisher sardonically classified as 'sheep', 'goats' or 'llamas' before scrapping them or reducing them to non-combatant training or accommodation roles and reassigning their crews to more useful jobs.[16] 'The first duty of the Navy is to be instantly ready to strike the enemy,' he explained, 'and this can only be accomplished by concentrating our strength into ships of undoubted fighting value, ruthlessly discarding those that have become obsolete.'[17]

Finally, by 1914 both Britain and Germany were building a new class of small, versatile cruiser, able to operate independently or with the battle fleet according to need. They were characterised by their very high speed, often produced by the installation of new turbines instead of the older reciprocating engines. To foster popular support for expensive naval construction pro-grammes, both countries named these new 'light cruisers' after towns and cities, and they feature prominently in this narrative.

As a direct result of Tirpitz's desire to build battleships to confront the British in the North Sea, when war broke out Germany had just twenty-four 'armoured' or 'protected' cruisers, and twenty-five light cruisers, with only fourteen additional ships planned or under construction. Most of these were concentrated in home waters. In contrast, the Royal Navy alone had thirty-four armoured and fifty-two old protected cruisers, fifteen small 'scout' cruisers, and eighteen of the new light cruisers: a staggering total of 119 ships with another forty or so planned or building.[18] The British could also count on the support of French, Russian and, eventually, Japanese cruisers. Ship for ship, German cruisers could hold their own; in fact, the German ships were often newer, faster and better armed than many of their older opponents. But they were far too few.

The Kaiser's Pirates
When war broke out, the Germans had one battlecruiser, two armoured cruisers and seven light cruisers stationed outside home waters, supported by a number of old colonial gunboats and sloops. Several ocean-going passenger

liners had also been earmarked for conversion into auxiliary cruisers, should the opportunity arise to bring them home. The principal overseas formation was still the *Kreuzergeschwader Ostasien* at Tsingtao. At its heart since 1909 and 1910 respectively were the armoured cruisers *Scharnhorst* and *Gneisenau*, obsolescent but impressive ships of some 11,600 tons and carrying eight 210mm guns as their main armament, along with torpedo tubes and a plethora of secondary weapons. Manually served weaponry and steam engines meant that ships of this era required huge complements of men, some 850 in the case of *Scharnhorst* and *Gneisenau*.[19] It is telling that, with no naval tradition to draw on, both ships had been named after Prussian generals. Supporting the armoured cruisers were the light cruisers *Nürnberg*, *Leipzig* and *Emden*. Identical in all but minor details, they displaced some 3,500 tons and were armed with ten 105mm guns, two torpedo tubes and smaller secondary guns. Like the two armoured cruisers, they were capable of speeds of around 23 knots on a good day.

Vizeadmiral Maximilian Graf von Spee, one of Germany's longest-serving and most distinguished naval officers, had commanded the *Kreuzergeschwader* since 1912. Although born in Copenhagen, von Spee was from an old and aristocratic Rhineland family: an unusual background for a naval officer as Germany's junior service tended to recruit officers from the middle classes. A gunnery specialist, he had joined the naval service in 1878, aged just 16, and had since amassed some thirty-five years of experience overseas, in home waters and ashore. He was a tall man, with broad shoulders and a distinguished, upright bearing, coupled with a piercing stare beneath heavy eyebrows, and a pugnacious pointed beard reminiscent of an Elizabethan merchant adventurer. A confident, aggressive commander with the gift of confiding in subordinates without compromising his authority, he was the perfect appointment for an isolated command far from home. According to one author, 'he was at all times a true gentleman. A Catholic and happily married, he had a warm humanity, a sense of fair play that endeared him to his subordinates [and] the fatalistic outlook characteristic of many seamen.'[20] His subordinate commanders were *Kapitän zur See* Felix Schultze (*Scharnhorst*), *Kapitän zur See* Julius Maerker (*Gneisenau*), *Kapitän zur See* Karl von Schönberg (*Nürnberg*), *Fregattenkapitän* Johann-Siegfried Haun (*Leipzig*) and *Korvettenkapitän* Karl von Müller (*Emden*).

On the eve of war von Spee's squadron was widely scattered. He had taken his two armoured cruisers on a tour of the Kaiser's Pacific possessions, and they were lying at Ponape (modern Pohnpei), in the Caroline Islands, purchased by Germany from Spain in 1899. Haun's *Leipzig* was operating independently off the west coast of Mexico, protecting German citizens caught up in the turmoil of that country's revolution and civil war. Von Schönberg in

Nürnberg had been sent to Honolulu in the Hawaiian Islands. *Emden* remained at Tsingtao, where von Müller was senior naval officer.

The Kaiser's second most powerful force was *Konteradmiral* Wilhelm Souchon's *Mittelmeerdivision* in the Mediterranean, a small force which packed a big punch in the form of the 22,640-ton battlecruiser *Goeben*, supported by the modern light cruiser *Breslau*. Launched in 1912, *Breslau* boasted twelve 105mm guns, a 70mm armoured belt and turbine engines that gave *Fregattenkapitän* Paul Kettner's command a theoretical maximum speed of 30 knots. *Kapitän zur See* Richard Ackermann's *Goeben* was a different order of magnitude altogether. Armed with ten 280mm guns, well armoured and capable of up to 29 knots, Germany's third battlecruiser was arguably the most capable warship in the Mediterranean at the start of the First World War. Short, dark, occasionally moustachioed and of middle-class Huguenot extraction, the Leipzig-born Souchon was almost the diametric opposite of the aristocratic von Spee, but shared the latter's confidence and independence of thought; one near-contemporary observer described him as 'a veritable corsair', however unwarlike he might have appeared on first meeting.[21]

Although Germany had no bases in the Mediterranean, her Triple Alliance partners Austria-Hungary and Italy were important regional players. The German squadron had been despatched to the station two years earlier, to show the flag in peacetime, and to interdict the troopships that were predicted to stream across from French North Africa should hostilities begin. Souchon had taken over command in Trieste on 23 October 1913. But by the following summer *Goeben* and *Breslau* were operating at nowhere near peak efficiency. The battlecruiser was long overdue a refit, her bottom was badly fouled and her boilers desperately in need of overhaul.[22] Souchon admitted that whilst *Goeben* might once have been 'the most powerful and fastest warship in the Mediterranean', by the time the storm clouds gathered over Europe his flagship had 'a greatly reduced speed and radius of action'.[23] When Souchon heard of the assassination of the Austrian Archduke Franz Ferdinand, heir presumptive to the sickly Dual Monarchy, on 28 June 1914, *Goeben* was lying off Haifa, in Syria. Understanding the implications, he left as soon as the conventions of diplomatic good manners allowed him, and made for the Austrian naval base at Pola in the Adriatic as fast as his ailing boilers could take him. At the same time he urgently requested that new boiler tubes and the skilled workmen required to install them be sent there to meet him.[24]

As soon as the ship arrived, crew and contractors worked around the clock for nineteen days in the sweltering July heat, replacing tube after tube until *Goeben* was back to operating at something approaching the capabilities for which she had been designed. On 29 July, fearing that he would be bottled up in the Adriatic by British and French warships should hostilities begin, and still believing that he could rely on support from Italy, Germany's now-wavering ally, Souchon decided to relocate to a southern Italian port, giving him access to most of the Western Mediterranean. Closeted in his day cabin as his darkened ship steamed south, he contemplated his limited options: 'the order of the day was "take action, get at the enemy, lose no opportunities, fight today even if it means death with honour"'.[25] Kettner in *Breslau*, anchored off Durazzo (modern Durrës) with an international flotilla monitoring civil unrest in Albania, was ordered to join his admiral, cutting short his crew's regular water polo tournaments with the men of the British cruiser *Gloucester*. When the two ships met again, it would be more than cap ribbons that they would be trying to exchange.

The Kaiser's sole representative on the North American Station was *Fregattenkapitän* Erich Köhler's 3,650-ton light cruiser *Dresden*, identical sister to von Müller's *Emden*, although turbine engines gave her a slight edge in speed. Köhler had arrived in the Caribbean on 21 January 1914. Born in 1873 in the Saxon provincial town of Göttingen, he was a tall, serious man with thinning blond hair, blue eyes and the inevitable goatee beard, popular with his younger officers: 'We ... will always remember him as a friend and true comrade,' one of them recalled later. 'Still full of youth and vigour, he could understand the young and their ways.'[26]

Like Haun in the Pacific, Köhler's job was to protect German interests in war-ravaged Mexico, notably the oil installations at Tampico, and since arriving he had been operating out of the Mexican port of Vera Cruz. The role kept him busy, notably on 13 July, when he was unexpectedly ordered to Puerto Mexico to embark the embattled Mexican President, Victoriano Huerta, his War Minister Aureliano Blanquet and their families. Escorted by the British light cruiser HMS *Bristol*, Köhler was to take the soon-to-be ex-presidential party into exile. Steering close to the shore in deference to the sea-sickness of his guests, for whom *Dresden*'s officers gave up their cabins and the ship's band provided daily entertainment, he brought them safely to Kingston, Jamaica, where a grateful Huerta presented gifts to all the officers.[27] It is strange and jarring to read about this bizarre journey, with the European powers carrying out their customary roles of global policemen, just days away from a war which would overturn the accepted world order for ever. Still more striking are the cordial relations which existed between the German and British navies as they carried out their worldwide duties. *Dresden* even had a British 'chummy' ship, the armoured cruiser *Berwick*, whose captain signalled Köhler on 25 July to congratulate him on his new appointment. Recognising the importance of retaining an officer who was familiar with the region, Berlin had decreed that when *Dresden* was relieved by the new cruiser *Karlsruhe*, the experienced Köhler and his adjutant *Kapitänleutnant* Hubert Aust would take command of the incoming ship.

At 17:00 on 26 July *Dresden* dropped anchor alongside the brand-new *Karlsruhe* at Port au Prince in Haiti, and the two captains exchanged ships shortly afterwards. Although *Karlsruhe* was bigger, faster and better armed than *Dresden*, other aspects of the new ship did not make such a good impression: 'The captain's cabin on the *Karlsruhe* was red hot, so that he immediately announced that he would move to the chart house on the bridge ... the same temperature prevailed in the rooms of the navigator and the paymaster and in the offices, while in the officers' rooms, which were below and further aft, it was not much better.'[28]

The two ships parted on the same day, Köhler taking his new command to Havana, whilst *Dresden* proceeded to the Danish outpost of St Thomas in the Virgin Islands to take on coal before making for home. Her new commanding officer was a 41-year-old Prussian *Fregattenkapitän* named Fritz Lüdecke, a gunnery specialist with extensive technical experience ashore and at sea. *Dresden* was his first seagoing command. Variously described as 'a tranquil man of few words, gentlemanly and a good sailor' and 'a professional staff officer ... a serious, thoughtful officer', of all the Kaiser's scattered cruiser commanders Lüdecke was perhaps the least likely pirate.[29]

On 31 July, three hours into his homeward journey, with his crew anxious to see their families after nearly a year overseas, Lüdecke was ordered to reverse course. With the international situation deteriorating rapidly, Berlin had decided that he could best serve his country by remaining at sea and harrying enemy trade to the best of his ability. Köhler, lying at Havana and consequently better informed of developments, had taken *Karlsruhe* to sea the previous day, the younger members of the crew possessed by 'the fever for adventure and the feeling that something great and new stood before us', and cheerfully albeit tunelessly bellowing out *'Die Wacht am Rhein'* and *'Deutschland über alles'* as the cruiser picked up speed.[30]

On the other side of the world the last pirate was also preparing for war, at Dar-es-Salaam in German East Africa (modern Tanzania). An older light cruiser, SMS *Königsberg* had been built in 1907 and was similar to *Emden* and *Dresden*, if marginally smaller and slower, and was armed with ten 105mm guns and a pair of torpedo tubes. She had only been on her station since June 1914; slim, graceful and shining in her white overseas service livery, she was a source of considerable pride to the local German colonists. The posting was perhaps less welcome to the 350 sailors who made up her crew. Germany had conquered this sweltering tropical outpost in the 1880s and although Dar-es-Salaam was another little piece of Germany abroad, with its cathedral and its *Kaiserstrasse*, Tsingtao it was not; for Europeans, the climate left a great deal to be desired. Situated on the shore of a vast natural harbour in the Indian Ocean, close to the equator, the town was hot and humid for most of the year, with two torrential rainy seasons. Malaria was widespread, and the atmosphere inside *Königsberg* must have been fetid when the ship was not under way.

Königsberg's commanding officer was *Fregattenkapitän* Max Looff, a cheery, well-built father of three from Strasbourg with a spectacular Wilhelmine moustache. Although *Königsberg* was Looff's first command, he had extensive seagoing experience, in everything from torpedo boats to the battleship *Wettin*. He had just turned 40 when he brought his ship into Dar-es-Salaam, welcomed by a huge crowd of cheering, flag-waving locals. Just two months later he was stripping out the few fripperies available in a warship on an overseas station and preparing for war. At 18:00 on 31 July, unwilling to risk being blockaded in port should war break out, Looff assembled his crew for a rousing speech culminating in three cheers for the Kaiser, and then took his ship to sea, his men jettisoning the last superfluous gear overboard and priming ammunition. As *Königsberg* steamed into open water, she passed the elderly British cruisers *Astraea* and *Pegasus*, stationed off Dar-es-Salaam specifically to watch for Looff's ship and shadow her if she came out. But the two British veterans, launched in 1894 and 1898 respectively, were no match for *Königsberg*, which increased speed and effortlessly left them behind. After dark, steaming without lights, Looff encountered the third ship of Admiral Herbert King-Hall's Cape Squadron, the marginally newer *Hyacinth* (completed 1901) but *Königsberg* proved just as capable of showing her a clean pair of heels, King-Hall later recalling how 'she bolted off at full speed and ... soon disappeared out of sight!'[31] Four days short of war, Germany's principal naval asset in the Indian Ocean was at large.

Königsberg in the Indian Ocean; *Karlsruhe* and *Dresden* in the Caribbean; *Leipzig* off the west coast of Mexico and *Nürnberg* at Honolulu; von Spee with his armoured cruisers *Scharnhorst* and *Gneisenau* at Ponape; Souchon at Messina with *Goeben* and *Breslau*; and *Emden*'s von Müller in sole charge at Tsingtao. Ten ships, ten captains and two admirals, against the world's only naval superpower and her allies. What, exactly, were they hoping to achieve?

Most German naval strategists with a modicum of common sense could see the precarious position of their small overseas forces. Germany simply did not have enough cruisers, a weakness that *Admiral* Reinhard Scheer, Commander-in-Chief of the Kaiser's High Seas Fleet, admitted after the war was 'particularly deplorable'.[32] In essence, the German strategy was for every ship to achieve as much as possible before it met its inevitable end, and the tactic they were to employ was clearly spelt out in the *Kreuzerkrieg*, or cruiser warfare, War Orders issued to commanding officers: 'In the event of a war against Great Britain, or a coalition including Great Britain, ships abroad are to carry on cruiser warfare ... the aim of cruiser warfare is to damage enemy trade; this must be effected by engaging equal or inferior enemy forces if necessary.'[33]

The War Orders clearly illustrate the priorities of the Imperial German Navy's godfather, Tirpitz; all this piratical harrying of trade, whilst useful, was not seen as an end in itself. Rather, the raiding cruisers were to occupy as many Allied warships as possible, and so assist the main event, 'the conduct of the war in home waters'. In the end, for the Germans it was all about the battleships, and '*Der Tag*', the great day when they would smash the British in the North Sea and wrest control of the oceans for the Fatherland.

How the cruisers went about this somewhat doomed enterprise was left to individual commanders. The Germans recognised the inadvisability of attempting to micromanage the movements of ships that were thousands of miles away from home. Quite the reverse: the Kaiser's pirates were largely left to write their own rule books, and whether they succeeded or failed was going to be in no small part down to the personalities of individual officers. The Kaiser seems to have recognised that his overseas skippers were about to become an object lesson in the loneliness of command, and personally drafted a more general set of instructions which were presumably intended to be inspirational but rather missed the mark:

> Much more will depend on an officer, when he is in command of a ship operating independently in foreign waters, than is usually the case. The constant strain will exhaust the energy of the crew; the heavy responsibility in command will be increased by the isolated position of his ship; rumours of all kinds ... will sometimes make the position appear hopeless.[34]

Successful commanders, Wilhelm concluded, were assured of his 'Imperial favour', which was doubtless of great comfort.

International Law

The would-be pirates also had to operate within the constraints of an arcane set of rules, the 'Prize Code', governing the practice of war at sea. The German Prize Code gave captains 'the right to stop and search enemy and neutral vessels and to seize and, in exceptional cases, to destroy the same, together with enemy and neutral goods therein'.[35] So far, so clear. However, their behaviour was also supposed to be compatible with 'the honour of the German Empire' and 'the Law of Nations', and the latter could be extremely complicated.[36] Foremost among the sporadically observed and almost impossible to enforce pieces of legislation underpinning the Prize Code was the 1909 'London Declaration concerning the Laws of Naval War'.

The London Declaration was the outcome of a conference called by Great Britain, and was intended to provide a framework within which belligerent powers could operate the time-honoured strategy of maritime trade blockade – a vital tool for the British in particular for almost as long as they had possessed a navy. At the same time it was intended to protect the rights of neutral countries to practise commerce, either by using their own ships to trade with belligerents or by employing belligerent merchant ships to carry cargoes for them, by specifying which cargoes were considered war material or 'contraband'. True contraband was easy to identify, and embraced weapons and ammunition, explosives and other military equipment, although the declaration does include some potentially contentious entries under this category, notably 'saddle, draught and pack animals suitable for use in war' and 'clothing and equipment of a suitable military character'.[37] Similarly, non-contraband was fairly clear, consisting largely of unfinished goods whose purpose was hard to prove, such as textiles and raw materials, or undeniably peaceful luxury goods like china, glass or 'fashion and fancy goods'. The problem lay in the enormous grey area that lay in between, grouped under a potentially bewildering heading: 'The following articles, susceptible of use in war as well as for purposes of peace, **may** [author's emphasis], without notice, be treated as contraband of war, under the name of conditional contraband.' Under this heading could be found foodstuffs, fuel, finished clothing, gold and silver bullion and a host of other cargoes.

One way for a cruiser skipper to identify contraband legally was to board a suspicious merchant ship and examine the cargo manifest. But even if the cargo was contraband, this did not guarantee any right to seize or destroy it. This was only conferred if the ship's papers confirmed that the cargo was 'documented for discharge in an enemy port or for delivery to the armed forces of the enemy'. Having risked his ship by standing by his prize until the cargo was proved to be contraband and bound for an enemy port, if the offending vessel was neutral the cruiser skipper then in theory had to remove and destroy the cargo, or send the ship into port under guard, whereupon the cargo could be legally dispersed through a process of condemnation (in a court) and sale. The ship could only be sunk if doing otherwise presented a clear risk to the warship. Belligerent merchant ships carrying contraband could be sunk, as long as the cargo was not owned by a neutral, but no ship could be sent to the bottom until all those aboard had been safely evacuated. Under the German Prize Code, the crews were not considered prisoners of war if they signed an agreement 'not to undertake any services connected with the belligerent operations of the enemy' for the rest of the war.[38] Neutrals and passengers had to be released as soon as possible.

This brief examination cannot do justice to the pitfalls inherent in interfering with legitimate trade on the high seas. The Declaration illustrates just how difficult it was to create international law in an age characterised by the rapidly accelerating globalisation of trade and the increasingly impersonal, industrialised nature of war. For a pithier summary of its limitations, we need look no further than Jackie Fisher, who in 1913 wrote to Churchill that 'the essence of war is violence, and moderation in war is imbecility'.[39] This was perhaps why, after spending two months discussing the issue and drawing up the Declaration, the British government refused to ratify it. As a consequence neither did any of the other signatories, including all the principal belligerents of the First World War, further muddying the waters. Despite this, the Kaiser's pirates generally abided by its provisions, although the British reluctance to ratify was perhaps on the mind of one disgruntled German officer when he wrote in 1917 that 'the history of marine law, or, I might say, marine lawlessness, is an indelible witness to the unbridled selfishness and greed of the English people and of their government'.[40]

Supply

The tangled web of international law was by no means the only impediment to the successful prosecution of *Kreuzerkrieg*. Unlike their predecessors, whose ships were powered by wind, a free and unlimited resource, the Kaiser's pirates relied on steam power. They were thus not quite so subject to the vagaries of the weather, but early twentieth-century steamships were powered by coal, and consumed it voraciously. In addition, their crews needed fresh water, food and other stores. The British, with their long-established empire and traditional reliance on naval power, had developed an efficient worldwide network of bases and coaling stations. Germany's overseas territories were few and far between and, thanks to Great Britain's almost limitless capacity to transport expeditionary forces around the globe, they were all vulnerable to instant seizure in the event of war.

The *Admiralstab* (German naval staff) knew this, and established the so-called *Etappen* system to support the cruisers if the bases fell. The oceans were divided into zones, known as *Etappen*. Each *Etappe* was controlled by a communications centre, ideally in a German embassy or consulate in a neutral city, safe from Allied attack, run by a naval officer with a Telefunken wireless transmitter. One of the most famous and active was *Kapitänleutnant* Karl Boy-Ed, in Washington DC. German merchant ships carried Telefunken sets and sealed orders placing them under the command of the local *Etappe* if war broke out; the Hamburg–Amerika Line had already signed a contract committing it to providing 75,000 tons of coal a month to overseas cruisers.[41] The *Etappen* could relay orders from the *Admiralstab* to the cruisers and supply ships, organise meetings at sea, and pass messages back from the ships at sea to Germany. It was a sophisticated system, but it was not complete. The distances involved were huge, and powerful relay stations were required to pass signals to the furthest-flung *Etappen*. Not enough relay stations had been built, and most were in Germany's vulnerable colonies. And the whole fragile infrastructure depended on the goodwill of neutral countries, whose enthusiasm might wane if Great Britain, the global superpower, indicated its disapproval.[42] If the *Etappen* system broke down, the pirates would only have two practical choices left, both unreliable, complicated and potentially risky undertakings. They could 'live off the land', taking coal from enemy ships they seized, or they could enter neutral ports, where under international law belligerent warships could remain for twenty-four hours and take on non-military stores, including coal.

The Opposition
It is worth emphasising just how many opponents the pirates faced, even after Fisher's rationalisation of the British fleet. Fisher had withdrawn the Royal Navy's Mediterranean Fleet as part of his policy of concentrating in home waters, but Souchon's small squadron still faced three British dreadnought battlecruisers, four large, modern armoured cruisers, four modern light cruisers and sixteen destroyers. If this were not enough, he was also up against the French Mediterranean Fleet, the *1ére Armée Navale*: twenty-one battleships, including four dreadnoughts, fifteen cruisers and forty-three destroyers.

On the North American station *Karlsruhe* and *Dresden* faced four old armoured cruisers, the modern light cruiser *Bristol* and two French cruisers. Further south, off the South American coast, lurked another light cruiser, *Glasgow*. In addition the four armoured cruisers of the 5th Cruiser Squadron were cruising in mid-Atlantic and were available if needed, and another six cruisers at Gibraltar could either enter the Mediterranean or cross the Atlantic as required.

Von Spee faced the British China Squadron of four modern cruisers operating in the western Pacific and around the Dutch East Indies (modern Indonesia), and the East Indies Squadron, an old battleship and two modern cruisers operating in the Indian Ocean. These two relatively small forces could if necessary call upon the fledgling Royal Australian Navy and its powerful flagship, the battlecruiser *Australia*, and were also supported by a scattering of French and Russian ships. Worse still, less than three weeks into the war Britain's ally Japan declared war on Germany, bringing into play that country's large, modern fleet. Only *Königsberg* at Dar-es-Salaam was relatively weakly opposed, the British Cape Squadron at Simonstown consisting of just a handful of small, old ships, but the Indian Ocean could be quickly reinforced from the Mediterranean through the Suez Canal if required.

The 'pirates' did enjoy two significant advantages. First, and importantly, they had an inconceivably vast area in which to hide, they could choose when and where to strike, and there were plenty of targets. In 1913 the Board of Trade's 'Annual Statement of the Navigation and Shipping of the United Kingdom' counted more than 8,000 British merchant ships, totalling over 11 million tons, nearly half of the world's tonnage. Britain was a net importer, dependent on trade for her economic survival; the home islands were not even self-sufficient in food. So more than half of these ships were engaged in 'foreign trade', far from home waters, steaming independently along the recognised shipping lanes that linked the world's great trading ports.[43] If a raider appeared on the junctions of the shipping lanes, he was virtually guaranteed to find prizes, and the British, for all their impressive resources, could not hope to protect every possible target all the time.

Secondly, the *Admiralstab* had delegated to their far-flung subordinates almost complete freedom of action, and they only had one job to do. The British, on the other hand, faced a myriad of often contradictory tasks at the start of the war. As well as tracking the pirates, Royal Navy cruisers had to patrol millions of square miles of ocean (a singularly flawed policy) defend dozens of overseas stations and seize Germany's remoter island colonies. Most importantly, they had to implement the government's strategic priority of 'Imperial concentration'. This involved bringing home Imperial troops from scattered garrisons around the world to reinforce the tiny British Expeditionary Force in France, transporting the Canadian Expeditionary Force safely across the North Atlantic to Britain and shipping the Australian and New Zealand Army Corps (ANZAC) to reinforce Egypt. Remarkably, this immense and complex operation was carried out without serious incident, but for the Royal Navy the political commitment to a continental alliance meant that scarce warships had to be diverted to escort precious and vulnerable troop convoys returning from as far afield as India, Australia, Canada and South Africa. The Royal Navy faced perhaps the most complex and challenging range of tasks in its history, but it was still wedded to a command and control system passed down from the Napoleonic Wars. Although a fairly rudimentary staff had been created in 1912, it has been described as 'deficient in all characteristics that are necessary for staff work', and decision-making still rested largely in the hands of the Navy's operational head, the First Sea Lord, and his political equivalent, the First Lord of the Admiralty.[44] This worked perfectly well in the 'age of sail', when distance and imperfect communications limited the range of possible orders to the broadest of general instructions. With the advent of almost instant communications using first telegraph and later wireless, the temptation to overrule the commanders on the spot became correspondingly greater. The extent to which this took place reflected the personalities of the men who occupied these key posts.

Fisher had retired in January 1910, and in August 1914 the First Sea Lord was Prince Louis of Battenberg. A distant cousin of the king, he was a heavy-set, distinguished-looking man with a legendarily voracious appetite, whose appearance belied his talents; a notable sailor-scholar, he was an ambitious career naval officer, an instinctive sailor and a gifted tactician. Battenberg was 60 when the war broke out. His political superior, the First Lord of the Admiralty, was just 39 but had already been in the Cabinet for six years, first as President of the Board of Trade and then as Home Secretary, before moving to the Admiralty in 1911. He was, of course, the controversial 'wunderkind' of British politics, Winston Churchill: an energetic moderniser with a restless, enquiring mind, gifted, intelligent and tireless. Churchill had immersed himself thoroughly in his new brief, in part by consulting Fisher, with whom he had formed a close if tempestuous friendship. But he was also impatient, overbearing and an instinctive micromanager who found it hard to leave subordinates alone to get on with their jobs; he once described his own leadership style as to 'pester, nag and bite'. If Battenberg, the professional, could handle Churchill, the visionary, they were potentially a 'dream team', but early signs were not good; one historian has written that Churchill appointed Battenberg for his 'malleability' rather than his professional abilities.[45]

Churchill summed up Admiralty policy with regard to the pirates with robust clarity. 'The first security for British merchant ships must be the superiority of the British Navy,' he wrote in a memorandum in April 1914, 'which should enable us to cover in peace, and hunt down and bring to battle in war, every enemy's warship which attempts to keep the seas ... [The] enemy's cruisers cannot live in the oceans for any length of time.'[46] It remained to be seen, as the clock ticked down towards war, just how quickly the strong-willed Churchill, the talented but docile Battenberg and their commanders overseas would be able to fulfil this confident promise.

Chapter 2

Fate of Nations:
the Pursuit of *Goeben*

'Personally I should have shot Sir Berkeley Milne!'

Jackie Fisher, 18 August 1914

Konteradmiral Wilhelm Souchon concentrated the *Mittelmeerdivision* on 1 August at Brindisi, where he learned that Germany had declared war on Russia, and that Italy's loyalty was suspect. The Italian authorities refused to allow the German ships to coal, citing bad weather as an excuse, and Souchon continued along the Italian coast like a vagabond. He was turned away again at Taranto before finally anchoring at Messina, on the north-east tip of Sicily, on 2 August, the day the Italians finally declared neutrality, claiming that the Triple Alliance was a purely defensive agreement which Austria-Hungary had broken in spirit by attacking Serbia. Souchon was furious, writing later that 'the Italian government in its betrayal was shameless!'[1]

The Messina authorities also refused to provide coal, but Souchon had other options: several German merchant ships were sheltering in the Sicilian port to await developments and his sailors descended upon them like locusts, tearing them apart with axes and crowbars to extract some 2,000 tons of fairly poor quality fuel.[2] Dissatisfaction with cheap civilian coal was a recurring feature of the pirates' war. It was very smoky, and over time wrecked the sophisticated machinery of warships; merchant ships were usually simpler, and owned by companies which prioritised profit over performance. Nevertheless, beggars could not be choosers, and officers and men turned to in the lighters and bunkers, derrick crews competing with each other to haul the heaviest loads. Souchon recalled later that he had been 'hard put to it not to seize a shovel and bear a hand myself'.[3]

Among the assembled freighters Souchon spied the 8,063-ton Deutsche–Ostafrika liner *General*, which he had earlier recalled by wireless on her way to Dar-es-Salaam. Sweeping aboard energetically, Souchon ordered the unfortunate passengers ashore, brushing aside their understandable concerns about being stranded in a foreign port without funds on the eve of a world war with

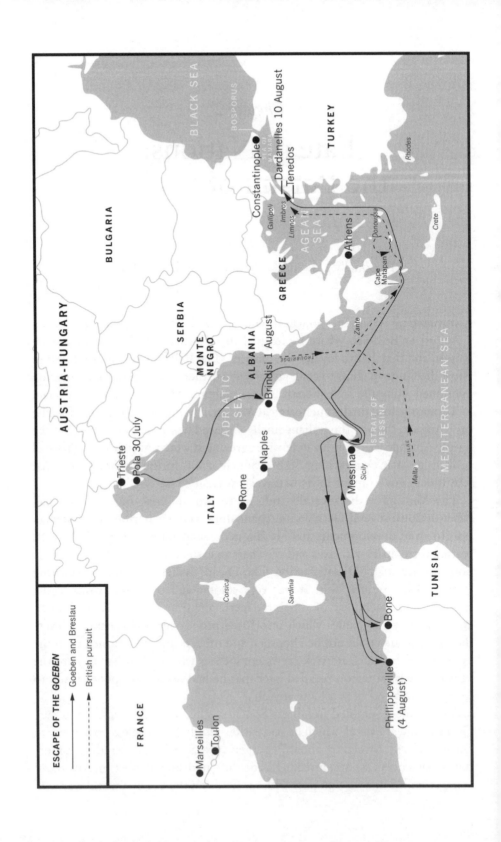

a lavish distribution of gold from *Goeben*'s war chest, and 'they were soon shouting hearty farewells to us from the ferry to Reggio'.[4] Captain Fiedler of *General* was then told that his ship was a naval auxiliary – to his credit, the merchant skipper appears to have embraced his changed status.

It was obvious to Souchon that war with France must inevitably follow war with Russia, and he had no intention of being interned in a neutral port; by 01:00 on 3 August the squadron was back at sea. True to his primary objective, Souchon planned to bombard the Algerian ports of Bône and Philippeville (modern Annaba and Skikda), from where the French XIX Army Corps would embark for home. As the German ships ploughed westwards through the dark Mediterranean, *Goeben*'s wireless operators intercepted a faint message from a sympathetic Italian station at Vittoria, on Sardinia. Germany was at war with France.

Souchon was catastrophically outnumbered, but he had two advantages. Unaware of his mechanical problems, his 'defect at the fatal hour, when the Kaiser called us and our comrades looked towards us full of trust', his enemies still considered *Goeben* superior to any French ship in the Mediterranean, stronger than the pre-dreadnought battleships that formed the backbone of the *1ére Armée Navale* and fast enough to escape the first-generation dreadnoughts that might accompany them. The French also had to keep half an eye on the Austrians and the vacillating Italians; both nations operated battle fleets and might take advantage of an opportunity.

The Allies were further hampered by poor leadership, lack of coordination and an obsession with central control. Recognising that the French priority was to protect their North African troopships, the British decided to deal with *Goeben* once they joined the war, and in the shape of Admiral Sir Archibald Berkeley Milne's three battlecruisers *Inflexible*, *Indomitable* and *Indefatigable* they had ships with the appropriate combination of speed and firepower to do so. On 30 July Milne received a warning order from Churchill. After summarizing the international situation, the First Lord went on to instruct Milne that:

> Your first task should be to aid the French in the transportation of their African Army by covering and if possible bringing to action individual fast German ships, particularly *Goeben* ... You will be notified by telegram when you may communicate with the French Admiral. Except in combination with the French as part of a general battle, do not at this stage be brought to action against superior forces.[5]

Churchill thus instructed Milne to help the French, but by implication forbade him from talking to them without permission from Whitehall. The vague reference to avoiding action against 'superior forces' would also come back to haunt the British protagonists once the *Goeben* affair had ended; Churchill probably had the Austrian fleet in mind rather than *Goeben*, but the meaning became less clear as it was passed down the chain of command. Finally, in instructing Milne to 'cover' *Goeben* when he apparently meant 'shadow', the message betrayed what one naval commentator has called 'Mr Churchill's faulty judgement on naval matters'.[6]

For one thing, nobody had thought to ask the French. The 1906 Anglo-French *Entente Cordiale* was not a formal alliance and, although the two Admiralties were in communication, no mechanism existed for commanders at sea to cooperate. *Vice-Admiral* Augustin de Lapeyrère, commander of the *1ére Armée Navale*, was no fool, and decided to delay the troopships until they could proceed in convoy escorted by his battleships, giving Souchon no choice but to engage the entire French fleet. Quality would be matched against quantity: the French battleships might be old, but there were a lot of them. In fact, when Captain Kennedy of *Indomitable* communicated the British plan to the French port admiral in Valetta, Malta, on 6 August, the latter replied, 'Does your admiral not know we have all our fleet with the transports? They are quite safe.' De Lapeyrère even offered Milne four armoured cruisers to help hunt for *Goeben;* the British were speeding to the rescue of a damsel who was not in distress.[7]

Nelson might have disregarded the order and contacted the French, possibly turning an embarrassing humiliation into the war's first naval victory. Unfortunately, Milne, 'Old Arky-Barky' to his contemporaries, was no Nelson. A stocky, neat little man of 59, whose photographs exude an unmistakable air of smugness, his seniority almost certainly owed more to the connections at court he had previously acquired as Flag Officer, Royal Yachts than it did to any pronounced leadership qualities. The great naval historian Arthur Marder described him, devastatingly, as 'an officer of inferior calibre, utterly lacking in vigour and imagination'.[8] Fisher was even less charitable. Milne was a protégé of his great rival, Lord Charles Beresford, and had once offered to testify against Fisher in an Admiralty proceeding. The former First Sea Lord, who could turn grudge-bearing into an art form, had pathologically loathed Milne ever since, raging that he was a 'backstairs cad, a sneak [and] a serpent of the lowest type' and accusing Churchill of treason when he appointed Milne to command the Mediterranean Fleet in 1912.[9]

Over the next week Milne received a relentless stream of signals from the Admiralty, micromanaging his every move. He seems to have accepted the effective emasculation of his authority, conforming where possible and occasionally requesting clarification when the flow of ultra-specific orders became too bewildering or contradictory. It was 2 August before he was permitted to talk to the French and by then de Lapeyrère was at sea and hard to contact.

Later the same day another Admiralty signal outlined specifically how Milne was to do his job. Two battlecruisers were to shadow *Goeben*, while cruisers and destroyers watched the Adriatic in case Souchon attempted to join the Austrians. Milne himself was ordered to remain at Malta in his flagship *Inflexible*, removing one of the most powerful ships from the hunt to ensure that the strings joining the Commander-in-Chief to his puppet-masters in London remained firmly tied.

Micromanagement from London, coupled with Milne's supine personality, fatally hampered the British campaign, leaving the Royal Navy constantly one step behind the Germans. *Goeben*'s last reported position was at Brindisi, so Milne sent *Indomitable*, *Indefatigable* and Rear-Admiral Ernest Troubridge's 1st Cruiser Squadron to the Straits of Otranto, from where they could cover the port and block the entrance to the Adriatic. By the time they arrived, Souchon had left for Messina, so Milne sent Captain Sidney Drury-Lowe's light cruiser *Chatham* to watch the Sicilian port. When Drury-Lowe arrived, he reported that the harbour was empty and the bird had flown again, much to the relief of 18-year-old sailor Albert Masters: 'Fortunately for us they'd gone,' he recalled. 'We were in no position to make an attack on the *Goeben*, 11-inch guns, Christ, she'd have blown us clean out of the water!'[10]

The Admiralty intervened again, leaping to the conclusion that Souchon was heading west for the French troop convoys and then the Atlantic, and ordering Milne to send his battlecruisers to Gibraltar to prevent the Germans from breaking out of the Mediterranean.

In the meantime Souchon, operating largely free of interference from his superiors, was approaching the Algerian coast, *Goeben* making for Phillippe-ville and *Breslau* for Bône. At dawn on 4 August they opened fire, Souchon recalling with perhaps understandable exaggeration how 'the first German shells fell on the quays and transports ... spreading death and panic among the troops assembled there'.[11] *Goeben* in fact fired just fifteen shells and no French personnel were killed, although one shell hit a magazine, causing a spectacular explosion.

Souchon then reunited his ships and took them back out to sea, but heading east, not west. Two hours earlier a signal had arrived ordering him to Constantinople (modern Istanbul), the capital of the Ottoman Empire. *Konteradmiral* Wilhelm Souchon was to provide the fuel to fan the flickering embers of Turkish political instability into a conflagration that would engulf the Middle East and help define the modern world.

The declining Ottoman Empire was flirting with both of the great armed camps which dominated Europe before the First World War. It was nominally ruled by the 35th Sultan, Mehmed V, an ineffectual figurehead who had spent the first thirty years of his life confined to the palace harem, but real power rested with Enver Pasha, the War Minister and leader of the revolutionary Young Turks movement, which had governed the Empire since 1908. Enver favoured Germany, and a German military mission under *Generalleutnant* Otto Liman von Sanders had been training the Turkish Army since 1913. The Navy Minister, Djemal Pasha, leaned towards France and Britain, and a British naval mission under Rear-Admiral Arthur Limpus was helping to develop the Ottoman Navy. Two new dreadnoughts, *Sultan Osman I* and *Reshadieh*, were nearing completion in British yards, after a patriotic fund-raising campaign had raised £7.5 million by public subscription from the Empire's largely impoverished peasant population. On 31 July 1914 Winston Churchill requisitioned both ships for the Royal Navy for the duration of the war. *Reshadieh*, fitting out at Armstrong's on the River Tyne, was almost complete and her Turkish crew had already arrived, so armed guards were posted at the yard gates, completing what one author has called 'a breathtaking essay in provocation'.[12] Although Churchill wrote later that Turkish negotiations with Germany began on 24 July, seven days before he requisitioned the ships, the diplomatic situation was extremely delicate, and riding roughshod over Turkish sensibilities at such a time cannot have helped.[13] Certainly the Turkish people were furious. One startled British Embassy official recalled how 'a large number of Turkish ladies drove up to the Embassy at Therapia ... to protest against our action in holding the ships up, and made impassioned speeches to the Councillor of the Embassy, to the effect that they had given up their jewels to buy these ships'.[14]

Two days later Enver signed a secret treaty with Germany, and two days after that Souchon received new orders taking him straight into the middle of this political dogfight. But before he could make for Constantinople, he desperately needed fuel: *Goeben*'s worn boilers were burning the poor quality coal from Messina at a spectacular rate. Souchon decided to chance a return to the Sicilian port to top up, but at 11:00 look-outs high in *Goeben*'s spotting tops observed two large warships on the port bow, steaming on the opposite course, their foaming bow waves indicating that they were closing at high speed. The great tripod masts indicated that they were not old French battleships but modern British battlecruisers. The *Mittelmeerdivision* had, as Souchon later recalled, 'run straight into the British lion's jaws'.[15]

HM ships *Indomitable* and *Indefatigable* were heading for Gibraltar as per the most recent Admiralty instructions. One day later this encounter might have brought about the war's first naval action, but Britain had not yet declared. Instead, the two powerful forces passed each other sedately on opposite courses, before the British ships turned about, heeling over under the blue Mediterranean sky to take up a shadowing position 5 miles astern of the Germans. It was an anxious time for both sides. Souchon did not give the order to open fire, unsure whether his country was at war with Britain, but concerns about 'perfidious Albion' were at the forefront of his mind: 'England has invariably commenced war by attacking her foes before any declaration, frequently in peace time.'[16]

Much the same thoughts were passing through the minds of the British as they watched the low, sinister profile of *Goeben*. In this bizarre interlude, poised between peace and war, it was the normal courtesies that caused the greatest concern. Anxious eyes searched *Goeben*'s masts to see whether an Admiral's flag flew there. For one of *Indomitable*'s officers, the adornment constituted both threat and opportunity: 'If *Goeben* had been flying an Admiral's flag we should have had to salute it, and a salute would very likely be the cause of the Germans replying by shot and shell, for which we were fully prepared. But there was no such luck.'[17]

Although both ships' companies were at action stations, the huge turrets remained resolutely trained fore-and-aft and the British ships swung in behind the Germans, triumphantly signalling Milne a sighting report which was textbook perfect: 'Enemy in sight 37° 44′ N., 7° 56′ E., **steering east** [author's emphasis], consisting of *Goeben* and *Breslau*.'[18] Milne in turn reported this to the Admiralty, but incomprehensibly failed to report the most important fact: the direction the Germans were heading. It was perhaps this ludicrous and unforgivable error that later provoked Jackie Fisher to call for Milne's execution. Back in London, Churchill was still clinging resolutely to his mistaken conviction that *Goeben* would strike first at the French convoys and then make for the Atlantic. He therefore assumed the German battle-cruiser was west-bound, and his subsequent orders reflected that fact. When the First Lord made up his mind, nobody in the Admiralty was going to make him change it. But Souchon was still heading east, as another hectoring signal arrived from the Admiralty: 'very good, hold her, war imminent'. 'What a waste of w/t. The less one puts it to use the better,' grumbled one *Indomitable* officer, doubtless reflecting the views of many sailors about micromanage-ment across the ether.[19]

At 14:45 the British light cruiser *Dublin* joined the pursuit, taking station on *Goeben*'s beam as a hazy mist built up to the east. Finally Souchon, desperate to maintain *Goeben*'s illusion of superior speed, ordered his engine room staff to give him every possible revolution and the German ships drew ahead, *Goeben*'s stokers shovelling frantically while her engineers patched up her failing boilers. The British were no better off: it was a long time since the battlecruisers had been docked, and both were desperately short of stokers. Just after 16:00 *Goeben* and *Breslau* pulled away out of sight, steering in close company and zig-zagging into the mist. Captain John Kelly's *Dublin* hung on gamely until 20:55, following the German funnel smoke until it was too dark to see before signalling that she too had lost touch.[20]

Neither Milne nor the Admiralty seem to have considered the possibility that Souchon might be bound for Messina; even if they had, there was little they could do about it. Italy had declared her neutrality and Churchill was unwilling to risk jeopardising it. At 18:00, apparently after taking advice from Battenberg, he sent Milne the following uncompromising signal: 'The Italian government has declared neutrality. You are to respect this neutrality rigidly and should not allow any of HM ships to come within 6 miles of the Italian coast.' He later conceded in *The World Crisis* that this 'was destined to complicate the task of catching the *Goeben*'.[21]

It certainly did, as it prevented Milne's ships from passing through the Straits of Messina, even though international law actually permitted him to do so. However, Churchill's signal had nowhere near as catastrophic consequences as one sent by Milne at 18:50. Slavishly adhering to his orders, which stated that *Goeben*'s ultimate objective could only be the French convoys, he ordered Kennedy to turn *Indomitable* and *Indefatigable* back to the west, despite the fact that, unlike Churchill and Battenberg, he was fully aware that *Goeben* was now heading **east**. Loyally convinced that his Commander-in-Chief must be better informed about German intentions than a mere captain, Kennedy turned his ships about and they ploughed their way back through the darkness.[22] At 20:15 he received notice that hostilities would commence at midnight following the expiry of the British government's ultimatum to Germany. The signal reiterated the order to join *Inflexible* and the light cruisers *Chatham* and *Weymouth* west of Sicily. The force most capable of bringing *Goeben* to action and sinking her was thus effectively out of the hunt. Only the light cruiser *Gloucester* was detached to make a fast run to the southern entrance of the Straits, in case the Germans appeared there.

In the meantime Souchon was making his way to Messina, rightly confident that the Italians would honour their obligations under international law, which allowed belligerent warships to pass through their waters or enter their ports for twenty-four hours, both of which options would, of course, have also been open to Milne. As they neared the Italian coast, *Goeben*'s wireless crackled into life and the friendly wireless operators at Vittoria passed on the unwelcome news of Britain's declaration of war. Souchon and his men had had a narrow escape, and they knew it. As the two ships crept into Messina, every man was slumped at his post, bone-weary from hours at action stations, manning the guns, peering through the gloom for enemy ships or carrying out the endless, back-breaking work of stoking the boilers and trimming the ship's diminishing coal supplies to keep the battlecruiser from capsizing. One young seaman was found dead from exhaustion in one of *Goeben*'s bunkers.[23]

But there could be no rest for the hunted. As soon as *Goeben* and *Breslau* dropped anchor, almost every officer was ashore, moving heaven and earth to obtain coal in the face of mounting Italian hostility; soon after the ships arrived, a deputation of Italian officers had come aboard with a letter from the Governor of Messina, warning Souchon not to stay longer than twenty-four hours. While the German naval attaché in Rome exploited every friendly contact he knew in the Italian government to wangle permission for one last coaling, the local representative of the German millionaire industrial magnate Hugo Stinnes obtained several lighter loads with no questions asked, and loyal merchant skippers fell over one another to provide coal and supplies. According to Souchon, the prize for coal-scrounging went to his able and energetic Chief of Staff, *Fregattenkapitän* Basse, who 'even succeeded in coaling us from a British steamer, although he did not, as is alleged, personally drink the British skipper under the table to achieve this'.[24]

Somehow, the Germans begged, borrowed or stole some 2,000 tons of coal, a wealth of other supplies and even 400 volunteers from the crews of the merchant ships, who gravely presented themselves before the warships' officers, anxious to serve their country. The youngest was just 15, and took his tearful entreaties to Souchon himself; the *Konteradmiral* sent him ashore but two days later he was pulled half-dead from his hiding place in one of *Breslau*'s coal bunkers.[25] By noon on 6 August it was clear that no more supplies would be forthcoming, and Italian patience was wearing thin. Worse still, Souchon's weary sailors, shovelling coal in the broiling August heat and besieged by yelling, jostling boatloads of Sicilian peasants desperate to extract souvenirs and every last *pfennig* from the 'doomed men', were reaching the limits of their endurance; much more, and they would be completely incapable of fighting a battle:

> The hauling and tipping grew slower every hour and neither rousing band tunes, extra rations, encouraging words, the example of the continually labouring officers nor jokes on my part could keep the men going. They were literally collapsing from exhaustion and were taken in rotation on board the steamer *General* and turned in for some hours in the passengers' cabins, extravagantly refreshed with cool drinks and baths, but all in vain; cases of fainting and sunstroke became more frequent.[26]

Reluctantly, Souchon stopped coaling and began his preparations for sailing. Some of his officers wrote their wills. Men not on duty rested, curling up in quiet corners to write last letters home, or busied themselves stowing away treasured personal possessions. Others tore down any unnecessary fittings which might prove a handicap in action by catching alight or breaking into lethal splinters. All the comforts appreciated by sailors on foreign stations were thrown over the side or transferred across to the *General*, from carpets and curtains to wooden furnishings, toiletries and personal effects. At 17:00 on 6 August *Goeben* and *Breslau*, stripped back to the bare, efficient war machines they were designed to be, raised anchor and made for the southern entrance to the Straits of Messina, the cheers of watching Sicilians ringing in the ears of the crews as they busied themselves on deck. Although the *Admiralstab* had warned Souchon that the situation in Constantinople was volatile, suggesting he make for the Adriatic instead, the *Konteradmiral* was determined to adhere to his original plan. 'I . . . made up my mind to carry the war through the Dardanelles and the Bosporus,' he wrote later, 'if not with the connivance of Turkey, then against her wishes.'[27] Until dark, *Breslau* was to steam 5 miles astern of *Goeben* and both ships were to follow a false course indicating that they were making for the Adriatic, but as soon as night fell Souchon planned to close up and run hell-for-leather for the Dardanelles. He ordered Fiedler to wait two hours and then take *General* directly to a rendezvous at the Aegean island of Santorini, staying inside Italian territorial waters for as long as possible.

Outside the southern entrance to the Straits of Messina, Captain Howard Kelly, brother of John Kelly of *Dublin*, was still patiently patrolling in his light cruiser *Gloucester*. At 15:35 on the afternoon of 5 August he had correctly deduced from the strength of *Goeben*'s Telefunken signals that she must be at Messina, and had broadcast the news to the fleet. The information was corroborated by the British Embassy in Rome at 17:00, but Admiral Milne made no changes to his dispositions, still certain that Souchon's objective had to be the troop convoys far away to the west, or perhaps to break into the Adriatic. Vital time was lost; one informed naval commentator argues convincingly that had Milne acted as soon as he received Kelly's intelligence, his battlecruisers could have had both ends of the Straits of Messina blocked some four hours before Souchon sailed: 'a golden opportunity to force the enemy to fight or submit to internment'.[28] But Milne did nothing.

The only significant force south of the Straits of Messina was Kelly's parent formation, Rear-Admiral Ernest Troubridge's 1st Cruiser Squadron, comprising the armoured cruisers *Defence*, *Black Prince*, *Duke of Edinburgh* and *Warrior* and eight destroyers. Troubridge was a rugged-looking officer, who had just celebrated his 52nd birthday; his mane of snowy white hair had earned him the nickname 'the Silver King'.[29] A descendant of one of Nelson's famous 'Band of Brothers', Troubridge had seen more action afloat than many late Victorian naval officers, having served as an observer aboard Admiral Togo Heihachiro's flagship *Mikasa* during the Russo-Japanese War, where according to one account he had earned a reputation for 'cool courage under the most searching conditions'.[30] Fate would grant Troubridge the Royal Navy's last opportunity to bring *Goeben* to action. Unfortunately, although no coward, he was no Nelson; for Troubridge, at least, experiencing at first hand the devastating power of modern naval gunnery would arguably turn out to be more of a handicap to decision than an advantage, particularly when the 'Silver King' was further hampered by vague instructions. On 4 August Milne had signalled him, repeating Churchill's fuzzy general order: the 1st Cruiser Squadron was to 'remain watching at the entrance to the Adriatic and ... not to get seriously engaged with superior forces'.[31]

The signal log from Troubridge's flagship, *Defence*, has survived, and provides a fascinating, if clinical account of the events which unfolded on the night of 6/7 August 1914. It reveals his concern that, although outnumbered four to one, *Goeben* was still a 'superior force', as was made clear in a signal to his captains that was sent before he even knew that the Germans were 'out': 'From RA 1 CS to Captains. In event of *Goeben* coming through Messina ... the squadron will give him battle. But as the *Goeben*'s guns outrange our guns at least 4,000 yards, I shall endeavour to retreat at full speed to a position just inside Paxos Island where I would endeavour to fight at a range that permits of our gunfire being effective.'[32]

'What-if' history is a dangerous game, and we should avoid passing judgement so long after the events on individuals who were operating under stresses that we can barely understand. Nevertheless, Troubridge's reservations and the subsequent decisions he made were highly controversial, so in this instance it seems timid not to venture an opinion. There is no doubt that Troubridge's cruisers were smaller and less formidably armed than *Goeben*. *Black Prince* and *Duke of Edinburgh* mounted six 9.2-inch and ten 6-inch guns, *Warrior* six 9.2-inch and four 7.5 inch and *Defence* four 9.2-inch and ten 7.5-inch. *Goeben*'s ten 280mm weapons comfortably outranged them all, and just one of her huge shells could tear through the cruisers' flimsy armour like paper.[33] But, crucially, *Goeben* was fighting four ships, not one. Handled well, the cruisers could attack from all sides, and *Goeben*'s defective boilers meant that she could probably not rely on any significant speed advantage for longer than a few minutes at a time. To be fair, as far as Troubridge was aware, he was still facing the fastest ship in the Mediterranean, but he should also have been aware that his cruisers' combined weight of shellfire was actually marginally superior to *Goeben*'s: 8,480 pounds (3,846kg) to 8,270 pounds (3,751kg). He should also have been aware that engaging four targets would have posed serious fire control challenges for Captain Ackermann. Finally, although sinking *Goeben* might have been impossible, Troubridge did not have to sink her. Delaying her until the battlecruisers arrived, forcing her to expend irreplaceable ammunition and perhaps even damaging her and forcing her to run into a neutral port would have had exactly the same result, and would have been worthwhile, even if it cost him half his squadron to achieve it. By any definition of the term, *Goeben* was not unquestionably a 'superior force', although Churchill's vague, amateurish use of the term in the first place did not help the situation. To Troubridge's credit, he did not rule out fighting *Goeben* altogether; in a general signal sent at 16:54 on the 5th he stated that he would try to fight a night action if possible. But by inference, he clearly believed fighting the battlecruiser in open water in daylight would be little short of suicide.[34]

Troubridge's squadron was the last line of defence. When Souchon broke out, he was cruising between Capo Colonna and Kefallonia, from where he could interdict both the Straits of Otranto and the southern entrance to the Straits of Messina. At 17:10 Kelly in *Gloucester* signalled that *Goeben* and *Breslau* were coming out, heading north, and that he intended to shadow them. An hour later and far away to the west, Milne began to bring his battle-cruisers east, belatedly realising that Souchon's course ruled out a raid on the French convoys. But he was forced to steer southwards around the Sicilian coast, hamstrung by the Admiralty instruction to stay out of Italian waters. This was not finally lifted until 19:40, and the signal did not reach Milne until midnight on the night of 6/7 August, far too late to be of use. Milne compounded the problem by heading south at a glacial pace and making an unnecessary coaling stop at Malta.

The evening was still and clear. Kelly clung tenaciously to Souchon's tail, *Gloucester* forging gamely through the swell a few miles off *Goeben*'s beam. At 19:30, aware that he was starting to lose the German ships against the Calabrian coast, Kelly courageously turned *Gloucester* straight at the *Mittelmeerdivision*, in an effort to get inshore of them and silhouette them against the moon when it rose. The doubtless startled Germans made no attempt to intervene with Kelly's daring manoeuvre and *Gloucester* slotted neatly in to a new position on *Goeben*'s port beam, Kelly's wireless operators patiently sending a steady stream of position reports in defiance of German attempts to jam them. And so the chase continued through the night, as the German warships made their way steadily towards the Adriatic and Troubridge's cruisers closed at their best speed.

Aboard the British cruisers the mood was bullish. The Royal Navy was, after all, the strongest on earth, defender of the greatest trading empire the world had ever seen and keeper of the 'Pax Britannica' since 1815. 'I knew little or nothing about foreign policy', one junior officer on board *Defence* wrote years later, 'beyond the fact that the Mediterranean belonged to us ... everybody [was] in a great state of excitement and completely confident that, although *Goeben* had heavier armaments and could engage us outside our gun range, we should see her off.'[35]

Everyone hoped to get in the fight. At 20:14 Captain John Kelly of *Dublin* signalled his intention to join his brother. 'I could search vicinity by half an hour after daylight. Have altered course accordingly,' he sent, waiting to be forbidden rather than meekly requesting orders.[36] Milne gave his blessing to Kelly's decision a few minutes later, placing him under Troubridge's orders until the situation was resolved. Troubridge, in the meantime, was still heading resolutely north, hoping to engage the Germans before dawn in the confined waters around Corfu, as they ran through into the Adriatic.[37]

Souchon's deception came to nothing. When he turned south towards Cape Matapan, the southern tip of mainland Greece, at around 22:45, the tenacious Howard Kelly was still with him, painfully aware that the battle-cruiser could send *Gloucester* to the bottom in minutes. Kelly signalled Souchon's course alterations to Troubridge but the rear-admiral, convinced it was a ruse, did not turn to intercept until midnight. Shortly afterwards, John Kelly in *Dublin* detached his accompanying destroyers *Beagle* and *Bulldog*. The two destroyer skippers pushed on with all possible speed and at 13:00 they sighted the German ships careering through the night. Leading Telegraphist Albert Baker was aboard *Bulldog* as the German ships came into view: 'We could see them quite plainly as the moon was showing us up … when steaming full speed we always flame at the funnels and no doubt they thought half the British fleet was after them, but what a terrible agonising time it is waiting for the first shot.'[38]

The two tiny destroyers began to steam in circles, creating a thick smoke-screen from which they could spring out to deliver a mortal blow with torpedoes, but someone had misjudged the speed at which the German ships were travelling; when they emerged, the *Mittelmeerdivision* had gone. 'The enemy seemed to have been gifted with wings,' Baker remembered, 'they could hardly be seen in the distance and we steamed in their direction but they left us behind.'[39] Another slim opportunity had passed by.

The British had been outplayed, although *Defence*'s signal log dispassion-ately records how Troubridge's desperate attempts to catch the enemy con-tinued into the small hours of the morning. As late as 02:10 he was still optimistic that he could bring Souchon to action before daylight, broad-casting a general signal to his squadron which outlined his intentions. 'I am endeavouring to cross the bows of *Goeben* by 6.00am and intend to engage her if at all possible,' it read. 'Be prepared to form on a line of bearing turning into line ahead as required. If we have not cut him off I may retire behind [the Peloponnese island of] Zante to avoid a long-range action.'[40] Troubridge, it appears, was still ready to show he had the 'Nelson touch', even at such a late hour. Or was he? At 03:33 the log records the following brief, melancholy note: 'RA 1 CS to *Gloucester*, *Dublin*: Am obliged to give up the chase.'[41] At 03:49 Troubridge signalled Milne with a little more detail: 'Being only able to meet *Goeben* outside the range of our guns and inside his, I have abandoned the chase with my squadron ... *Goeben* evidently going to Eastern Mediterranean.'[42] Souchon was just 67 miles away. The news was greeted with despair and even fury around the fleet: in *Inflexible*, one officer noted in his diary that Troubridge should receive a white feather, the notorious symbol of cowardice.[43]

Captain Howard Kelly of HMS *Gloucester* had no doubts about where the duty of a fleet cruiser skipper lay in such circumstances: shadow, shadow and keep shadowing. Ignoring his dreadful vulnerability, lack of support and a direct order by Milne at 04:53 to 'drop astern [and] not be captured', Kelly stuck with *Goeben* until the following day, when he took the bold decision to engage *Breslau* in the hope of delaying the enemy's escape and allowing Milne time to catch up. At 13:35 Souchon serendipitously ordered *Breslau* to turn back to drive *Gloucester* away, and Kelly took his chance, opening fire on the German cruiser with his 6-inch guns at long range and scoring one inconsequential hit. Stung, *Fregattenkapitän* Kettner turned his ship broadside-on and engaged, startling Leading Stoker Jack Cotterell: 'a shell went straight through one of our lifeboats hanging on its davits, which was a shock because I was sitting in the "heads" at the time. I've never moved so fast in my life.'[44] Shortly afterwards *Goeben* turned and opened fire, and Kelly wisely retreated. At 16:40, with his stokers rummaging around in his echoing and almost-empty bunkers for the last few tons of coal, and Milne signalling him not to proceed any further east than Cape Matapan, the redoubtable Kelly reluctantly gave up the chase. Milne, still at Malta, congratulated him for his 'splendid work', but failed to instruct anyone to relieve him and continue the chase.[45] Kelly was one of the few officers to emerge from the *Goeben* affair with his reputation enhanced, and was rewarded with the Companionship of the Bath for his efforts. The official historian called his conduct 'the one bright spot in the unfortunate episode'.[46]

For the first time in twenty-four hours Souchon was free from his pursuer, but he too desperately needed fuel and his men were exhausted. Conditions in the boiler rooms and coal bunkers had become progressively more dreadful during the long chase; the temperature had risen to 125 degrees Fahrenheit and four stokers had been scalded to death.[47] *Goeben* and *Breslau* entered the Aegean during the night and separated at dawn on 8 August to hide among the islands, steaming at their most economical speeds until it was time for a pre-arranged rendezvous with a collier. In the meantime Souchon ordered *General* to Smyrna to act as a signal relay station between the admiral and the

German naval organisation in Turkey. Fiedler's first signal was an urgent request to the local naval transport officer, *Korvettenkapitän* Hans Humman, who had grown up in Turkey and was a friend of Enver Pasha. 'Do your utmost to enable me to enter the Straits,' Souchon urged via Fiedler, 'with the permission of the Turkish government [but] if necessary without their formal sanction.'[48]

As the wheels of German clandestine diplomacy began to turn, the weary sailors slumped at their posts and slept, the adrenalin of pursuit draining away. For more than twenty-four hours the two warships slipped quietly though the calm, sun-dappled Aegean waters with barely a man visible on deck. Finally, as the sun rose on 9 August, *Goeben* dropped anchor in a sheltered bay on the east coast of Donoussa, a tiny rock at the eastern end of the Cyclades group, barely 100 miles from the Turkish coast. *Breslau* arrived three hours later, Kettner reporting to general relief that he had located the collier and she was following him. There followed an unexpectedly long, nerve-wracking wait, the seconds, minutes and then hours ticking by as the two ships lay motionless under the strengthening sun, steam raised and ready to slip their cables at the slightest sign of trouble, every man tensed for action. Finally, late in the afternoon, the German steamer *Bogador* lumbered into view, thinly disguised as the Greek *Polymitis* by the addition of a false name and some fetching cap ribbons. Smiling apologetically from the bridge was one of *Breslau*'s officers, *Reserve Leutnant-zur-See* Oscar Hildebrandt; sent across to pilot the collier in, he had been unaware that his new charge could barely make 8 knots until the cruiser had sped over the horizon.[49] *Bogador* was laden with coal, piles of it covering her decks as well as filling her holds, and *Goeben* and *Breslau* made fast on either side. Their crews heaved coal throughout the night, each ship keeping steam up, poised for flight like wary pheasants, while look-outs scanned the horizon from the summit of a nearby hill.[50]

Nothing was coming. Milne did not leave Malta until 12:30 on 8 August, eight hours after *Gloucester* finally lost the enemy. At this point a high-speed dash into the Aegean might still have brought Souchon to action, but Milne never exceeded 12 knots, still seemingly convinced that Souchon would eventually turn back west. His glacial progress was interrupted at 14:30 by a signal that would finally end any remaining chance of catching *Goeben*. It read, simply, 'Commence hostilities against Austria.'

In the event of war with Austria-Hungary, standing orders required Milne to concentrate his force and watch the Adriatic. He therefore obediently turned north to rendezvous with Troubridge, never questioning, trying his hardest not to think. Unfortunately the signal was an error. According to Churchill, 'at this juncture the Fates moved a blameless and punctilious

Admiralty clerk to declare war upon Austria. The code telegram ordering hostilities to be commenced ... was inadvertently released without any authority whatsoever.'[51] The mistake was not corrected until 12:30 on 9 August, when Milne sent a routine position report and a shocked Admiralty realised he had been steaming steadily in the wrong direction for the best part of a day. Souchon coaled in peace, and at daybreak on 10 August he set off for the Dardanelles.

Souchon was still unsure whether Humann's overtures had been met with fraternity or hostility when he arrived off Cape Helles, at the mouth of the Straits, at 17:00 on 10 August. Everything was still, the coast shimmering in the heat of a Mediterranean summer evening. The warships went to action stations and Souchon consulted his flag lieutenant, *Oberleutnant-zur-See* Wichelhausen, who had served in the region aboard the German embassy tender *Lorelei* back in 1911 and knew the Turkish minefields well. Wichelhausen believed that the German ships could slip through if they hugged the European side of the Straits. As the two officers conferred, the mounting tension was broken by a signal from *General* in Smyrna, but frustratingly it was badly garbled: 'Sign of interrogation ... enter ... demand surrender of forts ...' was all that could be made out.[52] Would the Turks fire or not? At 16:00 Souchon made his decision. Going back was unthinkable: already his look-outs had sighted suspicious smoke on the horizon behind him, and there was nowhere else to go. The *Mittelmeerdivision* must enter the Dardanelles: 'With every nerve straining and the crews at action stations, ready to open fire, we steamed in. I signalled to the signal station at Cape Helles, asking for a pilot to be sent at once.'[53]

For a few seconds nothing happened, and then two Turkish torpedo boats hurtled out of the tiny harbour at Cape Helles, thick black smoke pouring from their stubby funnels, flying the signal for 'Follow Me'. Enver Pasha had made his choice, and *Goeben* had found sanctuary. 'The *Mittelmeerdivision* had burst its bonds and was now free to fight for the Fatherland,' Souchon wrote exultantly. 'The excellent German preparedness for war, a little daring and a good deal of luck had achieved a great deal of success.'[54] By nightfall *Goeben* and *Breslau* were anchored under the guns of the old fortress at Chanak (Çanakkale), where they remained for three days before passing triumphantly into the Sea of Marmara and arriving off the decaying but still magnificent capital of the Ottoman Empire, Constantinople. T.M. Whittle was aboard a British merchant ship at Constantinople when the low, menacing battle-cruiser slipped into the harbour:

> One early morning I see this dirty great big black object coming into harbour. 'Oh my God!' I thought, 'what's happening now?' This *Goeben*

fella was different from the ordinary spit and polish and everything of peacetime, everything was a dirty black grey colour. Up she came. Well the Bosporus is not very wide at that part, at the maximum a mile or so from where we were lying ... and *Goeben* came up and anchored close by, maybe half a mile away. Well, well, well, I called the captain, and he said 'All right, that's all right, we can't do anything about that!'[55]

A few days later *Kapitän zur See* Ackermann underlined the menace his ship posed by training the battlecruiser's guns directly at Whittle's ship, 'looking down into our eyes'. Admiral Milne finally arrived off the Dardanelles with the three battlecruisers and the light cruiser *Weymouth* on the night of 11 August. Resolutely slamming shut the stable door after the horse had long since bolted, the Admiralty ordered him to establish a blockade and destroyer patrols across the mouth of the Straits.

The full implications of Souchon's gambit were not immediately apparent, and at first the British treated the affair as something of a triumph: the Ottomans remained neutral, and eventually, it was believed, *Goeben* and *Breslau* would be interned. Unfortunately Souchon was well aware that his duty was to bring matters to a conclusion that was satisfactory to Berlin. After five days of frantic diplomacy the two warships were 'sold' to Turkey, in ostentatious compensation for the battleships requisitioned by Churchill. Watching anxiously from his ship, T.M. Whittle observed the arrival of a group of Turkish sailors: 'Before the day is out there are landing parties together of Germans and Turks, they go ashore singing and enjoying themselves.'[56]

As Turko-German relations warmed, attitudes to any Britons unfortunate enough to be in Constantinople deteriorated. When Whittle chanced a stroll ashore, one local resident lifted her *yaşmak* (veil) and spat at him, and shortly afterwards a party of Turkish sailors tried to hustle the unfortunate sailor off the pier. In due course the atmosphere aboard *Goeben* changed from pleasure to business:

> Later on ... they lowered boats, towed targets, fitted some sort of miniature rifle to their big guns, towed these targets round about and had night firing, always the Germans were training the Turks how to use their guns. And then we realised that instead of getting our *Sultan Osman* battleship, they were going to get the *Goeben*.[57]

On 16 August 1914 the German ensign was hauled down and replaced by the Turkish crescent, and the German sailors solemnly replaced their white caps with fezzes and accepted Friday as the new day for church parades. Renamed *Yavuz Sultan Selim* (*Goeben*) and *Midilli* (*Breslau*) the two ships changed the balance of power in the Black Sea at a stroke, as well as posing a constant, malevolent threat to the eastern Mediterranean.

On 23 September Souchon was appointed Commander-in-Chief of the Ottoman Navy. Just over a month later, frustrated at the Turks' continued refusal to join the war, he took his new command and bombarded Odessa, Sevastopol and Novorossiysk, causing extensive damage and loss of life. A week later Turkey was at war with Russia, Great Britain and France. Russia, isolated from her allies, eventually collapsed into revolution, defeat and decades of miserable oppression. The Ottoman Empire vanished into a shadowland of war and genocide, before finally emerging as a modern secular democracy in 1923. France and the British Empire were dragged into months of bloody stalemate on the Gallipoli Peninsula, a cauldron of slaughter, albeit one in which the nascent states of Australia and New Zealand found their souls. As Churchill wrote later, *Goeben* carried with her 'more slaughter, more misery and more ruin than has ever before been borne within the compass of a ship'.[58]

As the dreadful consequences of Souchon's escape became apparent, calls for a scapegoat grew louder. In truth, blame lay everywhere: with Churchill, the arch-micromanager who always knew best, imperiously overruling Battenberg and his other professional advisers, directing every move his ships made from a smoke-filled room in Whitehall; with Milne, the archetypal Victorian peacetime sailor, obsessed with spit, polish and social conventions, a man wholly devoid of initiative, who once famously said 'they don't pay me to think, they pay me to be an admiral'; with Troubridge, who agonised for hours over the precise meaning of his orders instead of damning the consequences and, to paraphrase Nelson, 'putting his ship alongside that of the enemy'. Ultimately, Milne and other officers like him welcomed Churchill's centralisation of control, allowing him to ride roughshod over their judgement to spare them the effort of thinking. Years of peacetime service which fetishised polishing brass and painting coal and sacrificed tactical training in case it made a mess had left its mark on the service that had swept Napoleon's fleet from the seas.

Milne was never formally censured, but he was ordered to strike his flag when he returned home and remained on half-pay until his retirement in 1919. He turned vindictively on his former subordinate, Troubridge, who took the inevitable fall; with the cold clarity of hindsight, his decision to disengage was almost certainly wrong. Troubridge faced first a court of enquiry and then a full court martial. Although he was honourably acquitted, he never served at sea again. During the enquiry Troubridge in turn rather disgracefully attempted to pass much of the blame on to a subordinate, his flag captain Fawcet Wray, who was a gunnery expert and supposedly told Troubridge that the action would be 'the suicide of your squadron'.[59] Wray, in turn, maintained that he had not advised Troubridge to abandon the chase, just his plan to cross *Goeben*'s bows in open water, and that he had been 'astounded' by Troubridge's decision to give up altogether.[60]

Perhaps the most lamentable aspect of the *Goeben* affair was the failure of both Troubridge and Milne to lead. Milne was Troubridge's superior; had he ordered the latter to engage, Troubridge would surely have done so. Equally, Troubridge was Wray's superior; while the flag captain could give advice, Troubridge was under no obligation to take it. Vice-Admiral Kenneth Dewar served as a staff officer under Churchill, and was at sea in the battleship *Prince of Wales* when *Goeben* escaped. Years later, he was damning in his criticism of Milne:

> The virtue which Admiral Milne attached to unquestioning obedience, as opposed to intelligent cooperation, was the natural corollary of a pseudo-disciplinary system of command and training which ignored the principle of functional responsibility ... Admiral Milne did not seem to realise that he, and not the Admiralty, was the appropriate authority to conduct naval operations in the Mediterranean.[61]

Nonetheless, Dewar concluded robustly that the ultimate responsibility for Milne's lack of initiative lay with the system, and with Churchill: 'High Authorities [i.e. Churchill] who encroach on the functions of their executives become responsible for their mistakes ... the country suffers and the Navy is discredited.'[62] Elsewhere, the Kaiser's other pirates would also try to take advantage of these weaknesses.

Chapter 3

Phantom Raider:
the Cruise of *Karlsruhe*

Fregattenkapitän Erich Köhler's *Karlsruhe* was the newest pirate loose on the high seas at the start of the First World War. Completed in 1913 and commissioned on 15 January 1914, her tour on the American station was her first operational cruise after months of training and working up in the Baltic. At nearly 5,000 tons, she was a lithe and graceful representative of the ship-builder's art, her slim silhouette marred only by the four oversized smoke-stacks which characterised ships of the coal-burning era. With twelve 105mm guns, two torpedo tubes and turbine engines giving her a speed of more than 27 knots, she was potentially a formidable commerce destroyer and Köhler, who had served on the American station since January as commanding officer of *Dresden*, knew the waters well.

Karlsruhe was in Havana when Germany declared war on Russia on 2 August. The mood among *Karlsruhe*'s unblooded crew was tense, *Kapitän-leutnant* Hubert Aust recalling how 'the men remained on deck until late at night, discussing the affairs in more or less loud tones depending on their individual temperaments'. War with Russia, it was generally felt, must inevitably be followed by war with France and Great Britain. In the meantime, with no Russian ships anywhere near, all the Germans could do was wait, as Köhler took his darkened ship north through the Florida Channel at 16 knots. In the wireless cabin the airwaves crackled with the transmissions of the British cruisers that surrounded him.

The nearest of his potential pursuers was Captain Lewis Clinton-Baker's county class armoured cruiser *Berwick*, formerly *Karlsruhe*'s 'chummy ship'. Although old and slow, *Berwick*'s armour and 6-inch guns made her a dangerous adversary; Köhler was under no illusions about what greeting Clinton-Baker would give him if they met in wartime. *Berwick* was based at Jamaica, but was said to be making her way to Havana. Further afield lay the rest of Rear-Admiral Sir Christopher 'Kit' Cradock's 4th Cruiser Squadron, responsible for the Royal Navy's North American and West Indies station. Cradock had three more 'Counties' and the modern light cruiser *Bristol*. *Essex* and *Lancaster* were at Bermuda, more than 2,000 kilometres away in the western Atlantic. Cradock was at Vera Cruz on the Mexican coast in his flagship *Suffolk*, accompanied by *Bristol*. To complete the ring of steel surrounding Köhler, Rear-Admiral Archibald Stoddart's 5th Cruiser Squadron controlled the central and southern Atlantic from its base at the Cape Verde Islands, and two French cruisers, *Condé* and *Descartes*, were also close by, protecting French interests in Mexico. Köhler was heavily outnumbered. But the Atlantic was a big ocean, with plenty of sea-room in which to hide.

Clinton-Baker was the immediate threat. *Berwick* arrived at Havana on 1 August to find *Karlsruhe* gone and, after taking on coal as fast as his sweating sailors could shift it, the 48-year-old captain made for the Florida Channel, rightly surmising that this was Köhler's most likely route. According to the Canadian Sub-Lieutenant Victor Brodeur, as Clinton-Baker left Cuban waters he mischievously signalled Köhler, inviting the German captain to dinner aboard *Berwick* the following day. Köhler, still lurking around Havana at this point and no fool, supposedly replied courteously, 'I regret that we both will be otherwise engaged tomorrow.'[1]

The airwaves were not just alive with British transmissions. The *Etappen* had sprung to life with the onset of war, despatching Germany's warships and auxiliaries across the globe. One signal, from Boy-Ed in Washington, was directed at Köhler, ordering him to rendezvous with the Norddeutscher–Lloyd liner *Kronprinz Wilhelm* at a grid square in the middle of nowhere, where *Karlsruhe* was to arm and equip her as an auxiliary cruiser.

War with France came on 3 August, followed by the inevitable involvement of Great Britain the following day. Opening his sealed orders in his cabin, Köhler read that he had been placed in command of all commerce raiding on the US east coast until further notice.[2] As he worked through the thick bundle of closely written papers, his men took in the news. Some thought of their families, thousands of miles away, or worried that they would not get a chance to contribute to the war, so far from the fighting front. Others welcomed the opportunity to put their training and their expensive new ship to work on behalf of the country which paid for them. 'The report relieved the tension,' Hubert Aust noted in his diary. 'We now knew where we stood. The suspense that grew more excruciating each hour had finally ended. We could now come forth from our hiding place and all hands looked forward with great eagerness to the coming events.'[3]

At 07:00 on 5 August *Karlsruhe* made her first interception. To general disappointment, the steamer was the Italian *Mondibello*, bound from Messina to Galveston in ballast; after a quick search, she was released. *Mondibello* had no wireless, and her captain was astonished to discover that since he had exchanged the warmth of a Sicilian summer for the grey Atlantic, the world had gone to war. Later that day Köhler established radio contact with *Kronprinz Wilhelm*. Events were starting to move fast. As *Karlsruhe* knifed through the swell, some of her crew tossed her peacetime paraphernalia overboard, while others hung precariously over the side, slapping a crude coat of camouflage grey over the cruiser's dazzling white hull. By 07:00 on 6 August, when look-outs sighted first a smudge of smoke on the horizon and then the faint outline of a large ship, *Karlsruhe* was ready for war.

Karlsruhe's look-outs soon recognised *Kronprinz Wilhelm*'s massive slab-sided hull and four huge funnels and within the hour the two ships were wallowing side-by-side in the swell, the cruiser dwarfed by the liner's 25,000-ton bulk. As the two ships' bands vied with each other to produce the most rousing tunes, two 88mm guns, ammunition and small arms were slung across between the ships, along with most of *Karlsruhe*'s boats. Köhler crossed in a cutter to give *Kapitän* Kurt Grahn the unwelcome news that his precious ship would be handed over to *Karlsruhe*'s navigating officer, *Kapitänleutnant* Paul Thierfielder, although Grahn would remain aboard as executive officer. Thierfelder would take fifteen gunners and other specialists, turning the liner into a warship.[4] In exchange three reserve officers, including *Kronprinz Wilhelm*'s navigator, would join *Karlsruhe*.

By 10:15 the work was almost complete, and Köhler was back aboard his own ship, when look-outs sighted the twin masts, three spindly funnels and high bridge of a British county class cruiser on the horizon, heading northeast and apparently unaware of the presence of the two German ships. The two crews rushed to action stations, casting off the lines that tied the two ships together, while the officers and men that were exchanging ships shouted hasty goodbyes before jumping frantically across the widening gap between them. Köhler ordered full astern and water foamed under *Karlsruhe*'s counter, while the great liner surged ahead in the opposite direction, both bands still playing patriotic tunes and every unoccupied sailor cheering as hard as he could.[5]

On the horizon the British cruiser had altered course towards them. This time it was not *Karlsruhe*'s old nemesis *Berwick*, but Kit Cradock's flagship, the marginally newer *Suffolk*. Cradock's presence was wholly coincidental; although he had intercepted wireless traffic between *Karlsruhe* and *Kronprinz Wilhelm*, he had been heading for Nantucket to protect trade in the North Atlantic when his look-outs spotted the two German ships lashed together and stationary. The combative admiral altered course immediately, *Suffolk*'s engineers desperately trying to work the old cruiser up to her best speed.

Phillip Francklin, Cradock's flag captain, later exuberantly related the affair for the assembled journalists of Halifax, Nova Scotia: 'As soon as the Germans sighted us they took to their heels,' he recalled. 'The *Karlsruhe* did not even stop to pick up her boats. Her men clambered aboard as best they could and she hustled away.'[6]

Rightly identifying *Karlsruhe* as the more serious threat, Cradock set off after the faster cruiser, while summoning the rest of his squadron. Captain Basil Fanshawe in HMS *Bristol* responded, speeding down from the north to intercept, but *Berwick* was miles away, searching the Windward Passage before heading for Jamaica to coal. For now at least *Suffolk* was alone, in a stern chase that lasted for hours. *Karlsruhe* was faster and unless she suffered some sort of mechanical failure it was unlikely that Cradock would ever catch her, but he hung on, Köhler's look-outs haunted by the constant, sinister spectre of the British cruiser's smoke on the horizon until nightfall, when *Karlsruhe* finally dropped out of sight: 'Our only hope was that she was short of her fuel and could not keep up her steam,' Francklin remembered ruefully, 'but this hope proved fruitless'.[7]

But just as Köhler finally felt able to slow down and conserve his dwindling coal stocks, another threat emerged from the darkness. Racing southwards, Fanshawe had brought *Bristol* into position to make a perfect interception some 260 miles off San Salvador, before assembling his men on the quarter-deck and giving them a rousing speech emphasising the superiority of British men and guns. Able Seaman Henry King recalled heading below for dinner in high spirits afterwards, although some men joked that it might be their last meal.[8] At 20:15 Fanshawe's look-outs sighted *Karlsruhe* knifing due north through the moonlit water towards *Bristol*, just off the British cruiser's port bow and completely unaware of her presence. Fanshawe turned to port, cutting across *Karlsruhe*'s course and bringing his starboard battery to bear. Shortly afterwards, he signalled Cradock that he was engaging the enemy and opened fire at a range of 6,400 metres. Startled, Köhler turned *Karlsruhe* sharply to starboard before returning fire, Henry King writing later that 'we could tell by the length of time it took her to reply that she was taken by surprise'.[9] The two cruisers careered through the night on almost parallel courses, exchanging broadsides and reaching speeds of up to 25 knots as each captain tried to draw ahead and cross his enemy's bow.[10] At one point the hurtling cruisers passed within 3 miles of the American steamer *Loveland*, Captain Terjesen reporting how the 'the vibrations of the guns made our ship tremble' and several shots fell close enough to cause consternation among his crew.[11]

In theory, Fanshawe should have been able to keep *Karlsruhe* in sight until Köhler's meagre coal stocks were exhausted and reinforcements arrived.

Some 100 kilometres astern, *Suffolk* 'raced on for all we were worth,' Captain Francklin remembered. 'We were all sure that our fellows could whip the *Karlsruhe* easily at close quarters, but we wanted to be in at the finish ourselves.'[12] But it was not to be. *Bristol* was running on very poor coal and gradually her speed dropped away. *Karlsruhe* drew ahead, turned south-east, and vanished behind her own smoke. By 22:30 the frustrated Fanshawe had lost her.

Köhler had no intention of fighting an uncertain night action against an opponent who might prematurely end his commerce-raiding career. But he was not out of trouble yet. Intercepted wireless transmissions indicated that *Lancaster* and *Essex* were lurking to the north, and *Suffolk* and *Berwick* were still closing from the south. *Bristol* was not far away, and *Karlsruhe* was almost out of coal. Reducing speed to an economical 16 knots and darkening his ship, Köhler turned for the neutral Danish island of St Thomas, known as a sympathetic host to German ships. Köhler remained on his bridge, a steady, calming influence, snatching a few hours' sleep in an old cane chair, while his gun crews dozed beside their weapons and the cruiser slipped quietly through the night.

At dawn on 7 August Köhler called his men to action stations and posted extra look-outs, every man aboard anxiously scanning the horizon as 'the blood-red sun ball shone over the quiet surface of the ocean'.[13] But the ocean was clear. Köhler reduced speed to 12 knots, the coal in his bunkers diminishing with every mile he covered. At 07:00 the tense silence was torn apart by *Suffolk*'s strident wireless tranmissions; Cradock's flagship was just 20 miles away to the west and closing fast.[14] For three hours the Germans listened anxiously as the enemy transmissions rose to a crescendo, then gradually faded away.[15] Cradock had inadvertently turned across *Karlsruhe*'s stern, just out of sight, and 'missed her by a bare sea chance', as the official historian later eloquently recorded.[16]

Later that afternoon Köhler's grimy, exhausted chief engineer told him that, despite his best efforts, the cruiser did not have enough coal or machine oil left to make St Thomas, and the captain reluctantly altered course for Puerto Rico. Throughout the following day, 8 August, his stokers scraped the last lumps from the darkest corners of the bunkers. As each watch ended, the exhausted, filthy, half-naked men staggered up into the daylight and collapsed on the deck, spread-eagled like corpses under the cruiser's awnings, while Köhler's wireless operators continued to report British cruisers, sometimes near, sometimes far, circling like hawks. The Royal Navy never came closer to bringing *Karlsruhe* to action, but the gods continued to smile upon him, and at daybreak on 9 August he brought his ship into the peaceful harbour of San Juan de Puerto Rico. It was Sunday and not a soul was in sight as *Karlsruhe* dropped anchor with just 12 tons of coal left, barely enough for a few hours' steaming time at her most economical speed.

With absolutely no idea where *Karlsruhe* had gone, Cradock resumed his journey north to guard the busy north-west Atlantic sea-lanes from the armed German liners that were expected to emerge from US ports. The events of 6–9 August had a lasting effect on both men. Köhler, aware of how near he had come to disaster, was determined never again to come so close to running out of fuel, a priority that defined much of his subsequent raiding career. Cradock, furious that the sluggish *Suffolk* had cost him *Karlsruhe*, transferred his flag to the recently arrived armoured cruiser *Good Hope* at Halifax, Nova Scotia, a few days later, considering that her very marginally superior speed and armament compensated for her age, poor design and woefully inexperienced crew of reservists. The dreadful consequences of this decision will become apparent in Chapter 5. He did not return to the South Atlantic until 23 August, and neither he nor any ship under his command sighted *Karlsruhe* again.[17]

As San Juan awoke, a curious crowd started to drift down to the beach to inspect the surprising new arrival, reports of whose 'defeat' by *Bristol* had reached Puerto Rico the day before. One elderly American, a retired general, stridently insisted that the cruiser could not be *Karlsruhe*, maintaining, in the face of all evidence to the contrary, that she was her half-sister *Strassburg*.[18] International law permitted Köhler only twenty-four hours in San Juan, and the British and French consuls immediately lodged protests with the local US authorities, arguing that the German cruiser was not entitled to take on coal, only to repair any damage that was non-action related. Köhler countered by claiming his right under a recent proclamation by US President Woodrow Wilson to take on enough coal to make for the nearest home port; in his case, he optimistically claimed, this was Hamburg.[19] The American authorities shrugged their shoulders and left him to it, while frustrated allied officials looked on, glowering impotently. The Hamburg–Amerika Line steamer *Odenwald* lay in the harbour but she had almost no coal left, although her captain did send over five reservists and thirteen volunteers, including an enthusiastic gap-toothed 16-year-old named Hans Türs.[20] Instead, Köhler crossed the harbour to roust the German consul out of his prosperous suburban home. Like many of his kind, the consul was a local expatriate businessman whose diplomatic role was merely a part-time diversion. Nevertheless, assisted by the local Hamburg–Amerika Line agent, he rose to the challenge and by 09:00 two lighters full of poor-quality coal were alongside the cruiser. By 19:00 *Karlsruhe* had taken on 500 tons, along with cigars, cigarettes and fruit donated by the local German colony. Köhler had also instructed the

Hamburg–Amerika steamer *Patagonia* discreetly to depart, take on coal at St Thomas and rendezvous with *Karlsruhe* south of Barbados.[21]

Alarmed by rumours about approaching British warships, and aware that both the local American wireless station and the British and French cable relay offices were broadcasting his presence to the world, Köhler slipped back out to sea soon after sunset, taking advantage of a pitch black night and a sudden tropical rainstorm and heading east along Puerto Rico's long northern coast. At 22:00 *Karlsruhe* rounded Cape San Juan, the island's north-eastern tip, and turned south, the moon rising and weather easing just in time to help Köhler thread his way through the treacherous waters to the east of Puerto Rico. 'Twice in one night did the heavens favour us,' Hubert Aust gratefully recorded.[22]

Köhler was bound for the Dutch island of Curaçao; *Karlsruhe*'s bunkers were nowhere near full and what coal he had obtained was pretty poor-quality stuff. It took two days to get there, the off-watch personnel gathering on the quarterdeck en route to witness the formal enlistment of Hans Türs and the other *Odenwald* recruits. At dawn on 12 August the cruiser slipped into the harbour at Willemstadt, the capital of the Netherlands Antilles, a small, sweltering island group less than 100 miles off the coast of Venezuela. Her arrival was not without incident. The little colonial town was quiet at first, its colourful and traditionally Dutch waterfront buildings jarring against the searing blue tropical sky: 'Willemstadt is so clean and European that we would have thought that we were back in Holland', Hubert Aust wrote later, before bluntly concluding, 'had it not been for the many negroes.'[23] But as the cruiser approached, signal flags flew up and the forts sprang to life. 'Soldiers swarmed out along the beach and from behind the quay walls ... here and there they peeped with curiosity from behind the rocky blocks and the corners of the sea wall.'[24]

In the inner harbour lurked the modern Dutch coast defence ship *Jacob van Heemskerk* and her elderly half-sister *Kortenaer*, their heavy guns trained menacingly at the German cruiser; either ship was perfectly capable of blowing *Karlsruhe* out of the water in such a confined space. Köhler's men watched from their action stations, checking and rechecking their weapons, until a pilot boat carrying *Jacob van Heemskerk*'s captain came alongside and ended the tension. As *Karlsruhe* tied up alongside the wharf of Maduro & Sons, the manager of which was the local Austrian consul, Köhler's sailors gratefully stood down and stowed the cruiser's ammunition back in the magazines.

Coaling began at 08:00. The Dutch governor was helpful, but blunt. He had received no orders for days and the only news he had been able to obtain emanated from British and French sources, and based on this he expected to receive notice any day that his country was at war with Germany. *Karlsruhe* could take 1,200 tons of coal, but she needed to do it quickly and then leave. Köhler needed no encouragement. Assisted by sailors from the German steamers in harbour and a crowd of willing if relaxed local labourers, *Karlsruhe* had completed coaling by 20:00 and was under way. Before leaving, Köhler again quietly identified another tender, *Stadt Schleswig*, and ordered her captain to coal and follow him to sea. The German skipper would never again allow himself to come so close to running out of fuel; he was rapidly learning what it took to be an effective pirate.[25]

Rightly concluding that the Caribbean and north Atlantic were far too well protected by allied warships to make commerce raiding possible, Köhler had notified the *Admiralstab* that he intended to head south for 'Zone III', around Pernambuco on the Brazilian coast. The *Admiralstab* supported his decision, and the local *Etappen* ordered colliers and supply ships southwards to support *Karlsruhe* in her new hunting ground. But the writing was already on the wall for the German system. The supply ships were slow and vulnerable, and their effective deployment depended on wireless traffic, which was susceptible to interception. Almost as fast as the Germans could deploy them, the British could round them up or move into their rendezvous areas; Cradock had already caught the oiler *Leda* near Bermuda as he made his way north.

In the meantime *Karlsruhe* steamed slowly eastwards along the Venezuelan coast. At first the ocean remained disappointingly free of enemy shipping; for the first ten days or so of the war the German raiders exerted an influence wholly disproportionate to the threat they posed, as British ship-owners, unable to obtain insurance and fearful that their valuable cargoes would be lost, kept their vessels tied up in port. However, three days before war broke out the government had taken the 'drastic and unprecedented' step of introducing state insurance for war risks.[26] As the effect of this started to filter through, and it became apparent that the impact of the raiders was nowhere near as devastating as anticipated, the great wheels of British maritime trade began to turn once more. The steamers emerged from their refuges just as *Karlsruhe* embarked on her new career.

Köhler kept his men sharp with endless drills and exercises throughout the day, and during their off-duty hours they amused themselves by trying to interpret British news reports emanating from Trinidad, spreading maps out in the mess decks, every man trying to discover what Hubert Aust wryly called his 'latent strategical talent'.[27] The tedium was broken on the morning of 18 August south of Barbados, where *Karlsruhe* met *Patagonia*, whose captain had managed to obtain some 2,000 tons of coal. 'Even the most lowly fireman knew from the experience of the past days what this meant,' recalled Hubert Aust, 'she certainly lifted a heavy load from the captain's mind.' The steamer fell in behind the cruiser, providing a handy target when Köhler exercised his gun crews.[28]

At 16:00 the day improved still further when *Karlsruhe* sped off in pursuit of a single-funnelled steamer flying what Aust called 'the blood-red English commercial flag', almost every unoccupied man lining the rails to watch.[29] After forty minutes *Karlsruhe* drew near enough to fire a blank round, the stranger hove to and Köhler sent over an armed boarding party commanded by *Oberleutnant zur See* Wilhelm Schroeder. *Karlsruhe* had caught her first prize, the steamer *Bowes Castle*, bound for St Lucia carrying a cargo of silver dust and saltpetre, which was used in the production of gunpowder. Although she was a belligerent ship, carrying a military cargo, the situation was legally complex, exposing the perils of applying eighteenth-century 'Prize Rules' in an age of global trade; the cargo was mainly American-owned and, although bound for a British colony, her ultimate destination was New York. Nevertheless, Köhler believed he was entitled to sink her and, once the crew had been taken aboard *Patagonia*, Schroeder's boarding party opened *Bowes Castle*'s discharge valves and condenser head to the sea, set explosive charges in her hold and ran for their boat.

The reality of life as a raider dawned upon the suddenly rather reflective German sailors who lined the cruiser's rails to watch *Bowes Castle* slowly settle. 'The joy aroused by the chase had passed away,' wrote Hubert Aust, 'and even among the men we heard murmurs: "Too bad. Such a fine ship." It is not a very fine feeling to have to destroy a work of art such as a large, modern steamer.'[30]

For the next two days, *Karlsruhe* and *Patagonia* headed south, the dirty yellow water and powerful current indicating that they were passing the mouth of the Amazon far away to the west. On 21 August they slipped into the delta and anchored in a quiet bay, where 'thick jungles covered the coast as far as the eye could see [and] swarms of red and white birds, probably parrots, flew over us and fell into high ferns not far from the water ... When the tide came in great fish swam against it, often jumping a metre out of the water.'[31] Although the setting was beautiful, the heat and mosquitoes made coaling dreadfully hard work; during the afternoon the tide turned, the powerful current dragging the two ships across the bay despite their anchors, and eventually wrenching them apart. It was three days before *Karlsruhe* could depart.

On 25 August the cruiser crossed the equator, the traditional rituals postponed until peacetime by general assent, and met *Stadt Schleswig* near a small island off the Brazilian coast, another idyllic spot dominated by miles of stunning, golden beaches, where Köhler topped up with coal yet again, his narrow escape continuing to influence his decisions quite dramatically; never, perhaps, was a naval officer blessed with quite such an appropriate name. After sending away the empty *Stadt Schleswig* with the prisoners, he coaled yet again at Lavandeira Reef on 30 August before finally reaching his hunting ground the following day.

British shipping was moving again, and Köhler was on the crossroads of two major shipping lanes, running from Europe to South America and from South America to North America and the West Indies. Moreover, his opponents were badly distracted by the far more serious threat posed by Admiral von Spee's *Kreuzergeschwader*, at large in the Pacific and possibly heading west. British naval forces had been restructured to meet this threat, and to respond to a fundamental assumption that the *Admiralstab* would try to send *Dresden* and *Karlsruhe* around Cape Horn to meet von Spee. Admiral Cradock was sent to South American waters to watch Cape Horn, while Rear-Admiral Archibald Stoddart formed a new command in the north. Stoddart's myriad responsibilities included guarding the approaches to the newly opened Panama Canal, protecting North Atlantic trade and keeping the German liners safely bottled up. But in assuming that the Germans would be ordered to concentrate, the Admiralty greatly underestimated the extent to which the pirates were left to their own devices. Lüdecke eventually entered the Pacific, but Köhler had no intention of doing so and for him the coast was now quite literally clear, as nobody was watching the waters around the island of Fernando de Noronha, east of the great bulge of the South American continent jutting out towards Africa.

Karlsruhe had acquired another three auxiliaries, the Hamburg–Sudamerika Line ships *Asuncion* and *Rio Negro*, and Norddeutscher–Lloyd's *Krefeld*, when he sighted and intercepted his second prize, the battered, rust-streaked 4,336-ton British collier *Strathroy*, at 16:00 on 31 August. *Strathroy* was carrying 6,000 tons of coal; by the end of the day her largely Chinese crew had signed up to serve the Kaiser, and the collier was steaming in company with *Karlsruhe*, her lights doused and her colours struck. By 1 September Köhler was anchored with five tenders, *Patagonia* having rejoined at Atol das Rocas, another tiny speck in the Atlantic some 265km off the Brazilian coast. His luck was holding; just two days before, the British cruisers *Glasgow* and *Monmouth* had visited Atol das Rocas, but *Glasgow*'s captain, John Luce, had concluded that the islet was unsuitable as a coaling station and left. Köhler exchanged provisions and mail, detailed a German crew for *Strathroy*, now prosaically renamed *Kohlendampfer 1* (Steam Collier No. 1), and sent her and *Patogonia* away with instructions to rendezvous later.[32] *Krefeld* accompanied *Karlsruhe* as she headed north into the shipping lanes, the wireless-equipped *Asuncion* and *Rio Negro* fanning out on the horizon to port and starboard as scouts.

Shortly after dawn on the morning of 3 September, near St Paul's Rocks, *Karlsruhe* stopped the Nautilus Steam Shipping Company's *Maple Branch*, outbound for South America from Sunderland carrying general cargo and valuable cattle for a British-owned ranch in Argentina. She was a spectacularly rich capture, valued by Köhler at nearly a million marks, although the spider's web of ownership that encompassed her cargo graphically illustrated just how complex commerce raiding could be for a skipper who tried to obey inter-national law. The absence of purely military cargo meant *Maple Branch* required more sensitive handling than *Bowes Castle*, and the process took a full day:

> A steamer full of merchandise is a regular giant floating warehouse ... each firm sends special shipping papers with its goods and that makes a huge pile of documents which the captain hands over to the prize officer. Our captain laid great stress on the careful work of our prize pro-ceedings. A prize such as this ... makes more work than four ordinary steamers would.[33]

Once the paperwork was settled, *Karlsruhe*'s crew comprehensively looted *Maple Branch*, removing anything of any conceivable use; Köhler was learn-ing fast that the successful pirate must forage whenever he could. Tools and fittings, buckets and brooms, charts and navigational instruments, soap, typewriters (part of the cargo) and even gramophones were safely stowed away aboard *Karlsruhe*. The cattle were slaughtered for food, a grim process witnessed by Frederick Forbes, one of *Maple Branch*'s engineers:

> Five men were sent off from the cruiser to do the butchering, bringing along a "humane killer", a pole-axe, and some hand hammers. None of them had any experience of slaughtering and a more sickening sight I never hope to witness ... from 7 a.m. until 3 p.m., the butchers were soaking in blood and the ship was swimming with it.[34]

One spectacularly obese sheep was adopted by the German sailors and nick-named August; asthmatic and barely capable of standing, he provided amuse-ment for weeks before finally succumbing to the butcher's knife. Three live pigs were housed in a makeshift pen on the cruiser's upper deck, and hundreds of chickens, ducks and turkeys were brought across, prompting Köhler, in a rare burst of humour, to paraphrase King Henri IV of France, proclaiming that 'I want there to be no peasant in my realm so poor that he will not have a chicken in his pot every Sunday!'[35] Finally, with the orgy of pillaging completed and *Maple Branch*'s crew transferred to *Krefeld*, the increasingly efficient Schroeder blew a charge in her propeller shaft tunnel.

Karlsruhe's gunners sped her on her way with a few well-placed shells and she sank at 18:45, an object lesson in the art of raiding.

There followed another fallow spell. Over the airwaves wireless reports brought heartening reports of success from *Kronprinz Wilhelm*, commerce raiding in the same patch of ocean as *Karlsruhe*, and the liner *Cap Trafalgar*, now also at large and armed. Other radio traffic was less welcome; by now the crew of *Bowes Castle* had landed in Brazil, revealing exactly where *Karlsruhe* was operating. All around British warships were circling, but Köhler's luck held. Admiral Cradock, on his way to establish the new South American Station with the cruisers *Good Hope* and *Cornwall*, passed within 50 miles of *Karlsruhe* without spotting her when she was stripping the *Maple Branch*, and a few days later the newly arrived AMC *Carmania*, on her way to reinforce Cradock, narrowly missed catching the cruiser coaling from *Strathroy* on 7/8 September.[36] And still the ocean remained frustratingly bare of prizes. In desperation, Köhler stopped his ship altogether between 10 and 13 September, the cruiser wallowing in the swell while the men occupied themselves shooting sharks and watching in vain for smoke on the horizon.[37]

The drought ended at 03:30 on 14 September when look-outs spotted the running lights of a steamer ahead and Köhler rang down for full speed. *Karlsruhe* overhauled her quarry, the Nelson Steam Navigation Company liner *Highland Hope* just after daybreak. The steamer was in ballast, fitted with a brand-new refrigeration plant to collect South American meat, so the most valuable material aboard was her coal – and some British newspapers. It seems with hindsight quite incredible that it took so long to realise the wealth of useful intelligence that an isolated raider skipper could glean from captured newspapers: not just general war news, but commercial steamship schedules giving departure dates, destinations and cargo manifests, and news items detailing the arrival of new warships in friendly harbours.

Schroeder, commanding the boarding party, seems to have been in a foul mood, berating Captain J.B. Thompson for trying to evade capture and for the 'arresting caricature of the Kaiser' which graced his cabin. At first Schroeder threatened to have Thompson arrested, but eventually settled for ordering him and his men across to *Krefeld*, while 'the German seamen rummaged the ship, eating anything they could lay their hands on'. The transfer was not an elegant process: 'The engineer, weighing about seventeen stone, in climbing up the rope ladder while the ship was rising and falling in the swell, fell back on the captain, who was attempting to help him.'[38]

As *Karlsruhe's* officers perused the *Illustrated London News*, fuming over the more lurid propaganda excesses and noting down potentially helpful information, an intruder appeared over the horizon: the neutral Spanish steamer *Reina Victoria Elena*. Irritatingly, the intruder used her wireless to enquire loudly what *Karlsruhe*, *Krefeld* and *Highland Hope* might be doing, stationary in the middle of nowhere. This posed a dilemma for Köhler, as the question would have been heard by every British warship for a hundred miles. If he failed to answer, it would look suspicious, but if he answered, it might attract unwelcome attention. In the event, he sent back the terse reply 'Convoying British ships', which, as he feared, aroused suspicion.[39] Not far away, steaming sedately down the trade route, was Captain Heathcote Grant's old battleship *Canopus*. Grant, sure that no British warship was convoying merchant ships nearby, signalled the Spanish steamer, requesting her position. Köhler heard him, sank *Highland Hope* and made away with *Krefeld* and *Rio Negro*, his luck still holding, for now.[40]

Doubtless shaken by another narrow escape, Köhler took his ship far to the west, into the old sailing ship lane running up the middle of the Atlantic, where on 15 September he intercepted two Norwegian barques but allowed them to pass unmolested. Once again, he was growing concerned for the state of his bunkers, Hubert Aust noting that 'the coal supply was never permitted to fall below a certain amount, because we had to be ready for almost anything'.[41] Two days later the British collier *Indrani* wandered providentially into *Karlsruhe*'s path to answer Köhler's prayers; ironically, she was only in these waters because she was following Admiralty instructions to avoid the main shipping lanes until *Karlsruhe* was caught.[42] Only two years old and wireless-equipped, *Indrani* was carrying 6,700 tons of Virginia coal, which paradoxically had already been purchased by the German consul in Rio de Janeiro, presumably for the use of raiding cruisers. She was an ideal auxiliary and was taken into service as *Kohlendampfer 2*.[43] Once again, she was carrying newspapers that were scoured for intelligence; they were mostly North American, and Hubert Aust found their 'harmless sensationalism' far less offensive than what he called the 'low-down hatred' he felt characterised the British press.[44]

Keeping up with Köhler's regular shuffling of his support ships can be bewildering, even in the original accounts. Colliers met the cruiser at predetermined rendezvous, remained in company until they were empty, then left to try their luck in a neutral port, where they might either take on new supplies and return to sea, or be interned, depending on the whim and sympathies of the local authorities. By 19 September *Indrani*, *Krefeld* and *Rio Negro* had gone, and *Asuncion* was in company. By the following day the latter had gone, and *Krefeld* and *Rio Negro* were back. There is no doubt that Köhler had control of his supply situation.

The rhythm of the cruise was taking shape; coaling, searching and the occasional kill. The process of boarding, examining and scuttling became increasingly routine with every ship sent to the bottom. *Cornish City* and the old Dutch *Maria* were snared on 21 September, the latter considered fair game as her cargo of wheat was bound for Belfast and Dublin. Her unfortunate crew were 'a motley crowd of Greeks, Chileans and Arabs [who] had little time to make their final preparations; some of them arrived on board *Krefeld* in hard hats and wearing their best suits; others had no shirts or singlets, and were without stockings. Some of the firemen had been called straight from the stokehold, and were black with grime.'[45] The following day *Karlsruhe* caught the collier *Rio Ignassa*. *Cornish City* and *Rio Ignassa* were both carrying coal, but it was poor stuff, and Köhler apparently finally felt secure enough about his fuel supplies to sink them rather than take them along. He also stopped two neutrals, the 'dirty and very neglected' Italian *Ascaro* and the Swedish *Ingeborg*, but released both.

It is unlikely that Köhler would ever have had a better opportunity to make hay, had he known the movements of his enemies. With Cradock gone, only *Cornwall*, *Bristol* and the AMC *Macedonia* were still hunting for *Karlsruhe* in the Atlantic, and the northerly limit of their patrol area was far to the south; Köhler had his hunting grounds north of Fernando de Noronha all to himself. But in cruiser warfare, intelligence was everything; unaware of his golden opportunity, the German skipper chose to overhaul his ship. Between 23 and 27 September *Karlsruhe* wallowed stationary in the swell, clear of the main shipping lanes. Her crew hung over the rolling sides, chipping off rust and repainting steel plates which had been battered by days of coaling at sea lashed to colliers. Down below, engineers shut down and overhauled each boiler in turn or stripped the cruiser's engines. In the evenings off-duty men amused themselves shark-fishing, or gathered on the foc's'le to listen to the ship's band, while the officers exercised or 'promenaded' around what little deck remained free of coal sacks. Bizarrely, as the band played 'Deutschland über Alles', several hundred British and French prisoners crowded *Krefeld*'s rails to listen. For a few hours it was as if there was no war.[46]

By the time *Karlsruhe* returned to the fray, Köhler's best opportunity had passed. The Italian *Ascaro* reached St Vincent on 28 September and her captain went straight to the authorities, apparently irritated at being stopped and asked to explain himself. By the end of the day the British knew exactly where Köhler was hunting, although fortunately for him they still had precious few available assets they could deploy to find him, as *Karlsruhe* was terribly vulnerable: Köhler returned to the fray with so much coal on his decks he could barely traverse his guns. 'The entire main deck and quarter-deck were piled about one metre high with coal,' Hubert Aust later recalled, 'the ship did not ride the high seas very well vibrating as each large wave passed under her.'[47]

On 1 October *Asuncion* brought the welcome news that Cradock had gone south; less welcome was an account of *Cap Trafalgar*'s demise, and news that the secret coaling bases at Atol de Rocas and Trindade had been compromised. The Brazilian newspapers also described 'a great coal famine in Brazil', which the Germans put down to the pernicious British stripping Brazil of her coal reserves in defiance of a local government regulation banning its export. In fact, a cursory analysis of the ships taken by *Karlsruhe* alone reveal that most of the coal was bound *from* Britain *for* Brazil, and the 'famine' presumably resulted from Great Britain moving to a war footing and having less of this priceless strategic resource available for export.

Four days later, operating on the shipping lane from Las Palmas to Pernambuco with the *Krefeld* scouting 40 miles off his beam, Köhler overhauled the steamer *Farn* carrying 7,000 tons of the finest Welsh coal, while British prisoners aboard *Krefeld* supposedly lined the rails, cheering, making bets and urging the German cruiser on; those who bet on *Karlsruhe* won with ease, and by the end of the day *Farn* had became another *Kohlendampfer*.[48] The easy capture lulled Köhler into a false sense of security; by now *Bristol*, *Cornwall* and *Macedonia* had rushed north, and *Karlsruhe*'s wireless operators began to hear their signals all around, increasing in intensity. In fact, as Köhler went east out of the danger zone on 7 October, Captain Walter Ellerton brought his armoured cruiser *Cornwall* directly over the spot where Köhler had seized the *Farn* just thirty-six hours before.[49]

Fortunately for Köhler, the British sweep pushed him east, directly on to the track which most British merchant ships were following. Over the next three days he took four ships: *Niceto de Larrinaga*, carrying oats and corn to London, on the 6th; the Liverpool-bound *Lynrowan* on the 7th, carrying corn, sugar, tallow and hides, as well as twelve automobiles; and on the 8th the Lamport & Holts liner *Cervantes*, carrying fodder, wool, sugar and furs, and *Pruth*, which stumbled into *Karlsruhe* at around midnight, brightly lit and wholly unaware of the German cruiser's presence, carrying a cargo of saltpetre and barley. Between them they graphically illustrate the complex web of global maritime trade on which Britain depended in 1914 – there is nothing new about the concept of 'globalisation'.

The crew were taken off *Lynrowan* and transferred to *Krefeld*; they included the captain's sick wife and nurse, *Karlsruhe*'s first female prisoners. As they were rowed through the darkness towards the blacked-out auxiliary, any lingering fears about their ultimate fate were dispelled when Frederick Forbes and other British captives struck up a rousing chorus of 'Tipperary'. 'At the sound of our English voices the men sent up a cheer,' Forbes later recalled. 'They did not expect to find friends on a German prison ship.'[50]

Sinking prizes was not without hazard. Köhler used *Lynrowan* for target practice, but as the steamer made her final plunge at 15:00 the hatches sealing her holds burst open. Several hundred barrels of tallow shot to the surface, where they bobbed about accusingly in the water, a clear signpost reading 'raider at work'. Köhler drove *Karlsruhe* repeatedly through them at speed, but the persistent barrels bobbed back up time after time and were still there when the frustrated skipper gave up, leaving fat, terrified rats running over the slippery surfaces and a thrashing mass of sharks fighting over the fatty goo which leaked from their splintered sides.[51]

The next two interceptions were neutrals, the Spanish *Cadiz* on 9 October and the Norwegian *Bergunhus* the following day, but on the 11th, at about 15:00, Köhler's look-outs sighted three ships on the horizon at a prearranged rendezvous where *Karlsruhe* was due to meet the collier *Asuncion*. One was flying the Red Ensign and *Asuncion* herself was running for the horizon, signalling by wireless that she was under attack by a 'British' cruiser. Once Köhler had calmed the situation, he learned that the prize, *Farn*, had lured the British steamer *Condor* to the rendezvous by flying the Red Ensign and then held her in place, exchanging pleasantries by flag signal until *Karlsruhe* arrived. *Asuncion*'s nervous captain had arrived at the same time as *Karlsruhe* and, taking her for a British cruiser, had decided that discretion was the better part of valour and fled. *Condor* was a fine catch; her cargo manifest read like a shopping list of everything a raider captain needed to operate unsupported in hostile waters, including provisions, lubricating oil and even dynamite. Her unfortunate captain, well aware of the value of his cargo, had chosen a route well to the east of the general shipping lanes, only to stumble across Köhler's remote secret rendezvous.

By now, there were some 300 captives jammed into *Krefeld*, each a mouth to be fed, and a strain on the collier's rudimentary sanitary facilities; the old steamer was 'so crowded that we have heard the captains and officers have to have their meals on deck', but despite the challenges their treatment remained exemplary.[52] In a subsequent interview, Frederick Forbes remarked, 'I do not care what German soldiers may be doing on the continent, I must say that German officers, both of the navy and the merchant marine, are considerate, courteous and gentlemanly.' He went so far as to say that the Germans had treated their prisoners as brothers, and insisted that his interviewer record the gratitude felt by himself and other prisoners.[53] Hubert Aust compiled a list of the captives, broken down by nationality, which again illustrates the extraordinarily globalised nature of the 'British' merchant marine. As well as 223 citizens of enemy countries, most of them British, Aust lists 175 neutrals, including 107 Chinese, 22 Spaniards, 13 Swedes, 10 Dutchmen, 4 Americans,

4 Norwegians, 3 Chileans, 3 Swiss, 2 Italians, 2 Mexicans, an Arab, a Cuban, a Dane, an Ecuadorean and a Greek.[54]

Stripping *Condor* took two days, and it was 22:00 on 13 October before her sea cocks were opened to the ocean. Six hours earlier Köhler had ordered *Krefeld* to make for Tenerife, a neutral harbour which was distant enough to allow him to make a clean break and be miles away before the news broke of his new location. As the tender turned east and slowly made away, Köhler dipped *Karlsruhe's* ensigns and sent a signal wishing his former prisoners a safe voyage – one last courteous gesture of many.[55] The cruiser's band played sentimental ballads and her crew lined the decks, anxiously watching *Krefeld* go. The collier was carrying the first mail which they had been allowed to send since the outbreak of war and, if she made it to Tenerife, anxious relatives might finally receive confirmation that their sons, lovers, husbands or fathers were alive.

By now, Köhler's hunting grounds were fatally compromised. Stoddart, the newly appointed Senior Naval Officer North of Montevideo, had begun to consolidate his new command, which included seven cruisers and AMCs, as well as the old battleship *Albion*. The powerful, modern, armoured cruiser *Defence* was also joining him from the Mediterranean.[56] The odds were starting to stack up against Köhler. Sinister wireless intercepts warned him that British warships were drawing steadily nearer and the prizes started to dry up once more as Admiralty instructions started to trickle down to the steamer skippers. On 18 October he sank the collier *Glanton* and stopped three neutrals, but although he waited, drifting, in the same spot for another four days, the horizon remained clear. On 22 October Köhler relieved the monotony by organising a short service to mark the birthday of the Empress Augusta, the Kaiser's wife: 'He eulogised this Imperial Lady,' Hubert Aust sentimentally recalled, 'mother of her country ... a real German mother that had the same worries as other mothers had, in that she had six sons and one son-in-law all in the field.'[57] But the 'spirited and heartfelt "Hurrahs"' which rang out over the ocean could not wholly hide the widespread apprehension that passed through the more perceptive of the crew; by now, *Krefeld* would be at Tenerife, and all hell would shortly break loose. The following day Köhler seized the small steamer *Huntsdale*, carrying corn to Bristol; after sending her to the bottom, he decided it was time to leave.

Assuming that the British would converge on his present location, he planned to make for the West Indies, where he could raid what he assumed would be the now-unprotected British and French island colonies; Aust recalled that 'he especially had in mind a joke on the French island of Martinique and the English Barbados'.[58] He left on the 25th. The next day, while approaching the shipping lane from Trinidad to Brazil in the dead of night, he ran across a blacked-out steamer, which the next day turned out to be his final and most valuable prize, the big Lamport & Holt steamer *Vandyck*.

Köhler estimated *Vandyck*'s worth at 4,896,000 marks. She was only three years old, bound from Buenos Aires to New York carrying general cargo, 1,000 tons of frozen meat and 210 mostly neutral passengers. In this more innocent era passengers were a nuisance: if Köhler wished to sink *Vandyck*, both they and their luggage had to be brought to safety, which meant summoning his tenders. In the meantime a boarding party commanded by *Leutnant zur See* Frese, formerly the first officer of *Kronprinz Wilhelm*, notified Captain Anthony Cadogan of his fate. Cadogan informed his passengers, who were at lunch, that he was no longer in command of his ship; one witness recalled that they took the news calmly, unlike their stewards, who were 'so nervous they spilled the soup ... and got the courses sadly mixed'.[59] Later that afternoon, the laborious process of preparing the passengers and crew for transfer to the *Asuncion* began, under the cheery direction of *Leutnant zur See* Count Beissel von Gymnich, who gave everyone permission to take souvenirs from Cadogan's ship before she went down. 'One passenger took an electric clock, another carried away a bearskin rug ... Most were contented with silver spoons and forks. A very stout man said he did not wish a souvenir, but walked on the keyboard of the piano out of revenge for its having kept him awake during the trip.'[60] One passenger turned out to be Columbia's ambassador to Argentina, who nervously presented a letter confirming his status, signed by his German opposite number in Buenos Aires.

The transfer of the passengers began at 06:00 on 27 October. According to Aust, the steamer's boats were in poor condition and leaked, soaking the passengers and their baggage, a complaint that was repeated by several passengers but angrily rebuffed by Cadogan. 'It was a war seizure,' he told a *New York Times* reporter, 'and in my opinion the passengers got off very lucky. They were all transferred safely without any accident, and only a few pieces of baggage were damaged by water. The boats of the *Vandyck* were in A1 condition ... the heavy freight caused the boats to dip a little in the choppy sea and that was the water ... noticed by the passengers.'[61] This rather bizarre narrative emphasises the peculiar nature of commerce raiding carried out under the prize rules; later in the war passengers and crews of merchant vessels would have a great deal more to worry about than whether their baggage got wet.

The transfer took hours. At midnight another British steamer, *Royal Sceptre*, passed by, but her cargo of coffee appeared to be neutral-owned and Köhler's crew was fully occupied, so he reluctantly let her go. In fact, Captain W.H. Estill outwitted the German skipper, hiding evidence of his cargo's actual destination, which was Canada: 'After replying to the numerous questions re.

cargo, etc., in a way I thought suitable for the occasion, and, if not altogether truthful, quite in order considering the serious position I was in, he appeared satisfied ... at 12.30 a.m. on October 28th, I was informed I could proceed and at once ran full speed ahead again, thinking I was very lucky, which was the last remark the officer made as he left me.' *Royal Sceptre* was the last steamer to have the misfortune to run across *Karlsruhe*.[62]

At 06:30 on 28 October *Vandyck* was scuttled, her erstwhile passengers and crew watching her go from *Asuncion*'s rails, before the tender took them and the crews of *Glanton* and *Huntsdale* to safety. By sunset on 4 November *Karlsruhe* was 300 miles from Barbados. Köhler had coaled from *Farn*, which had left for eventual internment in Puerto Rico, and was proceeding in company with *Rio Negro* and *Indrani*. It was a beautiful evening and morale was high. On the other side of South America von Spee had scored a notable victory at Coronel, and *Karlsruhe* was off to give the British lion's tail a mighty tug. 'The sinking of steamers is very nice,' commented one young sailor, 'but ... it is high time that our guns got to do something!'[63]

Below, the officers were dining in the wardroom aft, newly decorated with pot plants and flowers 'liberated' from *Vandyck*, while the off-watch men had gathered on the foc's'sle to listen to the band. At 18:30, in latitude $10°\ 7'$ north, longitude $55°\ 25'$ west, a tremendous explosion tore through the forepart of the ship. Down below all the lights failed, and the ship took on a sudden list to port. Somebody yelled 'torpedo', and the rumour spread like wildfire as the officers raced for the upper deck.

It was no torpedo. The cause of the explosion has never been established beyond doubt, but the most likely explanation is the accidental explosion of unstable ammunition – a relatively common problem with warships of the period, and certainly one that would have been magnified by the climate and Köhler's circumstances, which made routine care and maintenance almost impossible.[64] The explosion vaporised the cruiser's forepart from her bows back to the first funnel, including the bridge, and Köhler vanished without trace, along with 262 of his men.

Hubert Aust raced on deck, to see the bottom of a sinking ship near *Karlsruhe*. It was some minutes before he realised it was the bows of his own ship. Elsewhere, alarm bells rang out and Köhler's well-drilled crew raced to their damage control stations, shutting watertight doors and sealing off the flood waters so fast that, miraculously, the cruiser's stern stayed afloat for another twenty minutes. But it was clear that it was all over. The survivors from the stern numbered 123 in total, including almost all of the officers. Safely aboard the tender *Rio Negro*, they watched, stunned, as the ship that had been their home for the last year slipped beneath the waves: 'We had hardly gone 100 metres from the ship when her stern lifted straight out of the water so that we could distinctly see her propellers and rudder ... when the rest of *Karlsruhe* shot suddenly to the depths all the men in the boats gave three "Hurrahs" to her and to our comrades.'[65]

It was a shocking, brutal end to the career of the 'phantom raider'. Aust and the other survivors assembled on board the *Rio Negro*, 'a heavy load of pain and sorrow' hanging over every man. After a brief discussion, the prize, *Indrani*, was scuttled and the survivors started the long journey north, back to Germany via Norway, under the command of *Karlsruhe*'s executive officer, *Korvettenkapitän* Studt. Thanks to an extraordinary combination of good luck and good judgement, they made it, *Rio Negro* dropping anchor in the Jade River on 6 December 1914. Excellent operational security, coupled with the swift posting of the survivors to the High Seas Fleet with the new cruiser *Regensburg*, enabled the *Admiralstab* to keep *Karlsruhe*'s loss secret, and her phantom haunted the thoughts of Allied planners and nervous mariners for months. In January 1915 Captain Barber of the steamer *Coamo* gave the *New York Times* correspondent in San Juan, Puerto Rico, a vivid account of how '*Karlsruhe*' had turned a searchlight on his bridge before disappearing into the darkness.[66] Another 'eyewitness' claimed to have watched the phantom being destroyed in a dramatic night action off Grenada, and then to have retrieved a life-buoy, an oilskin-wrapped sword and human remains from the surf. Much to his bewilderment, nobody else appeared to have noticed the breathless action.[67] The story of *Karlsruhe*'s loss did not finally break until mid-March.

In the end *Karlsruhe* sank seventeen ships totalling 76,609 gross registered tons, a record exceeding that of Karl von Müller's far more celebrated *Emden*, which was wreaking havoc at the same time on the other side of the world.

Chapter 4

Emden: Swan of the East

'Our first duty is to raid the commerce of the enemy.'

Kapitänleutnant Karl von Müller, 2 August 1914

At Tsingtao, von Müller was responsible for the torpedo boat *S90* and a ramshackle collection of gunboats and merchant vessels. On 22 July his small force was supplemented by the antiquated Austro-Hungarian cruiser *Kaiserin Elizabeth*, whose keel had first touched salt water in 1890. Her commanding officer, Richard Makowitz, had opted for at least the illusion of safety provided by a friendly harbour in the face of a rapidly deteriorating international situation. Despite the gloom, von Müller and Makowitz did their best to observe the usual courtesies, fostering exchanges between the two cruisers and organising parties and excursions into the surrounding countryside.[1]

The forced gaiety could not disguise the serious situation. *Emden* received a constant stream of messages from Berlin, for onward transmission to von Spee's cruisers out in the Pacific, and von Müller was well informed about European events. On 29 July, learning that Austria-Hungary had declared war on Serbia, he began to prepare for battle. Von Müller knew that Tsingtao was terribly vulnerable should Great Britain and her ally, Japan, join the war. The colonial outpost was too isolated and poorly defended to hold out for long against a full-scale attack, and von Muller's objective was to get to sea as soon as possible, to avoid being trapped in the harbour. In the meantime his crew loaded as much coal and ammunition as *Emden* could carry, and stripped out superfluous gear. Finally, at 07:00 on 31 July, von Müller took his ship and the chartered collier *Elsbeth* to sea, to rendezvous with von Spee's cruisers at Yap in the Caroline Islands. As he steamed out he ordered his crew to action stations, a precaution that inevitably increased the tension: 'We had been conditioned to expect that hostile ships would accost us as soon as we left Tsingtao,' Franz Joseph recalled. 'Were we now threatened with a premature demise?'[2]

As it happened, the young officer had nothing to fear. Just one day earlier Admiral Sir Martyn Jerram's powerful China Squadron had been operating in the Yellow Sea, where it could prevent *Emden* from breaking out and

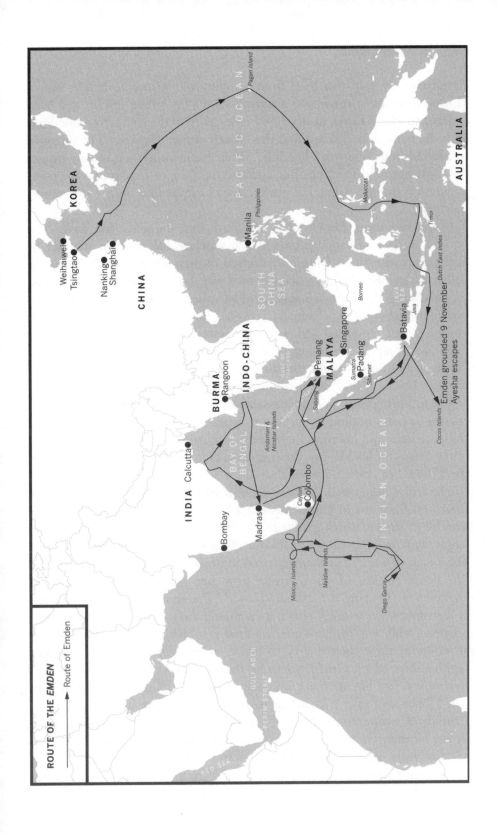

ROUTE OF THE *EMDEN*

→ Route of Emden

simultaneously stop von Spee from bringing the *Kreuzergeschwader* home. However, to his 'surprise and chagrin', soon after sailing Jerram had been ordered to Hong Kong, nearly 1,500 miles away to the south, to rendezvous with the battleship *Triumph* and the French cruiser *Dupleix*.[3] The directive originated from Winston Churchill.[4] While his intention was to concentrate the most powerful force possible against von Spee, in over-ruling the commander on the spot Churchill made *Emden*'s escape into open water almost inevitable.

In the meantime *Emden* made off south into the gathering dusk. The cruiser was darkened and her crew at 'war watches': half the men on watch or at the guns, the others lying fully dressed in their hammocks. At 09:00 the collier *Elsbeth* detached to make her own way, but otherwise the night, and the following day, proved something of an anticlimax, *Emden* cruising undisturbed in tranquil waters.[5] Finally, late on 1 August, von Müller learned that Germany had mobilised and war was inevitable. Exactly who the enemy might be occupied the thoughts of many aboard, including Franz Joseph: 'There could be no doubt that France and Russia were our enemies, but whether Britain would also participate remained an open question.'[6]

The following day von Müller assembled his crew and delivered a brief but rousing speech, outlining his plan to make for the Nagasaki–Vladivostok shipping lanes and interdict Russian trade. Finally, according to von Mücke, 'three cheers for his Majesty, the Emperor, rang out over the broad surface of the Yellow Sea', before *Emden* cleared for action.[7]

The cruise began well. At dawn on 4 August, as *Emden* emerged from the Straits of Tsushima in foul weather and heavy seas, her look-outs sighted a smudge of smoke, which gradually metamorphosed into 'a vessel somewhat larger than our own, which was also travelling with screened lights and looked like a man of war'.[8] The stranger tried to break for neutral Japanese waters, 'the dense column of smoke rising from her funnels indicating that her engines were working at maximum power'.[9] For an hour *Emden* pursued her at high speed, her wireless operators jamming the strange ship's radio transmissions, while von Müller's gunners fired first blanks and then live shells in an effort to force their quarry to heave to and submit to boarding. The fugitive ship, which turned out to be the Russian Volunteer Fleet steamer *Ryazan*, was fast, but not quite fast enough. As she wallowed in the heavy seas, von Müller sent over a boarding party commanded by Julius Lauterbach. Lauterbach's cutter came close to being crushed by the 3,500-ton *Ryazan*, but by late morning the two ships were on their way back to Tsingtao. *Ryazan* was just five years old and German-built, so von Müller had decided to convert her into an auxiliary cruiser using weapons from the old gunboats. Renamed

Cormoran, she cruised the South Pacific without success until she was eventually interned on the US island of Guam on 14 December 1914.

Monitoring the airwaves carefully, avoiding suspicious smoke and making the best speed they could, the two ships slipped back into Tsingtao at 05:30 on 6 August. By now signals had confirmed that Great Britain had declared war on Germany. Although the odds against her had just grown immeasurably greater, *Emden* had taken her first prize, and the mood on board was buoyant: 'we had enemies enough, but everyone in *Emden* knew that much could be endured among such cheerful companionship ... [Britain's] merchantmen promised rich booty'.[10]

Tsingtao was preparing for the worst, with the harbour already mined, defences dug and the port infrastructure prepared for demolition.[11] By the evening of 6 August *Emden* was heading for open water again, her band bravely striking up '*Die Wacht am Rhein*'. Thirty-four reservists had joined her, and she was accompanied by the collier *Markomannia* and the auxiliary cruiser *Prinz Eitel Friedrich*, a former Norddeutscher–Lloyd liner. This time von Müller was bound for Pagan in the Marianas Islands, and a rendezvous with von Spee.

It took six days to reach Pagan, the small force periodically separating and recombining to avoid arousing suspicion and to allow each ship to proceed at her best speed. *Emden* took no prizes, although the horizon was blighted by a seemingly endless procession of Japanese ships. Technically, they were forbidden under international law from reporting the presence of a belligerent warship if they wished to retain their neutral status, but evidence seems to suggest that at least one did so: Japan, after all, had been Britain's ally since 1901. By the end of the month it would all be academic anyway. Japan delivered an ultimatum to Germany on 14 August, and by the 23rd she had declared war. The journey was further enlivened by gunnery practice and lectures by von Mücke, who had decided to counter the inevitable shipboard rumours by updating the crew about the European war.

On 12 August *Emden* and *Prinz Eitel Friedrich* arrived at Pagan, where they found von Spee's armoured cruisers, the light cruiser *Nürnberg* and eight large merchant ships and naval auxiliaries. *Markomannia* arrived the following morning to complete the picture. Von Müller was summoned to a conference aboard *Scharnhorst*, von Spee's flagship, leaving his men to heave coal in the sweltering heat.

Von Spee had concentrated his force, but in the face of overwhelming enemy superiority his options were limited. Remaining in Asian waters was ruled out by the likely intervention of the Japanese, and moving south to Australia was precluded by the presence of the powerful battlecruiser *Australia* and her supporting light cruisers, which were more than a match for his force. Heading west to raid commerce in the Indian Ocean was attractive, but operating the *Kreuzergeschwader* in the British Empire's back yard was impractical, owing to the impossibility of obtaining the enormous quantities of coal required by the big armoured cruisers. Moreover, at heart von Spee seems to have found the possibility of a naval engagement more appealing than splitting up his force to stalk merchant ships and live like tramps from captured colliers. He decided to keep his force together and head east to South America, where a remote coastline and sympathetic neutrals might make supplying his ships easier. Always at the back of his mind was the hope of finding and defeating a small enemy force, or of getting home via Cape Horn and the Atlantic.[12]

Von Spee typically asked his officers for their opinion. Von Müller's response was forthright, asking 'would it not be right at least to send one light cruiser ... to the Indian Ocean, where conditions for cruiser warfare would be particularly beneficial?'.[13] Von Spee thought it over, and by late afternoon he had assented, privately, allocating von Müller *Markomannia* to act as her tender and collier. The *Kreuzergeschwader* cleared Pagan at 17:30, and at 20:00 *Emden*'s crew were delighted to see the flagship signal '*Emden* detached. Good luck!' Von Müller replied, 'Success to the squadron, and bon voyage', as the helm went over and the light cruiser heeled to starboard, her foaming wake streaming out behind her as she altered course to the south-west.

At this point the overstretched British had absolutely no idea where *Emden* had gone after she left Tsingtao; in the confusion and excitement it was easy for one ship to slip through the net. As von Müller headed west, his enemies assumed he was with von Spee. 'The surprise was complete,' the British official historian conceded. 'We had not a single cruiser in the Bay [of Bengal.] So complete was the sense of security ... that masters [of merchant ships], in spite of Admiralty instructions, were in this section keeping to the usual track and steaming with undimmed lights ... the *Emden* had an easy task.'[14] Churchill's commitment to cover and bring to action every German cruiser could not be met. After the war he recognised the error, writing that 'we ought to have had more fast cruisers in foreign waters'.[15]

Von Müller had a free shot at British trade in the Indian Ocean. By early September he had brought his ship undetected into the Bay of Bengal, provisioning from the Norddeutscher–Lloyd liner *Prinzess Alice* at the German outpost of Angaur and making several illicit rendezvous with colliers in the Dutch East Indies (modern Indonesia) on the way. Faint wireless signals indicated that the nearest British warships were far away. The only warship *Emden* encountered was friendly: the superannuated German colonial gunboat *Geier*, on 21 August.[16] By the time *Emden* arrived in what was to be her hunting ground, her crew had enjoyed nearly three weeks of non-stop training and the ship was sporting a fourth funnel made of canvas, intended to help her resemble the British light cruiser *Yarmouth*. *Emden* was now a pirate. 'Our once-elegant cruiser bore little resemblance to her pre-war nickname, "Swan of the East". Continual coaling had dented and ripped our flanks, while the paint was too scratched and blackened to remain swan-white ... seawater rusted the exposed metalwork.'[17]

Her first interception came on 9 September in the dead of night on the main Calcutta–Colombo trade route, but the vessel turned out to be neutral: the Greek steamer *Pontoporos*. By way of consolation, she was carrying 6,500 tons of British government coal. This was legitimate 'contraband', and the apparently practical Captain Polemis agreed to change employers; *Pontoporos* was now serving the Imperial German Navy.

It was not long before von Müller was rewarded for his patience. He had placed *Emden* squarely on the intersection of some of the world's busiest shipping lanes and at 08:00 the following morning the first legitimate target hove into view. The British transport *Indus* was making her way to Bombay to pick up troops for the European war, her decks fitted with specially designed stalls for artillery horses. Her assignment made the success even sweeter for the *Emden*'s crew; not just a British ship, but one which was intended to make a very direct contribution to the war against Germany. As a bonus, the troopship was packed with useful supplies, and *Emden*'s boats plied backwards and forwards between the two ships for hours, until the cruiser's upper deck resembled a country market: 'There were towels, soap, linen, tinned foods, fresh meat, live hens and ducks, drinks, nautical instruments, charts, pencils and some very welcome oilskins.'[18] Finally, her crew transferred to *Markomannia* and the hapless *Indus* was ready for sinking. A scuttling party opened the sea cocks and the troopship began to settle, helped on her way by a few carefully placed shells. An hour later she expired spectacularly, a disturbing sight for any sailor, even those responsible for her end: 'All at once *Indus* rushed gurgling into the depths. The spectacle was eerie. Escaping air made a loud bang, throwing up masses of debris, while the masts sprang several metres out of the water before splashing back audibly.'[19] *Emden* had made her first kill.

Now the floodgates opened. Between 10 and 18 September the cruiser intercepted another nine ships. Some were neutrals and released, but five went to the bottom. First to go was another troop transport, the *Lovat*, dispatched on 11 September after once again being first stripped of anything useful, including recent copies of Indian newspapers with their vital intelligence. Useful information was also gleaned from the indiscreet chatter of the captive crews, who had little to do aboard *Markomannia* apart from gossip. It is, however, hard to give any credence to the almost pathologically anglophobic von Mücke's assessment that the prisoners 'had an eye open to business' and deliberately revealed the courses and destinations of other British ships![20] Unlike *Indus*, *Lovat* was actually carrying 380 horses, which all drowned, apart from a particularly fine racehorse which the sentimental von Mücke 'spared the agony of death by drowning' with a bullet through the head.[21]

On 12 September SS *Kabinga* fell foul of the 'Swan of the East', almost running into her in the darkness before being stopped by a blast from *Emden*'s siren. However, *Kabinga* was spared, thanks to von Müller's strict observance of international law; although she was British, her cargo was largely American-owned. Instead, von Müller turned her into *Emden*'s *'lumpensammler'*, or rubbish dump, for captured crews. Once full, she would be sent into a neutral port. The work of transferring the prisoners was left until the following morning, by which time another victim had come by, the collier *Killin*. As the sun rose over the Indian Ocean the transfer work began, and by 10:00 *Killin* was on her way to the seabed and *Kabinga* was packed with disgruntled merchant seamen.

The next day, 13 September, could have been a red letter day for *Emden*, but of the three ships intercepted, two were neutrals. After intercepting the big British steamer *Diplomat* in a rain squall and poor visibility, and swiftly disposing of her by blowing out her bottom with explosive charges, von Müller came upon the Italian vessel *Loredano*. Franz Joseph and *Oberleutnant zur See* Ernst von Levetzow tried to persuade her captain to take the 200 prisoners incarcerated in the *Kabinga*, so that von Müller could sink the latter while still ensuring the prisoners were safely off his hands, but the Italian skipper was uncooperative, even when offered hard cash. Negotiations dragged on until dusk, when von Müller finally gave up, recalling his boarding party and sending the Italian ship on its way. A few hours later *Emden* encountered another Italian steamer in the darkness, *Dandalo*, whose captain, bizarrely, proved to be the brother of *Loredano*'s skipper. Now observed by two neutrals, von Müller decided to move on, and altered course for the Madras–Calcutta shipping lane, where he sank Captain W.H. Ross's four-year-old collier *Trabboch* on 14 September. Afterwards he finally sent away *Kabinga*, by now bursting at the seams with nearly 400 prisoners who apparently gave *Emden* three cheers as they left.

Perhaps their gratitude merely reflected simple relief, but there is no doubt that von Müller's strict observance of the rules appealed to the British sense of fair play. Arthur Bray was a deck officer aboard *Emden*'s next victim, the steamer *Clan Matheson*, when she was intercepted later on 14 September. His story, recounted in a letter to his mother, is perhaps a reasonable illustration of the merchant sailor's perspective on what might be termed the '*Emden* experience' – the largely untold other side of the raider's tale. On watch in the dead of night, Bray was startled by 'two loud reports' astern and a curt morse signal 'stop immediately and do as you are told'. The young midshipman on the bridge could not read this signal, and, in an interesting demonstration of the standard of visual signalling on board some merchant vessels, neither could the captain, who according to Bray, did not 'know one morse letter from another'. *Clan Matheson* only stopped when a doubtless irritated von Müller instructed his gunners to fire a couple of live rounds into the sea close alongside her. These were undoubtedly warning shots, rather than an illustration of *Emden*'s 'rotten marksmanship', which was young Arthur Bray's interpretation![22]

Arthur Bray continued to hammer out his ship's name on the wireless until *Emden* ordered him to stop. Everyone aboard the British ship still believed that the abruptly signalling warship was friendly; it was pitch black, and the Bay of Bengal was after all a British lake. They were rudely disabused of this notion when Lauterbach's boarding party of twenty sailors and three officers climbed up the side. Spotting the gothic script on their cap ribbons, Bray called a warning to his captain: 'All he said was "My God!"' Lauterbach soon discovered that *Clan Matheson*'s valuable cargo, which contained everything from motor cars and railway locomotives to typewriters, was British-owned, Calcutta-bound and fair game. Arthur Bray and his colleagues were tersely instructed to collect their valuables and 'clear out'. Within forty-five minutes they had transferred across to *Markomannia* and *Clan Matheson* was on her way down.

Arthur Bray spent four days aboard *Markomannia*, and went as far as to say that he had 'a jolly fine time' on the collier, writing that 'they did all they could to make our enforced stay with them pleasant and turned out of their rooms to give us accommodation'. Thus was *Emden*'s reputation for fair play and 'sportsmanship' born and enhanced, prompting the *London Daily Chronicle* to muse sentimentally that 'we admire the sportsmanship of their exploits, as much as we heartily wish that the ship may soon be taken'.[23]

Shortly after *Clan Matheson* went down, von Müller's wireless operators intercepted a signal from the Calcutta lightship, broadcasting *Emden*'s presence in the Bay of Bengal to the world. The source of the information was the truculent captain of the Italian freighter *Loredano*. Italy was still technically Germany's ally, albeit one which had failed to join the war, and there was understandable resentment aboard *Emden*, Franz Joseph writing later of 'a breach of faith and rank betrayal'.[24] In fact, the Italian's supposed treachery hardly mattered, as a few hours later *Kabinga* made a similar broadcast once safely clear of the danger area. *Emden*'s secret was out: 'the whole field was astir, and the hunt was up.'[25] At Singapore Admiral Jerram ordered the armoured cruiser *Hampshire*, the light cruiser *Yarmouth*, the armed merchant cruiser *Empress of Japan* and the Japanese cruiser *Chikuma* to fan out across the Bay of Bengal in hot pursuit.

Von Müller had already decided to move on after coaling from the Greek collier *Pontoporos*. Coal was usually transferred in harbour, and the ships of the time were not really designed to carry out the procedure in open water. The work was filthy and occasionally dangerous: 'The great heat made the work arduous, but slack and dust from the poor-quality coal was all but unbearable ... we could hardly blame the men for the strings of oaths; indeed we were in full empathy with the cursing.'[26] Such was the lot of a twentieth-century pirate. But by 22:00 on 16 September the work was complete. *Emden* first made for the Burmese port of Rangoon, on the eastern side of the Bay of Bengal, but encountered no ships other than the Norwegian *Dovre*, which received Arthur Bray and the rest of the crew of the *Clan Matheson*. The Norwegians were well disposed towards Germany, agreeing to delay for as long as possible before landing the prisoners, but it was inevitable that *Emden*'s cover would be blown again. Von Müller turned about, and raced back westwards. He had decided to give the British lion's tail one last but thorough tweak before quitting the Bay for good. His plan was to bombard Madras (modern Chennai), over 1,000 miles away on India's east coast.

Topping up with coal on the way, and changing course to avoid the some-times alarmingly close wireless transmissions from enemy warships, most notably the call sign 'QMD' of the British armoured cruiser *Hampshire*, von Müller arrived off Madras on Tuesday, 22 September. The capital of the Madras Presidency was a swarming metropolis of over 500,000 people, as well as a vital communications centre with rail links across the Indian sub-continent and an important commercial port with dockyard facilities for the Royal Navy. Von Müller had chosen his target well for what he described as 'a demonstration to arouse interest among the Indian population, to disturb English commerce [and] to diminish English prestige'.[27] Throughout the day *Emden*'s crew prepared for battle, exercising the guns, stowing away captured stores and bringing up ready use ammunition. Afterwards the men bathed and changed into clean clothes as a precaution against infected wounds. The colliers *Markomannia* and *Pontoporos* were detached with instructions to rendezvous after the raid. Finally the ship's officers were called together for one last briefing before, as night fell, *Emden* made for the hostile shore. As they approached Madras at 20:00 the Germans were startled to see that the city was 'a sea of light'; clearly the war still seemed a long way from colonial India.[28] Von Müller intended to shake the city out of its cosy com-placency by shelling the storage tanks of the Burma Oil Company, south of the city. The huge tanks were painted bright white, with a red stripe pro-viding a convenient aiming mark.

At 21:00 *Emden* went to action stations and increased speed, hurtling into the harbour at 17 knots, steering straight for the tanks. By 21:45 she was about 2 miles offshore. Von Müller rang down 'all stop' to the engine room, and *Emden* glided silently to a halt, turning to port as she did so to bring all her guns to bear on the target. After a few heart-stopping seconds of silence, von Müller gave the order: 'Switch on for'ard searchlight. Open fire!'[29]

As *Emden* opened fire, the ship moved off again, keeping the target locked in her searchlight beams as she headed steadily south along the coast, firing some 250 rounds. The first salvo overshot the target, one shell exploding in the bedroom of the installation's manager, wrecking his bungalow although miraculously failing to injure either him or his wife and children. As the shocked family picked themselves from the wreckage of their home, the next salvo plunged down on target, right into the tanks: 'A quick upleaping of tongues of bluish-yellow flame, streams of liquid fire pouring out through the holes made by our shots, an enormous black cloud of dense smoke ... we had sent several millions' worth of the enemy's property up into the air.'[30]

As the tanks burned, the bombardment continued. Although most shells fell on the target area, overshoots continued to drop in the town. For all von Müller's undoubted efforts to avoid what modern commentators term 'collateral damage', it was perhaps inevitable during a rapid night bombardment in an age of relatively primitive fire control; 'smart weapons' were a long way off in 1914. One shell crashed into the elaborate facade of the National Bank of India, spraying steel fragments across the beach road, the offices of the *Madras Mail*, and the home of Mr and Mrs O. Wynne Cole, 'who had a very alarming experience when fragments spattered up against the upper storey of their premises, and even entered the drawing room'.[31] More fell around the lighthouse, damaging several bungalows.

As *Emden* moved down the coast, her guns flashing regularly, salvoes fell in the harbour, damaging staff quarters, workshops and the Sailing Club. Two shells hit the British India Steam Navigation Company ship *Chupra*, bursting among a group of young cadets. Several were wounded and one, 17-year-old Joseph Fletcher, received fourteen injuries and died shortly afterwards. He still lies in Madras, in a small Commonwealth War Graves Commission cemetery. Remarkably, he was the only merchant mariner to die as a result of *Emden*'s activities.

Three Indian policemen and a night watchman at the oil tanks were also killed, one unfortunate man being dismembered by a shell which apparently passed through a barrel of tar before striking him.[32] Twelve people were injured. The casualty rate was strikingly low, considering the number of shells fired and the rather counterintuitive response by the inhabitants of Madras, who, instead of looking for shelter, apparently saw the whole affair as some sort of entertainment laid on for their benefit, 'hurrying down to the beach in every possible way that they could – in motor cars, carriages, motor cycles, bikes, on foot, etc. For a couple of hours afterwards crowds of excited people were busy hurrying to and fro.'[33]

The entire operation took just ten minutes, and was almost unopposed, the antiquated muzzle-loading howitzers at Fort St George only firing nine shells before von Müller snapped off his searchlights and left, steaming with running lights showing on a northerly course to deceive the British before darkening ship entirely and altering course to the south. *Emden* left the Bay of Bengal in turmoil, with merchant shipping confined to port and press and public baying for action. At the Admiralty Churchill was forced to respond, ordering a concentration of ten British and Allied warships in the Indian Ocean. 'It is no use stirring about the oceans with two or three ships,' he wrote on 1 October, 'when we have got Cruiser sweeps of eight or ten vessels ten or fifteen miles apart there will be some good prospect of utilising information as to the whereabouts of the *Emden* in such a way as to bring her to action.'[34] For the British, *Emden* was becoming a serious threat, not just because of the ships she sank, but because of the millions of pounds' worth of cargoes she delayed, the warships she caused to be diverted from other operations, and the damage she did to British prestige in India. The raid also terrified the local moneylenders, who took their business inland and brought commerce to a standstill for months; even today the word '*emden*' apparently remains a Tamil slang term for 'streetwise'.[35] Truly, the '*Emden* effect', as one naval officer wrote, 'could by no means be measured by an armchair calculation of the tonnage sunk'.[36]

Leaving chaos behind him and a furious First Lord demanding solutions, von Müller headed south, linking up with *Markomannia* the following day. A two-day patrol, perilously close to the coast of Ceylon (modern Sri Lanka), yielded two near-misses with neutral Dutch and Norwegian steamers and a further three prizes, the last of which, Captain J.W. Steel's freighter *Gryfevale*, was retained for use as *Emden*'s next 'rubbish dump', under the command of Julius Lauterbach. With his new acquisition and the faithful *Markomannia* in company, von Müller turned west, to Minicoy Island in the Maldives.

Emden took three prizes in swift succession on 27 September, the first of which was the Admiralty collier *Buresk*, carrying a cargo more precious to the lonely raider than gold or jewels: 6,600 tons of Cardiff coal. 'Great was the joy aboard the *Emden*. At last we had some decent coal and better than Welsh we could not do. Most pleased of all was *Marine Oberingenieur* Ellerbroek, who hugged me enthusiastically,' wrote Franz Joseph, who had prophesied the capture of a collier some days before.[37]

Buresk was immediately taken over as an auxiliary, under the command of *Kapitänleutnant* Klopper, a reservist who had joined *Emden* from the liner *Prinzess Alice* when the two ships met briefly at Angaur. The collier's Arab crew were retained, as were, strangely, four Britons and the Norwegian ship's cook, all of whom asked to remain aboard, despite the fact that if they transferred to *Gryfevale* they would be free in a few days. Sunday service followed the capture of *Buresk*, after which came two more captures: the steamers *Ribera* and *Foyle*, both of which were swiftly sunk. *Gryfevale*, by now packed with three ships' companies as well as her own, was sent into Colombo at noon, marking the end of a good day's work.

Aware that he would now have stirred up another hornets' nest, von Müller left Minicoy on 28 September, bound for Diego Garcia in the remote Chagos Islands. On the way he took the last coal from *Markomannia*, which left to rendezvous with *Pontoporos*. 'It was hard to part from our faithful companion ... *Markomannia* had shared *Emden*'s joys and sorrows for more than two months. She had been faithful and diligent. Would we ever meet again?'[38]

Von Müller took almost two weeks to nurse his battered ship down to Diego Garcia. *Emden* had been at sea for nearly two months, and had steamed more than 16,000 miles. Her boilers and engines desperately needed overhauling, and her vulnerable condensers were encrusted with salt and needed to be stripped and cleaned. Repeated coaling at sea had left her sides and upperworks dented, rusty and in urgent need of repainting, not just for aesthetic reasons but to maintain the ship's structural integrity. Almost all of the linoleum deck covering had worn away, and her guardrails had been bent and broken by the unexpected pressure of hundreds of tons of coal stored on deck as a supplement to the ship's bunkers. Below the waterline the cruiser's bottom was encrusted with weed and shellfish, further reducing her speed. Sophisticated steam warships required extensive periods in dock, especially light cruisers, which were designed for speed above all else. *Emden* had no dockyard and the work had to be carried out at sea, hence von Müller's slow passage south, stopping when necessary, periodically heeling his ship over so her bottom could be scraped, or taking boilers out of service to replace key components. At the same time the men cleaned and serviced the ship's guns and her arsenal of small arms, and every sailor was given gunnery training. By the time she reached Diego Garcia, *Emden* was ready for action again, although her appearance still left much to be desired.

Diego Garcia was a surreal experience for von Müller and his men. In an age of instant communication, it is almost inconceivable to imagine that, two months into the 'war to end all wars', the remote British outpost was unaware that it had even begun. Diego Garcia had no cable link and was visited by a supply ship only once every three months, the last having left in July.

Consequently the German cruiser was greeted like a long-lost relative by the manager of the local palm oil plantation, a Mr Spender, who came out in a boat 'with his face beaming with the pleasure of seeing someone from the outside world ... bringing with him gifts of fresh eggs, vegetables, etc. He gave eager expression to the delight it afforded him to have the opportunity, after many years, once again to greet some of his German cousins, so dear to his heart.'[39]

The 'cousins' saw no reason to disillusion the locals, spending a pleasant two days plying them with captured whiskey while coaling from *Buresk*. Questions about *Emden*'s dishevelled appearance were airily waved away with talk of terrible storms and 'international fleet manoeuvres', and when *Emden*'s engineers repaired the plantation manager's motorboat, they were rewarded with a live pig, piles of fresh fruit and a boat full of fish. When the cruiser finally left, she had made a friend for life. A few days later *Hampshire* arrived, in company with the AMC *Empress of Asia*. One of the latter's hastily seconded gunners, Edgar Mole of the Royal Garrison Artillery, tried to enlighten the hapless Spender and his staff about the war, 'but they only laughed at us when we told them'.[40]

It is not difficult to imagine the frustration of those hunting *Emden*: days of chasing phantom contacts and nights of near-collisions with ships that inevitably turned out to be harmless. After leaving Diego Garcia *Empress of Asia* spent an hour pursuing a mystery light in the dark: 'we chased her for an hour and lost her in the fog. There was plenty of wind up and a medal staring us in the face but "ND" [no dice].' Later, the AMC came close to being sunk by the Russian cruiser *Askold* after another night-time encounter, rendered even more dangerous by the language barrier.[41]

After a leisurely nine-day cruise, and two days of fishing and hospitality at Diego Garcia, *Emden* returned to the war on 10 October, heading back to Minicoy Island, where between 15 and 19 October she intercepted what Franz Joseph called 'an embarrassment of ships'.[42] The first, *Clan Grant*, was so full of urgently needed supplies that, after catching her at nearly midnight on the 15th, von Müller had her steam in company for days while boarding parties emptied her of everything from cigarettes and live cattle to furnace oil and fire bricks. While this work progressed, *Emden* caught perhaps the oddest of her victims, the 473-ton dredger *Ponrabbel*, on her way to Tasmania. She was the second such ship to be sent out, the first having foundered, and Captain Edwin Gore and his crew had sensibly insisted on payment in advance. They shed no tears for their uncomfortable and chronically unseaworthy charge. When *Emden*'s boarding party climbed over the side, *Ponrabbel*'s crew were apparently lined up by the rail, bags packed and broad grins on every face.

With *Clan Grant* stripped of anything useful, the two ships were sunk and their crews transferred to the captured collier *Buresk*. A few hours later *Emden* sighted lights on the port bow, and caught the 4,806-ton steamer *Benmohr*, which was boarded and despatched with almost unseemly haste. Over the next few days the prizes arrived in swift succession. A night-time encounter with the neutral Spanish steamer *Fernando Po* was followed the next day by what was possibly *Emden*'s most important catch: the brand-new, 7,562-ton cargo-liner *Troilus*, packed with valuable copper, tin and rubber, as well as several passengers, one of whom startled the normally bombastic Lauterbach into silence with a breezy greeting as she climbed over the rail. The lady concerned had been a passenger in Lauterbach's previous command, *Staatsekretär Kraetke*, and her tale provided an interesting illustration of the effect *Emden* was having on British trade:

> First of all, while on her way from Hong Kong to Europe, the ship on which she was travelling had turned back while still in the Yellow Sea upon learning that the *Emden* was near ... then she had managed to get as near as Singapore, from whence she had started out afresh, and again she had the experience of having her ship called back ... because it was reported that the *Emden* was in the neighbourhood. After a few more weeks of waiting ... she had met the *Emden* after all![43]

Taking *Troilus* in company until there was time to take off her passengers and strip her of supplies, *Emden* continued marauding. In the evening she took the freighter *St Egbert*, another British ship carrying a neutral cargo, ideally qualified to become a new 'rubbish dump'. Minutes later she overran the Admiralty collier *Exford*, whose valuable cargo, with that of *Buresk*, would allow *Emden* to continue her depredations for months. For the rest of the night *Emden* steamed in company with an unmanageable convoy of four captured merchantmen with wildly varying speeds and handling characteristics. 'It was', wrote Franz Joseph with typical understatement, 'a difficult night.'[44]

At 07:00 the following morning daylight gave von Müller an opportunity to sort out the shambles, transferring the prisoners to *St Egbert*, and sending boarding parties to strip *Troilus*. 'A fully laden rowboat was a comical sight. There were whole hams, sausages; tinned goods of every kind; sacks of table linen; whole baskets filled with plates, cups, teapots and coffee jugs, saucepans and frying pans, knives, forks and spoons. It was as though we were at a giant fair.'[45]

In the midst of the confusion *Emden* darted off to take the steamer *Chilkana* and relieve her of her brand-new wireless set, which was installed in the captured collier *Exford*. *Chilkana* and *Troilus* were sunk by gunfire, and *St Egbert* sent away. By now von Müller had made up his mind to raid Penang.

For the next few days *Emden* made her way carefully eastwards, avoiding shipping lanes and narrowly missing Captain Grant's *Hampshire* in foul weather on 20 October. At the Nicobar Islands von Müller coaled and sent away the captured colliers *Exford* and *Buresk*, with instructions to rendezvous west of Sumatra in a few days' time.

Exford, commanded by Julius Lauterbach, never found *Emden* again and was captured by the British AMC *Empress of Japan* on 11 November. Lauterbach later escaped from imprisonment in Singapore and returned to Germany.

At 04:30 on 28 October *Emden* began her assault on Penang. As she finally shook off the persistent French TBD *Fronde* six hours later, nobody aboard could imagine that she had almost reached the end of her career. Her nemesis was currently taking on coal and stores in the city whose name she bore, 5,000 miles away on Australia's west coast. Captain John Glossop's light cruiser *Sydney* was one of the newest ships in the Royal Australian Navy, a service that had only existed since 1911. The presence of *Emden* and her half-sister *Königsberg* in the Indian Ocean, and von Spee's *Kreuzergeschwader* in the Pacific, had forced Britain and her allies to radically change their strategy. Safety could no longer be taken for granted while the initiative lay with the pirates, as Churchill later wrote: 'The superior strength of the Allies was overwhelming ... [but the enemy] ... had only to hide and strike ... We could not possibly be strong enough every day everywhere to meet him.'[46]

On 24 October Churchill made a public statement spelling out the situation with cold logic: the German cruisers were few in number, they would eventually be caught and the risk of being sunk by them was small. 'Out of 4,000 British ships engaged in foreign trade', he said, 'only thirty-nine have been sunk by the enemy, or just under one per cent in all.'[47] This was absolutely correct. But just like those who fear air crashes or health scares today, nobody wanted to be part of that percentage, however derisory, and insurers did not wish to pay for their clients' unfortunate defiance of the odds. Too many ships remained in port.

Those that had to sail were put into convoys escorted by warships; this was a solution, but it was one which prevented yet more warships from taking an active part in the hunt. *Sydney* was preparing to escort a convoy carrying the most valuable cargo of all: nearly 20,000 Australian and New Zealand troops on their way to Europe to help defend the mother country. One was Hubert Billings of the Australian Engineers:

> The convoy assembled at Albany, West Australia, from where we sailed on 1st November. That was a sight I can still see quite clearly in my mind and what a sight it was! Forty troop ships, four warships, which

seemed to cover the sea to the horizon in every direction. All steaming along in three lines very slowly at ten to twelve knots per hour.[48]

As well as *Sydney*, the vulnerable troopships were escorted by her sister ship *Melbourne*, the armoured cruiser *Minotaur* and the Japanese battlecruiser *Ibuki*. *Minotaur*'s Captain Edward Kiddle was senior officer of the escort when what the British Official History calls 'the Great Convoy' left Albany, but a week later Admiral Jerram detached his ship to South Africa, where a Boer rising had broken out. This left Captain Mortimer Silver of HMAS *Melbourne* in command, as the transports made their way north into the Indian Ocean.

On 30 October *Emden* took her last prize, the British *Newburn*, but von Müller, in a typically humane gesture, spared the ten-year-old steamer and sent her into the Malayan port of Kota Raja with the French prisoners from *Mousquet*. The last French sailor left *Emden* later that morning; desperately wounded, he had died under treatment and was buried at sea with full military honours.

His location once more compromised, von Müller steamed south along the coast of Sumatra, meeting *Buresk* en route. By now, it must have seemed to those aboard that, like the mythical 'Flying Dutchman', *Emden* was doomed to roam the seas until Judgement Day. What they could not know was that Judgement Day was close at hand. On 1 November the cruiser marked the three-month anniversary of her cruise. She had steamed for 30,000 miles, in the course of which her engines had made 10 million revolutions and she had consumed 6,000 tons of coal. Her continued mechanical efficiency was a tribute to the skill and dedication of her engineering team.[49] But von Müller had not finished yet. He had already decided on his ship's next target, a vital cable relay station on Direction Island in the Cocos group, where three important submarine cables linking Australia to the rest of the British Empire met.

At 06:00 on 9 November *Emden* approached Direction Island, her false funnel in place and no colours flying. As her anchor splashed into the water, three boats made for the shore carrying a landing party commanded by *Kapitänleutnant* von Mücke. The locals were not fooled. Almost immediately Superintendent Dover Farrant of the Eastern Telegraph Company sent his wireless operator running to his equipment, where he started tapping out a warning that there was a strange ship in harbour. Von Mücke, resplendent in a pith helmet, ended the defiant broadcast by bursting into the wireless office with his pistol levelled, but the damage had been done.[50] Admiral Jerram had already identified the relay station as a possible target for *Emden* and, although he could not spare ships to guard it, his captains had been instructed to respond to any signal from the Cocos with alacrity. Far out in the Indian

Ocean, the big cruiser *Hampshire* began an outlandish race with the AMCs *Empress of Asia* and *Empress of Russia*, each captain desperate to be in at the kill.[51] Like most of Jerram's ships, they were too far away to catch *Emden* before she completed her work and slipped away again.

But unknown to von Müller, the ANZAC troop convoy was just 55 miles north of Direction Island, bound for Colombo. Captain Silver reluctantly realised that his own duty was to remain with the convoy, and that he needed to retain his most powerful ship, the Japanese *Ibuki*, much to the frustration of that ship's commanding officer. Instead, he despatched *Sydney* to intercept the 'strange ship', which he was convinced was *Emden*. Glossop peeled away from the convoy, heading south. Aboard the troopship *Karoo*, Hubert Billings watched apprehensively as the cruiser steamed away, belching black smoke as Glossop squeezed every ounce of power from his engines. As the other escorting warships shuffled into new positions, Billings and his mates unobtrusively slipped inside *Karoo*'s wireless room, where they crowded around the set.[52] *Sydney* should have comfortably outmatched *Emden*: she was newer, faster, armoured and better armed, boasting 6-inch guns to *Emden*'s 4.1s. But all von Müller needed was luck, and he seemed to possess that in spades.

At 09:15 Glossop's look-outs sighted Direction Island – and *Emden*. Von Müller had at first believed the approaching smoke cloud to be his collier, *Buresk*, but as the ship drew near she took on the unmistakable shape of a British cruiser. Abandoning his landing party ashore, he cleared for action and raised steam. At 09:30 the 'Swan of the East' raised anchor for the last time and headed towards her enemy.

Glossop was startled to observe that, although *Emden*'s guns were smaller, their range and elevation were superior, and *Emden* opened fire first, at a range of over 9,000 metres. It seemed that the veteran German crew had the measure of his men. 'Her first shots ... were all within 200 yards of the ship ... she began to fire very rapidly in salvoes, the rate of fire being as high as ten rounds per gun per minute, and very accurate ... a perfect hail of shots were falling all around the ship.'[53]

Two shells ploughed into the Australian cruiser's after control platform, wounding those inside, and another hit the range-finder above the bridge, killing the operator and wrecking the instruments. More shells burst on the open deck between two 6-inch mounts, killing or wounding most of the gun crews and setting light to the ready use cordite supply; a wounded gunner threw the flaming mass overboard and saved his ship from disaster. Below decks, 24-year-old Surgeon-Lieutenant Leonard Darby began his grim work as 'a constant stream' of wounded came below: a man so badly wounded in the chest that his still-beating heart could be clearly seen; another, shot through the abdomen, with his intestines hanging from the ghastly wound; men without limbs or eyes; men with multiple splinter wounds or terrible burns. After a few minutes Darby's sick berth attendant fainted; it was, after all, the first time any of this crew had seen action. Isolated from the outside world, Darby and his men wondered whether the fight was going against them, as their ship heeled sickeningly and the guns crashed.[54]

Battered and bruised, *Sydney*'s first broadsides were indeed ineffective and wayward; at his action station in the torpedo flat deep inside *Emden*, well below the waterline, Franz Joseph 'judged the British ship to be shooting badly.'[55] Confidence in the 'Swan of the East' remained high. Could von Müller pull off another victory against the odds?

The answer was no. After a shaky start, *Sydney*'s superior speed, man-oeuvrability and, above all, firepower began to tell. *Emden* was first hit at 10:00, and then a storm of 6-inch projectiles smashed into the German ship, most of them appallingly destructive lyddite rounds. Two burst beneath the pair of guns on her quarterdeck, wrecking them and rippling the steel deck into nightmarish waves. Another burst through the ship's side and exploded behind one of her lower-deck guns, smashing the unfortunate crew into the gun shield where 'they were all killed and horribly mangled'.[56] *Emden*'s forward funnel pitched overboard, and an uncontrollable fire started on the quarterdeck. Glossop later described how over the next hour the German cruiser was pounded into scrap metal: 'The next thing to go was the foremast which was carried away ... by a shell which also wrecked the fore-bridge and the superstructure around it ... the two remaining funnels went before long, and more fires broke out; in fact on one occasion she disappeared in the smoke for about five minutes.'[57]

At 10:45 von Müller realised that all his guns were disabled and almost everyone on the upper deck was dead. The after part of the ship was in flames and a lucky shot had smashed his steering gear forcing him to resort to the emergency helm position aft. *Emden* was losing speed as two boilers had burst, and she was starting to flood below decks. In a desperate attempt to use his last weapon, torpedoes, von Müller turned his disintegrating command towards *Sydney* but could not manoeuvre into a firing position; finally, at 11:00, Franz Joseph reported that a direct hit in the torpedo flat had caused flooding and the space had started to fill with noxious gases. With no options left, von Müller turned the labouring *Emden* towards nearby North Keeling Island: 'I decided to wreck my badly damaged ship ... rather than sacrifice needlessly the lives of those who survived.'[58]

Franz Joseph and his men had to escape from the stinking, waterlogged torpedo flat through a narrow torpedo loading hatch, a terrifying and laborious process, particularly for the wounded. A nightmare journey through the shot-perforated upper decks followed: 'Everywhere there were dead and wounded men – groaning, moaning and plaintively crying for help … wherever I looked I saw nothing but holes in the side, bent metal, burning rubbish and ashes … the worst part … was the stern, where the whole deck and the ship's sides glowed red.'[59]

Emden was now ploughing towards North Keeling Island at 19 knots (35km/h), a remarkable speed considering she had lost all her funnels and two boilers. At 11:15 she ran hard aground on a reef and von Müller ordered the engines stopped, fires drawn and sea cocks opened. *Emden* had fought her last fight. Confident that the cruiser's raiding days were over, Captain Glossop took *Sydney* back out to sea, where another suspicious smoke cloud had been sighted. As the Australian ship pulled away, Seaman Richard Broome watched *Emden* recede into the distance: 'She was a total wreck, on fire from the bridge to the stern, all three funnels, foremast and bridge gone, all her guns silent, her sides perforated with gaping holes, her upper deck a mass of twisted steel and her flag still flying.'[60]

The surviving Germans were left to their own devices. Land was still a tantalising distance away and *Emden*'s boats had been wrecked in the battle. Some tried to swim ashore, intending to rig a line back to the ship, but most drowned or were ripped apart on the jagged coral. Others tried to aid the wounded, using tablecloths instead of bandages, which had run out. Some men destroyed the ship's confidential documents or threw the gun sights over the side. There was no fresh water, and the heat soon became unbearable, particularly for the wounded. Sea birds 'hovered over the helpless men and tried to peck out their eyes', despite the best efforts of the survivors to shoot or bludgeon them.[61]

In the meantime Glossop had overhauled his suspicious smoke cloud, which turned out to be *Buresk*. Klopper managed to scuttle his temporary command before *Sydney* could capture her, and Glossop was perhaps frustrated by the time he returned to North Keeling Island late in the afternoon. According to his own account, the prisoners from *Buresk* advised him that von Müller would never surrender.[62] Whatever his mood, his subsequent actions remain hard to comprehend, even when every effort is made to avoid hindsight or judgement. Seeing *Emden*'s ensign still flying over the wreck, he ordered his gunners to open fire again, after the German ship failed to respond to repeated signals to haul it down. Two more salvoes crashed down on the defenceless *Emden*, causing, by Glossop's own admission, another thirty casualties, before the ensign was finally replaced by a white flag. *Sydney* then made for Direction Island, in an attempt to capture von Mücke's landing party, but delayed to rescue some *Emden* survivors who had been blown overboard during the fighting. This allowed von Mucke's party precious time.

Having smashed the wireless and cut what most accounts confirm were dummy cables, von Mücke commandeered a small sailing schooner, *Ayesha*, and escaped. After many trials and tribulations, most of his party eventually reached Germany, via Turkey.[63] Glossop did not return to the *Emden* wreck at North Keeling until the next day.

Nightfall at North Keeling brought relief from the heat and the birds, but not rest. The exhausted survivors were continually occupied fighting fires and burying the dead who could be reached; Franz Joseph found the pitiful remains of his friend von Levetzow, lying where he had been caught by a flash fire caused by exploding ammunition; only the 'shape of his head' and a solitary star from his rank insignia identified him.[64]

Finally, at 13:00 the next day, *Sydney* reappeared. A despondent von Müller finally conceded that the fight was lost and gave his parole, guaranteeing that his men would not interfere with the Australian warship if Glossop took them off. The painstaking work of transferring the survivors by boat in a heavy swell began. Once aboard, they were treated by *Sydney*'s surgeons, assisted by a civilian surgeon from Direction Island and the only surviving German medic, Johannes Luther. *Emden*'s casualties were truly horrific. No fewer than 128 men died, of 317 aboard. Twenty-four seriously injured sailors were brought aboard *Sydney*, of whom three subsequently died. The rest were mangled shadows of their former selves, the roll call of their wounds another litany of despair: severed or shattered limbs, fractures, sucking chest wounds, burns, splinter damage – and all made worse after lying in the shattered wreckage of their ship in the searing tropical heat for hours. Luther had been unable to offer much more than rudimentary treatment: 'the wounds ... were practically all very septic, with maggots a quarter of an inch in length crawling over them.'[65] The operations did not stop until 12 November.

There is a general misconception that naval battles are somehow 'cleaner' than their equivalent on land, particularly during the First World War. It is easily explained; after most naval actions, the grim evidence of their brutality slips quietly beneath the waves, leaving little or no trace behind. Surgeon Darby's clinical, matter-of-fact analysis of the damage wrought upon the sailors of both sides during the 'Battle of the Cocos', written for the *Naval Review* in 1917, dispels this myth: slaughter at sea was just as bloody as slaughter on land. Nor was this the end of the story. *Sydney* departed for Colombo, with German survivors crammed into every available space; von Müller and his men were eventually taken to Malta, where they spent the rest of the war as prisoners. HMS *Cadmus* was assigned the grim task of clearing the wreck. By the time the old sloop arrived, *Emden*'s dead had lain strewn across her twisted decks for nine days. Bertram Kiel was a member of the party sent across to the shattered cruiser. Instructed to 'bury the dead as reverently as possible', they soon discovered that this was simply impossible:

> We got hold of a bloke's legs and two arms, tried to carry him to the gangway, his legs came out, they'd been there nine days, and you can imagine the fumes that came from that body, we couldn't touch another body none of us ... we was just about done in with the fumes that came out that one body. They was twice the size of an ordinary man, blown out ... all the gases was inside the body.[66]

Emden's dead were eventually slipped over the rail for the blank-eyed Indian Ocean sharks, bringing to a dismal end the meteoric career of the Kaiser's most famous pirate, who sank fifteen ships totalling 66,023 tons. Her captain's humane behaviour in an age of total war had earned him the respect of friend and foe alike. 'It is almost in our heart to regret that the *Emden* has been destroyed,' mused the usually jingoistic *Daily Telegraph*. 'Von Müller has been enterprising, cool and daring in making war on our shipping.' It is not a bad epitaph for the 'Swan of the East'.

Chapter 5

Coronel: to the Bitter End

'I must plough the seas of the world doing as much mischief as I can until my ammunition is exhausted or a foe far superior in power succeeds in catching me.'

Vizeadmiral Maximilian Graf von Spee

When von Spee left the *Emden* to pursue her solo career on 13 August, in a froth of wakes and an idealistic flurry of signal flags, he had already decided to make for the west coast of South America, where enemy warships were few and enemy trade vulnerable. At first the squadron crept cautiously through the friendly Marshall Islands, heading generally eastwards, conserving coal and avoiding contact with anyone who might reveal its location. On 22 August *Nürnberg* was detached to Honolulu, to gather the latest war news.

Von Spee was painfully aware that away to the southwest lurked a powerful Australian squadron formed around the battlecruiser HMAS *Australia*, the one foe he really feared; he wrote to his wife on 18 August that '*Australia* ... by itself is an adversary so much stronger than our squadron that one would be bound to avoid it.'[1] He was right to be apprehensive. *Australia* was a 20,000-ton monster, almost brand-new, armed with eight 12-inch guns and yet capable of speeds that would far outstrip the German armoured cruisers. But what von Spee could not know was that, thanks to scattergun thinking at the Admiralty and the relentless micromanagement of assets that were thousands of miles from home, Rear-Admiral Sir George Patey, Commander-in-Chief of His Majesty's Australian Fleet, had been sent away on a fool's errand. Instead of hunting for the *Kreuzergeschwader*, by far the most significant enemy formation outside British home waters, *Australia* had been sent to capture Germany's vulnerable but arguably strategically insignificant Pacific island colonies. On 30 August *Australia*, accompanied by the light cruiser *Melbourne* and the French cruiser *Montcalm*, put ashore New Zealand troops to seize German Samoa. Two weeks later she landed an Australian force at Rabaul, the capital of German New Guinea and the administrative centre of Germany's island empire. Patey was then ordered back to Sydney. Only late in September, with von Spee already some 5,000 miles away, was he

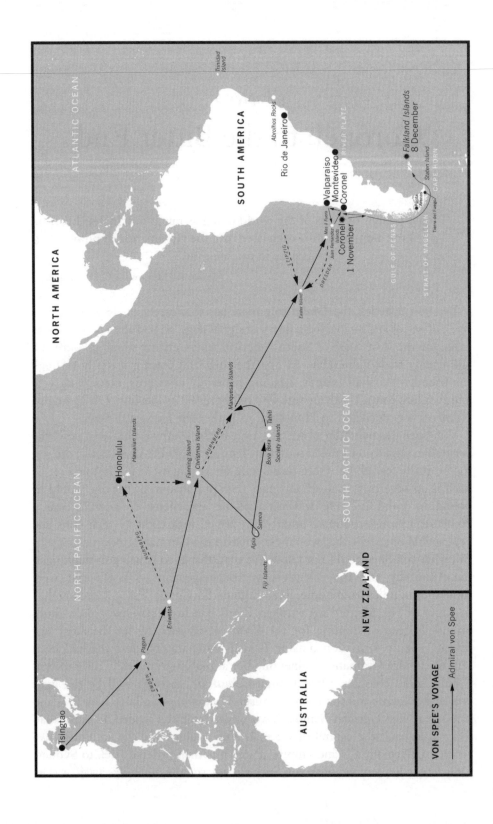

VON SPEE'S VOYAGE

→ Admiral von Spee

finally released to join the search, and by then it was far too late. The Admiralty was not wholly to blame for the poor decision-making which led to the most powerful warship in the south Pacific being used to attack a pair of defenceless and, above all, immobile, islands, rather than to bring the *Kreuzergeschwader* to action. The governments of New Zealand and Australia were equally culpable. They were eager to snap up this low-hanging fruit, and willing to pressurise London to let them use their own forces to do so, including *Australia*, which had been paid for by the Australian government. It was undoubtedly difficult for London to order the two vigorous young Dominions, on the verge of nationhood, to see the bigger picture, and it could be argued that seizing the islands did deprive von Spee of bases; the destruction of the wireless relay station at Yap by HMS *Hampshire* on 12 August was also particularly irritating. But is also hard to escape the impression that a youthful and inexperienced First Lord of the Admiralty, with what hindsight tells us was a deep-rooted preference for offensive action over the patient waiting game, might perhaps have found it an overly easy decision to make. Certainly the professional sailors in *Australia* found it incomprehensible, one observer remarking that 'the comments of the officers ... when they found themselves out of the hunt were pretty terse'.[2]

Political mischief also limited the Japanese contribution. Although the three Japanese dreadnoughts could have made short work of von Spee, their government did not even have to pay lip service to British hegemony, and they had their own agenda: seizing Tsingtao, and German possessions in the Marshall and Caroline Islands. Japanese warships did not join the search for the *Kreuzergeschwader* until October, by which time the Germans were thousands of miles away. The Battle of Coronel was arguably lost in smoke-filled rooms in London and Tokyo.

Churchill subsequently claimed that the Admiralty always predicted von Spee's likely destination.[3] This may well be the case, but does not explain why greater efforts were not made to bring him to action as soon as possible with the strongest available force. With hindsight, it is hard to escape the conclusion that the British response to the problem was incoherent and slipshod, 'governed', as one wartime German commentator noted, 'by no great unity of design ... too much was undertaken simultaneously, instead of concentrating on the one main military object'.[4]

In the meantime von Spee continued to slowly cross the ocean. On 6 September he rendezvoused with *Nürnberg*, which brought British and American newspapers and thirty-seven German-American volunteers who had crept aboard at Honolulu and stowed away until von Schönberg was well out to sea. The mood in the *Kreuzergeschwader* was buoyant. Against the odds, the Germans had evaded interception and were at large in the Pacific. One

sailor recalled how 'we were in the happiest frame of mind', although anxious
to make their mark on the war: 'What . . . are we doing here? The ocean is too
great to meet the enemy here.'[5]

On 6 September von Spee sent *Nürnberg* away again, to destroy the British
cable relay station on Fanning Island (modern Tabuaeran), a vital communications link between Canada and Australia, in retaliation for the destruction
of the Yap transmitter. The small British staff had no idea that German
landing parties were on the island until a grim-faced von Schönberg and
several of his men stepped into the telegraph office, one operator just having
time to tap out a quick message to the next station up the line 'before a
business-like gun pointed in his direction showed him the wisdom of taking
his hands from the ticker'.[6] Faced with a hundred armed German sailors in no
mood for pleasantries, Station Manager Bains and his staff gathered their
possessions and left the building, which the Germans blew up before combing
the island for other installations. They destroyed everything they found,
including the unfortunate Bains's home, 'whilst the little colony of white and
native residents huddled in a corner near the wharf with a guard over them'.[7]
The cable was cut and the end towed out and dropped in deep water. Finally,
von Schönberg's landing parties departed.

Forty-eight hours later, to the relief of Bains and his men, a cruiser flying
the French flag approached Fanning Island. Their relief was short-lived, however, as the ship was *Nürnberg* paying a return visit. A second landing party
marched straight to Bains's wrecked bungalow, where they forced open the
safe and remove the contents. 'We don't like to do this,' an embarrassed
German officer explained, 'but orders must be obeyed. This is the first time
we have been burglars, but you know how it is.' Maintaining a delightfully
stiff upper lip, the unperturbed Bains replied 'Quite so, old chap. No hard
feelings, I assure you.'[8] Von Schönberg then left for the last time, reuniting
with the *Kreuzergeschwader* at uninhabited Christmas Island on 7 September.

Nürnberg brought news of the New Zealand landings at Samoa, and
von Spee decided to make for the colony, hoping to surprise any ships which
might still be there, but when the German ships finally made landfall at Apia,
the capital, on 14 September, they found no enemy warships present, just a
garrison of 800 New Zealand troops. Wisely deciding against wasting time,
ammunition and lives carrying out a landing opposed by trained soldiers, von
Spee put to sea again, his frustrated crews still waiting for the chance to prove
themselves in action: 'We were very much annoyed, as we had done nothing
so far.'[9] As von Spee departed, he carried out a simple manoeuvre to deceive
the watching New Zealanders, first steaming northwest before altering course
to the east once out of sight of land. No one, least of all von Spee himself,

realised that this simple evolution would directly bring about his dramatic victory two months later. Most historians agree that the Admiralty was deceived by this time-honoured *ruse de guerre*; as von Spee was last seen steaming northwest, it was assumed he intended to return to Tsingtao, and there was no need to worry about him for a while.[10] Reassuring signals went out to British and Allied forces around the world, informing them of this appraisal. Among the recipients was the man who had been sent around Cape Horn to bring the *Kreuzergeschwader* to action in South American waters, Rear-Admiral Sir Christopher Cradock.

Kit Cradock was a 52-year-old Yorkshireman who had been at sea since he was 13. The Royal Navy was his life, and in many ways he seemed a typical 'sea dog' in the Elizabethan style, a man whose expressed wish was to die in action or on the hunting field.[11] But his portraits appear to challenge these preconceptions. The most famous photograph of him shows a rather gentle, thoughtful man, with deep laughter lines and a twinkle in his eye. He wrote three books, unusual for a man whose class and profession often despised any outward manifestations of intellectualism, and he was known as a friendly, sociable and popular officer.[12] Among his extensive array of medals was the Prussian Order of the Crown with Swords, presented to him by Kaiser Wilhelm II for bravery under fire during the Boxer Rebellion in 1900. Famously, on the outbreak of war he defaced the ribbon, claiming that 'I couldn't tear it out without ruining all the others ... so I got an ink bottle and made it look as unpleasant as possible.'[13]

Cradock's original 4th Cruiser Squadron had now been supplemented by another five elderly armoured cruisers, one of which, Captain Philip Francklin's *Good Hope*, Cradock took as his flagship on the grounds of a marginal superiority in armament and, above all, speed, after *Karlsruhe*'s escape on 6 August. But his new flagship was hardly a greyhound. Churchill described her as 'a fine old ship', but she had been launched in 1902 and even then had only been capable of some 24 knots.[14] Although armed with two single turret-mounted 9.2-inch guns on her upper deck, her remaining guns were elderly 6-inch weapons mounted in broadside batteries reminiscent of the era of the 'wooden walls', which were set low in the ship, making them hard to fire in heavy seas. Worse, *Good Hope* had been in reserve for years, having narrowly escaped being turned into razor blades in Fisher's purge of older ships, and had only recommissioned at the beginning of the war. Most of her crew were reservists, unused to one another or their ship.

Throughout August and early September Cradock's ships and men had expended time, energy and enthusiasm endlessly sweeping for *Dresden* and *Karlsruhe*, covering thousands of miles from Halifax, Nova Scotia, to the

River Plate. Then, on 3 September, Cradock was ordered to take his flagship further south and form a new command, in anticipation of the two German cruisers rounding Cape Horn into the Pacific. Most of his ships would remain in the north under Stoddart's command.

On 14 September, the day von Spee appeared off Samoa, Cradock received an Admiralty signal warning him that the *Kreuzergeschwader* might be making for South America. His instructions were typically specific, with little room for interpretation. He was to take his flagship and one county class cruiser to Abrolhos Rocks, a remote and secret coaling base off the Brazilian coast, where he would rendezvous with the armoured cruiser *Defence* and the pre-dreadnought battleship *Canopus*, which were being sent out from England. Cradock would also have three AMCs and the light cruiser *Glasgow*.

Glasgow had been the Royal Navy's sole representative in South American waters for nearly two years. Unlike the rest of Cradock's ships, she was fast, modern and well armed with two 6-inch and ten 4-inch guns – more than a match for any German light cruiser. *Glasgow* was blessed with a talented commanding officer, Captain John Luce, and an experienced, well-trained, regular crew, albeit one which had been preparing for home and leave. Maurice Portman, her navigating officer, recorded the sheer misery of patrolling in these waters at the onset of winter, in a ship whose supplies had been run down in preparation for the journey home:

> Admiral Cradock's lot are coming down our way and we push on to the south (Falklands) to see if they have gone that way. It is poisonously cold down here and we have had rain all the way down, but it is nothing to what we are going to get down south ... It will be awful. We have practically no food left ... if we had known we were stopping in commission another six months we should have had plenty of everything.[15]

Once Cradock had concentrated this force, he was to proceed to the Falkland Islands, where he could operate in the Atlantic against *Dresden* and *Karlsruhe*, or in the Pacific against von Spee. His orders concluded with an ambitious exhortation to 'break up the German trade and destroy the German cruisers'.[16] So far so good. Unfortunately, two days later the Admiralty signalled Cradock again, after von Spee's simple but effective deception at Samoa was taken as evidence that the *Kreuzergeschwader* threat had now receded. The new signal was an almost tragically casual instruction to take just *Good Hope* and one county class cruiser to break up German trade on the west coast of South America. The remainder of his force was to remain in the Atlantic, searching for phantom cruisers and watching US ports. Cradock was explicitly encouraged not to worry about concentrating his ships and, crucially, he was not told that the powerful *Defence* would no longer be joining him.[17]

Cradock's county class cruiser was already waiting. On 25 August *Glasgow* had been joined by Captain Frank Brandt's *Monmouth*, another recommissioned reserve fleet ship, most of whose fourteen 6-inch mountings were set so low down on the waterline that if the gun ports were opened in a heavy sea, there was a very real risk of flooding the ship; Fisher had sardonically written that the designer of the 'counties' had forgotten the guns altogether. Like *Good Hope*, *Monmouth* was manned by a hastily assembled, inexperienced crew. Her 43-year-old captain was a torpedo specialist who since 1906 had been mainly occupied in developing the Royal Navy's embryonic submarine force. Between September 1913 and February 1914 he had been on extended leave in Devon. One of *Glasgow*'s officers, on seeing *Monmouth* arrive, could not disguise his disgust: 'she had been practically condemned as unfit for further service, but was hauled off the dockyard wall [and] commissioned with a scratch crew of coastguardsmen and boys ... she is only half-equipped and not in a condition to come six thousand miles from any dockyard.'[18] Basil Cardew was the 19-year-old son of a Newark clergyman who served as Captain Brandt's clerk. In September 1914 he wrote home, describing the 'pretty average hell' of patrolling off South America in an old ship with inadequate ventilation and stores:

I had half an hour to join this ship and I only have one uniform and about two shirts and socks ... with any luck the war might be over soon. I'm afraid we shan't have time to catch the German ships out here ... there are hundreds of islands on the coast where they can hide and even if they stay at sea it is a thousand to one we should not run across them ... the worst of this game is that we darken ship every night, close all scuttles and hatches and of course block out all fresh air ... we are in the most awful fug. Being an old ship there are no ventilators or fans. We are running awfully short of provisions. No butter, very little jam and on corned beef all the time.[19]

Cradock's other only reinforcement was the pre-dreadnought battleship *Canopus*, yet another veteran only saved from the breaker's yard by the war. As with the cruisers, her crew was formed of reservists. She was also mechanically unreliable, and even the most optimistic of observers (including Churchill) were only willing to credit her with 15 knots. The only tactical advantage the ship provided was the firepower of her four 12-inch guns, the heaviest calibre weapons in South American waters, but even this was illusory: *Canopus*'s old guns were outranged by the smaller but more modern weapons in von Spee's armoured cruisers. Churchill believed that *Canopus* constituted 'a citadel around which all our cruisers ... could find absolute security', and repeatedly instructed Cradock to keep her with his force at all times, but the old battleship drastically limited his freedom of manoeuvre.[20] Another two cruisers, *Bristol* and *Carnarvon*, were nominally retained under Cradock's command, but they were in the South Atlantic and played no part in the disaster which followed. *Glasgow* was his only modern, efficient ship.

Cradock's South Atlantic command thus comprised one superannuated battleship and two obsolete cruisers, both manned by inexperienced crews, as well as *Glasgow* and three armed liners. This unlikely blend was perfectly adequate for sweeping the seas clear of German merchant shipping, as his latest instructions dictated. On 18 September Cradock signalled the Admiralty that he was heading for the Pacific as instructed, taking his three cruisers and the AMC *Otranto*. *Canopus* would remain at the Falklands 'to guard trade and colliers'.[21]

Back in the Pacific, von Spee had turned back east as soon as he was out of sight of the New Zealanders on Samoa. On 21 September he coaled at Bora Bora, in French Polynesia, where by accident rather than design his ships were once more mistaken for French. Even after the truth became apparent, 'provisions were readily supplied and paid for'.[22] Relations with the locals were less chummy when the *Kreuzergeschwader* arrived off Papeete, capital of Tahiti and the administrative centre for French Polynesia, at 06:00 on 22 September. According to a crew member from *Scharnhorst*, von Spee once again sent a boat, intending to obtain stores and coal, but this time 'we were ... doomed to disappointment', as the garrison had been warned by Bora Bora.[23] Von Spee's men were greeted by salvoes from a fort and the tiny gunboat *Zélée*. The French also began to burn the town's coal stocks, and block the harbour entrance. The Germans returned fire, sinking *Zélée* and silencing the fort, then wrecking substantial portions of the town and sinking the captured German merchant ship *Walkure*, but the spirited defence proved a point. Von Spee expended some 150 rounds of ammunition and revealed his location for no noticeable gain, beyond inflicting an estimated million francs worth of damage and killing two local inhabitants.[24]

News of the bombardment did not reach London until 30 September, by which time von Spee was coaling at the Marquesa Islands, 850 miles nearer to South America. By 12 October he was at Easter Island, where he met Fritz Lüdecke's elusive *Dresden*. Two days later Johann-Siegfried Haun in *Leipzig* arrived after a frustrating two months evading Allied warships off the US west coast, during which he had taken just two steamers. In his wake waddled three fat colliers from San Francisco, like a row of ducklings. Von Spee had managed to concentrate his maximum force, and his men were spoiling for a fight. 'Perhaps we may yet have a fight with four English cruisers,' wrote the anonymous correspondent from *Scharnhorst*. 'Let them come, we shall have something to tell them about.'[25] What the Germans could not know was whether anyone knew they were there.

As it happens, they finally did. Although news of the Papeete bombardment did not reach London until 30 September, four days later the Admiralty had a stroke of luck. Von Spee's signal to *Dresden*, instructing her to join him at Easter Island, was intercepted by wireless stations in Fiji and New Zealand. Finally, the gigantic, half-hidden chess board was starting to assume some sort of pattern. The Admiralty signalled Cradock on 5 October, instructing him to prepare to meet the *Kreuzergeschwader*. Cradock was still in the Falklands, but *Monmouth* and *Glasgow* had rounded Cape Horn with the AMC *Otranto* in typically filthy weather on 3 October: 'It blew, snowed, rained and hailed and sleeted as hard as it is possible to do these things,' recalled *Glasgow*'s Maurice Portman. 'I thought the ship would dive right under altogether at times.'[26] The elderly *Canopus* was still 2,300 miles away at Abrolhos Rocks. Cradock was on his way, but his inadequate force was badly scattered. He was also still calling in vain for the cruiser *Defence*, which remained at Gibraltar. No one had apparently seen fit to inform Cradock that she was not joining his command, although on 14 October, in a belated change of heart, Churchill had ordered her westwards to join HMS *Carnarvon* 'in forming a new combat squadron on the great trade route from Rio'.[27] Although still not under Cradock's command, the powerful armoured cruiser would at last be in the right hemisphere. The question was would she be in time?

It could not have helped that the Admiralty was in turmoil. The country was drifting into war with Turkey, which was declared on 5 November, and on 28 October Prince Louis of Battenberg resigned as First Sea Lord, following weeks of public and media attacks on his German ancestry, some of which would today be almost certainly regarded as libellous. Churchill had lost his senior professional adviser, much to his regret, although it has been argued that the pressure on Battenberg deflected attention from the First Lord's own disastrous handling of the defence of Antwerp earlier in the month; Marder calls his position at this time 'shaky'.[28] Nevertheless, days before the battle, instead of scouring the eastern Pacific for von Spee, he was scouring London for a replacement, and there was only one man he wanted – his friend and mentor, the septuagenarian Jackie Fisher. Fisher's rapport with Churchill had ebbed and flowed in the years before the First World War, from frosty silence to a state of mutual admiration. The relationship has variously been described as 'infatuation' and 'love',[29] and with hindsight Churchill was never going to look anywhere else: 'my mind had already turned in one direction and in one direction alone'.[30] Like Churchill, Fisher was a terrifyingly intelligent and determined leader, driven, and convinced he was right. Events would show how in these qualities lay the intrinsic flaw of their relationship; as Marder has pointed out, they were 'too much alike [which] made for a basic incompatibility in their official relations'.[31] But Fisher was Churchill's anointed. He took office on 29 October, too late to prevent disaster; on 1 November, thousands of miles away, Cradock met von Spee in the wild, remote waters off the obscure Chilean coastal town of Coronel.

In deference to his latest orders to concentrate, Cradock waited until *Canopus* arrived on 18 October, and then remained at the Falklands for another four days while the old battleship's engines were overhauled. Some eyewitness accounts claim that 'the strains of war' had undermined the mental health of Captain Grant's engineer commander, William Denbow, to the point where he invented problems to delay action, the unstated implication being that the unfortunate man's nerves had failed; one wrote that he was 'so unpopular with his stokers that he dare not go below in the engine room lest someone should drop a heavy spanner on his head ...'.[32] Be that as it may, when Cradock left the Falklands on 22 October, to round Cape Horn and join the rest of his squadron, he left *Canopus* behind, signalling the Admiralty four days later that '[I] consider it impracticable on account of *Canopus*' slow speed to find and destroy enemy's squadron. Consequently have ordered *Defence* to join me. *Canopus* will be employed as necessary escorting colliers.'[33]

Churchill called this message 'obscure', minuting that 'I do not understand what Admiral Cradock intends and wishes', but with the cold clarity available in peacetime a hundred years on, it could not be clearer.[34] Cradock did not view the firepower of *Canopus* as sufficient justification to accept the limitation in speed she imposed and had sent her away, because he still believed *Defence* was available to him. Churchill conceded that he was badly distracted at this point: 'I was gravely preoccupied with the circumstances and oppositions attending the appointment of Lord Fisher. But for this fact I am sure I should have reacted more violently.'[35] Be that as it may, the outcome cannot be disputed; thanks to what one commentator has dubbed 'vagueness and uncertainty' in the instructions coming from London, disaster was almost inevitable.[36]

Defence arrived at Abrolhos Rocks on 29 October, after a breakneck Atlantic crossing which one crew member recalled as 'one of the more curious missions in which I, at least, had ever found myself'. Tellingly, 'all our courses came directly from the Admiralty by wireless' and nobody on the lower deck, at least, seems to have had the faintest idea where the ship was bound.[37] Even the captain's clerk was in the dark, recalling how the ship was forbidden from using wireless and 'the number of times our orders have been cancelled and altered is legion'.[38] To his credit, Stoddart had already recognised Cradock's perilous situation and immediately sent *Defence* to join him, in defiance of orders, but it was far too late.

Cradock had finally concentrated his squadron, minus *Canopus*, at the Vallenar Islands on the Chilean coast, on 27 October, where a small landing party under Acting Mate Robert Roe went ashore from *Good Hope* to establish an observation post on a nearby mountain top. 'It took four hours to climb the mountain through dense and rotten vegetation', he recalled, 'and many an adventure we had before reaching the top ... they nicknamed me Robinson Crusoe and the Yeoman was Friday and the other three were cannibals.'[39]

Glasgow was immediately sent into Coronel, to transfer mail and collect the latest intelligence. She carried what would be Cradock's last message to the Admiralty: '*Monmouth*, *Good Hope* and *Otranto* coaling at Vallenar. *Glasgow* patrolling vicinity of Coronel. I intend to proceed northward secretly with squadron after coaling and to keep out of sight of land.'[40] As the light cruiser left, German wireless signals indicated that at least one enemy warship, *Leipzig*, was nearby, and the signals strengthened as *Glasgow* neared Coronel: 'We have been hearing her all afternoon', Maurice Portman wrote on the 29th, 'and she must be quite close somewhere.'[41] Wary of being blockaded in Coronel, the experienced Luce signalled Cradock, asking for permission to wait outside until the situation became clearer. Cradock agreed, instructing Luce to sweep for enemy ships, and took his other three ships to sea, hoping to pick off *Leipzig* if Haun became too curious. As he steamed out of Vallenar Roads on the 30th, he sighted the lumbering *Canopus* entering the anchorage, two colliers in company and her engines once more supposedly in need of attention. Robert Roe watched the squadron depart from his mountain top, feeling thoroughly miserable at being abandoned by his ship. His only consolation was a signal, which read that she would return in a few days and that '*Canopus* would look after me'.[42] The following day the old battleship hauled anchor again and left in pursuit of Cradock, collecting Roe and his four comrades before she left.

Luce, meanwhile, entered Coronel late on 31 October, after cruising outside for two days. Convinced that his presence would be reported by one of the German merchant ships in the harbour (which it was), he kept his visit short and soon left, arranging to rendezvous with Cradock at 09:00 on 1 November. As the ships sighted each other, the airwaves were humming ominously with strong German wireless transmissions. Cradock formed a patrol line, from west to east *Good Hope*, *Monmouth*, *Otranto* and *Glasgow*, each ship separated by 15 miles of storm-tossed ocean, and headed northwest by north at a steady 10 knots, in search of the apparently garrulous *Leipzig*. His force was still shaking out into this formation at 16:20 when alert look-outs on *Glasgow*'s starboard bridge wing spotted smoke on the horizon, almost invisible against the rugged Chilean coastline. Luce altered course to investigate. As he drew nearer, the black smudge turned into *Scharnhorst*, *Gneisenau* and *Leipzig*. The three German cruisers turned towards Glasgow, increasing speed, and Luce, in the words of one of his more flippant junior officers, 'hopped it' back to the squadron, urgently signalling that enemy armoured cruisers were in sight.[43]

Haun, of course, had never been alone. Von Spee left Easter Island on 25 October, the long delay in part occasioned by von Schönberg, who had to make a tricky repair to *Nürnberg*'s port propeller after colliding with a collier. Afterwards, he cruised in the vicinity of Isla Más Afuera, in the Juan Fernandez Group, today named Alejandro Selkirk Island after its most illustrious inhabitant.[44] On the 29th he arrived at Valparaiso, where von Spee received the encouraging news of *Emden*'s raid on Penang. Then, late on 31 October von Spee received a signal from the auxiliary cruiser *Prinz Eitel Friedrich*, relayed from the interned German steamer *Gottingen* at Coronel, indicating that *Glasgow* had just entered the port. The following morning the *Kreuzergeschwader* was making for the Chilean port at a steady 14 knots. Knowing the British were already aware of *Leipzig*'s presence in the eastern Pacific, von Spee instructed his captains to precede every signal with the light cruiser's call sign: another simple ruse had put the final seal on catastrophe. On sighting *Glasgow*, von Spee hoisted the signals 'full speed ahead' and 'clear ship for action', simultaneously recalling *Dresden* and *Nürnberg*, which had been detached to investigate neutral merchant ships. He also ordered his radio operators to begin what *Leipzig*'s wireless officer called 'invisible combat', using the powerful German Telefunken wireless sets to jam transmissions from the 'regularly bawling' British ships.[45]

At first contact Cradock's ships were protected by the light conditions, the low sun behind his squadron blinding the German gunners. But he had to act quickly: once the sun dipped, his ships would be beautifully silhouetted against the orange horizon, lending a significant tactical advantage to the Germans, whose ships would be correspondingly obscured in the murky coastal twilight. Von Spee also enjoyed a significant superiority in firepower. *Scharnhorst* and *Gneisenau* mounted sixteen 208mm, or 8.2-inch, guns, which were mounted on the upper deck and could be operated in the difficult conditions. Against this, Cradock could deploy just two upper deck 9.2-inch guns on board his flagship *Good Hope*. All the other guns aboard his two armoured cruisers, as well as being far lighter in calibre, were difficult to deploy in the prevailing heavy weather. Nevertheless Cradock had to close the range quickly and try to bring his smaller weapons into play if he were to stand anything like a fighting chance. One can only guess at his thoughts as he made this critical decision: fight or flee? Cradock opted to try to force an action before nightfall, rather than try to escape.

He was, perhaps, influenced by the suspicion that if he lost von Spee this time, it might be months before the German squadron appeared again. Maybe he had in mind the Royal Navy's long tradition of victory against the odds, and Nelson's famous dictum: 'No captain can do very wrong if he places his ship alongside that of an enemy.' Possibly he was consumed by thoughts of the opprobrium heaped upon Troubridge after *Goeben*'s escape. Whatever his motives, Cradock formed his squadron into line ahead and turned straight for the enemy, increasing speed to 17 knots and trying to outmanoeuvre von Spee by bringing all his guns into action as soon as he could to compensate for the German advantage in long-range weapons. At 18:18 he signalled *Canopus*, still 300 miles away but closing as fast as her labouring old engines could manage, 'am going to attack the enemy now'. Kit Cradock was not a man to run from a fight.

In poor visibility and worsening weather, the two squadrons slowly closed to effective gunnery range. Von Spee was no fool, altering course from time to time and refusing to allow Cradock to get too close. At 18.55 Cradock lost his race against the setting sun, which dipped below the horizon leaving the British ships silhouetted against the afterglow. Eight minutes later, with the squadrons steaming almost parallel courses in a generally southerly direction, right into the teeth of the strengthening wind, von Spee opened fire at a range of just over 10,000 metres. The lumbering steel behemoths ploughed steadily on in the gathering gloom, their bows dipping below the waves and vanishing in a shower of spray as they plunged into a heavy head sea, their guns flashing spasmodically. At first the two German armoured cruisers concentrated on *Good Hope* and *Monmouth*, while *Leipzig* fired at *Glasgow* and *Dresden* at *Otranto*. The poor light and foul weather were hardly ideal, as von Spee later reported:

> Spotting and range-taking were severely handicapped by the seas, which broke over the forecastle and conning tower, and the heavy swell so hid the target from the 15cm ... guns mounted on the main deck that they could not see their adversary's stern at all, and could only see the bows occasionally. However, the heavy guns of the cruisers could be used throughout.[46]

Von Spee's advantage in firepower was obvious from the outset in this uneven contest: a heavyweight fighting an elderly middleweight with one arm tied behind his back.

Otranto was a liability; her huge silhouette dominated the skyline, and she was poorly armed, unarmoured and slow – facts of which 19-year-old

Wardroom Steward A. Morris was painfully aware: '[The Germans] didn't half look a size, and I began to feel a nasty sensation in my stomach as the odds were against us and they were better ships. Of course you could not count on us as a fighting ship.'[47] Just a few months before, most of the men aboard, like stretcher-bearer A.A. Bushkin, had been employees of the Orient Steam Navigation Company, not fighting sailors:

> We were getting tensed up, full of excitement, wondering what was going to happen. I and others like me, merchant seamen, had no training whatsoever with regard to naval action or anything like that, we were very much worried. While we were thinking like that, suddenly a shell came screaming overhead with a rumbling screaming noise. We turned, 'Christ this is going to hit us! What's that?'[48]

Not long after the action opened, Cradock sensibly ordered the vulnerable AMC to stay out of range. She was nevertheless straddled by German fire: 'The escape we had was little short of a miracle, the shells falling within 30 feet of us, indeed, two went between the funnels, another dropped just in front of our bows and swamped all the men at the fore guns.'[49] Just after 19:00 Cradock signalled *Otranto* to leave altogether, and she played no further part in the action. Harry Spencer, her chief yeoman of signals, could not disguise his relief. A veteran sailor who had already survived the accidental sinking of the Mediterranean Fleet battleship *Victoria* in 1893, he was under no illusions about the lumbering AMC's chances if she stayed in the line of battle: 'We put our best leg foremost', he wrote after the battle, 'and legged it for all we were worth ... and never stopped till we arrived at Montevideo.'[50]

The German gunnery was excellent. In textbook style, as befitting the holders of the Kaiser's Prize for gunnery, the first salvo flew over, the second fell short, and the third produced a perfect straddle. Shells plunged into the water around the beleaguered British armoured cruisers, almost obscuring them among masthead-high plumes of filthy water. One shell smashed *Good Hope*'s forward 9.2-inch turret, setting her forepart on fire. Almost simultaneously, another hit *Monmouth*'s forecastle and her forward turret burst into flames, the roof flying into the air as the old cruiser heeled over and shuddered violently before hauling back into the line.

Maurice Portman and other horrified witnesses aboard *Glasgow* watched as the armoured cruisers were overwhelmed, their guns ceasing fire one by one and their hulls glowing from the fires that raged inside them:

> When she [*Good Hope*] was first hit she took fire and had hardly got the fire under control when another shot struck her in practically the same place and started the fire up again. She was hit all over and after the first

ten minutes had many guns out of action including … the fore 9.2″ which was one of the only two guns she could hope to do any damage with; she was on fire forward and all along her port [i.e. her engaged] side.[51]

Glasgow was hardly having an easy time of it, although her low silhouette made her harder to hit. With *Otranto* out of the line, she was engaged by both *Dresden* and *Nürnberg*: 'ears had become deafened to the roar of our guns and insensible almost to the shrieks of shell fragments flying overhead from shells bursting short'.[52] The two German cruisers were firing at extreme range, their guns at maximum elevation and the red-hot barrels almost perpendicular. Without the possibility of ricochets, the German gunners needed to score a direct hit, like the lucky shot which tore into *Glasgow*'s foretop spotting platform and ripped off a signaller's arm, leaving his comrades somehow to lower him to the cruiser's deck, under fire, the ship rolling and pitching in the heavy seas.

Retaliation was almost impossible. *Glasgow*'s gunners could hardly see their targets through the tumult of shell splashes, any form of directed fire was impossible and the gunners had to resort to independent fire, loosing off a shot at the flashes from the German guns whenever they blazed through the murk. At times the light cruiser's decks were awash and with her guardrails struck down in preparation for action, simply getting around the ship could be lethal for the unwary. *Glasgow*'s officers estimated that some 600 shells were directed at their ship; inevitably, some found their mark, one shell ripping through the cruiser's armoured deck, another punching a hole through her funnel and two more tearing open the ship's side before burrowing into her coal bunkers. A fifth impudently tore into the side of Captain Luce's personal pantry before crossing the passageway and wrecking his cabin. Even so, *Glasgow* escaped lightly, a fact which the more perceptive of her crew were perfectly aware of, one young officer later reflecting 'I cannot understand the miracle of our deliverance'.[53]

At 19:45, with dusk turning to dark and her sides almost glowing from the heat of the fires within her, *Good Hope* turned her bows to the enemy one last time, a few guns still firing sporadically. Whether this last act of defiance was through design or simply an accident caused by damage to her steering can never be known. Five minutes later a terrible explosion ripped though the tortured cruiser. To von Spee it 'looked like gigantic fireworks against the dark evening sky, white flames with green stars reaching higher than the funnels'.[54] Far away in the gloom von Spee was convinced the cruiser was still afloat, but on the British side it was clear no ship could survive such a catastrophic detonation. Able Seaman William Hawkes of *Glasgow* watched horrified as 'the whole of the midships part of the *Good Hope* blew right up in the air. The fire must have spread to her magazines.'[55] The dreadful shaft of flame lit up a terrible column of debris which reached still higher. *Good Hope* had been torn apart.

The shocked Hawkes watched the cruiser fire her after 9.2-inch gun twice more before she disappeared: 'that was the last I saw of her'.[56] Maurice Portman watched the column of flame reach up 200 feet before vanishing abruptly, leaving *Good Hope* 'a low black hull, gutted of her upperworks, and only lighted by a low red glare which shortly disappeared'.[57] No one saw the old cruiser finally give up the fight. She went down with all hands, from Admiral Cradock to 18-year-old Boy Roland Adams. Only Robert Roe and the other four refugees in *Canopus* remained of the 925 souls aboard. 'I cannot describe my feelings,' the distraught Roe later recorded in his diary: 'I feel I ought to have been in her and wish I was'. Aboard the fleeing *Otranto*, Wardroom Steward Morris knew what that awful pillar of fire signified, as the AMC ploughed into the darkness and the gathering gale: 'We gave up all hope of ever seeing that gallant admiral again ... a gloomy depression seemed to settle on the whole ship's company, but at the same time a great relief at being saved ... from what would have been sure death by fire.'[58]

It was now completely dark, both sides feeling for each other in the murk in a murderous game of blind man's buff. Only occasional flashes revealed the combatants, as nervous gunners blazed away at real or imaginary targets. At 20:05, recognising that *Glasgow*'s gunners were only drawing fire, the experienced John Luce ordered them to cease fire. Von Spee, unsure which British ships were still afloat, ordered his light cruisers to close and attack with torpedoes. In *Scharnhorst* and *Gneisenau* weary gunners secured their weapons and damage control parties assessed the cost, which was unbelievably small: *Gneisenau* had taken a few hits, one damaging the after 208mm turret and causing a jam which the turret officer, *Leutnant zur See* Freiherr von Lamezan, and the gunlayer put right in less than a minute using a couple of fire axes. Another shell passed right through the ship without exploding, wrecking the carpenter's store and the clothing store on the way. A few flesh wounds were the only casualties; the only fatalities were a parrot and a canary. *Scharnhorst* was only hit twice, one shell impacting harmlessly on the cruiser's armoured belt, the other penetrating an upper deck store room without exploding. So ineffective were the British shells that von Spee's men christened them 'jam pots'.[59]

As the gunfire faded, *Glasgow* drew near the battered *Monmouth*, seaman Edward Pullen recalling how the Royal Marines on her mangled quarterdeck cheered the light cruiser as she approached.[60] *Monmouth* was listing badly to port, her lower deck portholes lit by the macabre glow of her fires. Drawing as close alongside as he dared, Luce flashed a message, rendered almost ridiculous by the terse language of the naval signal book: 'Are you all right?' Whether Captain Brandt was still alive at this point is open to conjecture, but someone was still in command of the ailing cruiser: 'I want to get stern to sea,' came the reply. 'I am making water badly forward.'[61] As the lamps flickered, *Monmouth* painfully turned to the northeast, putting the wind behind her. Just as it seemed the wounded cruiser might yet be saved, the enemy reappeared, four ominous silhouettes approaching in line abreast. Luce signalled again, 'Can you steer north-west?', but received no reply. The 44-year-old captain was faced with an agonising decision: standing by *Monmouth* would almost certainly mean the destruction of his own ship, but living to fight another day meant abandoning *Glasgow*'s 'chummy ship' and the unfortunate souls who still lived inside her shattered hull.

Luce knew what he had to do. As well as his own ship, there was the lumbering *Canopus* to consider, now just 200 miles away. Captain Grant had cleared his ship for action after receiving *Glasgow*'s sighting report, extra rum had been issued and according to at least one gung-ho able seaman everyone aboard was 'rejoicing at the idea of having a go at the Germans'.[62] But the grim truth was that the old pre-dreadnought faced almost certain destruction if she ran into the *Kreuzergeschwader* in the prevailing dreadful weather conditions. One of her junior officers recalled that 'the lower deck 6-inch guns could not be fought and it is doubtful if we could have done much with the after 12-inch turret as the quarter deck was mostly awash'.[63] Someone had to turn her back, so Luce reluctantly ordered his helmsman to put the wheel over and the burning *Monmouth* slipped astern and out of sight. At 20:50 Luce lost sight of the enemy, and half an hour later he observed '75 flashes of fire' which he rightly surmised meant *Monmouth*'s end.[64] According to one (unsubstantiated) account, the distraught Luce was all for turning back to help the stricken armoured cruiser, but was talked out of it by his officers, who told him 'it would only be murder to his own men as well'.[65] *Glasgow* ploughed on alone.

It was a bit-part player, hurrying on from the wings at the end of the final act, that brought matters to a close. Karl von Schönberg's *Nürnberg* had begun the action 25 miles away to the north, where she had been investigating a brace of Chilean merchant ships, and ever since had been pursuing the squadron at high speed. Von Schönberg missed most of the action, seeing only gun flashes and the terrible explosion when the *Good Hope*'s death spasm tore apart the night. He arrived in time to receive von Spee's order for the light cruisers to attack. All was chaos: 'I had no idea which was friend and which was foe. The water breaking over us caused a short circuit, and our compass lamps went out. I made for the nearest column of smoke, but this ran away from me; then for the next one, which was moving at high speed parallel to us. We saw three funnels ...'[66] At first the poor visibility and heavy seas made identification difficult, as did the flames and smoke shrouding the mystery ship. Finally, after closing to around 500 metres range, von Schönberg was sure of what he was looking at: he had stumbled upon *Monmouth*. Seeing her ensign still fluttering, he fired a few shots before ceasing fire to allow the British time to strike; it was clear that *Monmouth* was helpless. Rather than haul down her colours, *Monmouth* turned agonisingly slowly towards *Nürnberg*. As with *Good Hope*'s last defiant gesture, this may have simply been a mechanical failure in a ship that had been battered almost beyond recognition, but von Schönberg could not be sure. If *Monmouth* could turn through 180 degrees, the undamaged guns on the cruiser's disengaged side could come into action. She might even try to ram. Von Schönberg had no idea whether other British ships were still present, and he could not take the risk of being surprised when almost stationary; even as he waited, his look-outs spotted smoke clouds on the horizon, drawing near. He gave the order to open fire again and watched the 105mm shells tear into *Monmouth*'s unprotected sides again and again, until the British cruiser finally gave up the unequal fight:

> I continued firing until *Monmouth* had completely capsized ... she heeled over in a very slow and stately way. The brave fellow went down with flags flying. An indescribable and unforgettable sight, as the masts with their great flags at the trucks slowly sank into the water, and then the red bottom of the ship became visible.[67]

Nürnberg's gunnery officer, *Korvettenkapitän* Robert Keydell, was a markedly less reluctant executioner: 'I came into my own at last,' he later related, 'a brief order to my gunlayers and then a hail of shell flew towards her ... almost every shot found its mark. It was a wonderful sight how the target simply flew in pieces.'[68]

There were no survivors. The weather was foul, von Schönberg's boats had been struck down and filled with water in preparation for action, and in any case the German captain saw his first duty as being to investigate the possibly hostile smoke on the horizon. All 738 men perished in the fiery wreck of their ship, or in the freezing waters of the South Pacific. *Monmouth*'s death agony brought to an end what would eventually be called the Battle of Coronel by the British, and the Battle of Santa Maria by the Germans.[69]

Glasgow escaped, running south at her best speed in *Otranto*'s wake, her crew patching up her wounds as she went and her wireless operators filling the airwaves with desperate calls to *Canopus*. Von Spee made for Valparaiso to take on supplies, rest his men and proclaim to the world the Kaiser's Pirates' most important victory.

Chapter 6

'Instruments of Nemesis': the Combination against von Spee

'He was a cut flower in a vase; fair to see, yet bound to die.'

Winston Churchill, writing about Admiral von Spee[1]

Von Spee's junior officers descended upon Valparaiso like footballers after a Cup Final win. In 1914 Chile's foremost seaport was a vibrant, multicultural hub of international trade, with a large and fiercely patriotic population of expatriate Germans. The *Kreuzergeschwader* dropped anchor at midday on 3 November, and the German sailors rushed ashore, proclaiming the news of their victory. One *Gneisenau* officer recalled a happy interlude dining at the city's German Club and riding with local ladies, his first such encounter since the outbreak of war, before returning to his ship laden with gifts. The squadron was besieged by enthusiastic reservists, anxious to sign up and bask in the reflected glory, fifty-five joining *Gneisenau* alone.[2]

Von Spee was less sanguine, gloomily concluding in his report to the *Admiralstab* that the victory 'might not mean much ... in view of the enormous number of the English ships'.[3] His squadron had revealed its location, and handing the Royal Navy its first defeat in over a hundred years could only bring about the most terrible retribution, to which his weary men and worn-out ships were ill-equipped to respond. The two armoured cruisers had expended nearly half of their 208mm shells, with no hope of replenishment. Small wonder, then, that when asked to drink to the damnation of the British Navy by a drunken civilian during a reception at the German Club, von Spee refused and angrily left the building. Outside, when a well-wisher tried to present him with a bouquet of flowers, the German admiral grimly accepted them, saying 'these will do nicely for my grave'.[4] Thirty-six hours later the *Kreuzergeschwader* was on its way back out to sea, to the sound of rousing cheers from thirty-two blockaded German merchant ships; that these valuable ships were still 'confined to the harbour by the sea-power of England' was an irony that was not lost on the more perceptive German sailors.[5]

Von Spee still believed *Good Hope* might have survived, albeit badly damaged, and also knew that *Glasgow* and *Otranto* had escaped. Ashore, he had learned that a powerful Anglo-Japanese squadron was coming from the north, formed around the armoured cruiser *Izumo* and the old battleship *Hizen*.[6] He remained determined to keep his squadron concentrated, a policy to which he had been committed since early 1913.[7] Returning to East Asian waters was still not an option: with *Emden* at large that region was a hotbed of Allied naval activity. Only the Atlantic offered the chance of continued survival and, perhaps, another success against the odds, so it seems likely that von Spee decided fairly quickly to take his squadron around Cape Horn. Then he could consider his options again: either to attempt to break through for home, to reinforce Germany's beleaguered African colonies or to carry out cruiser warfare.

Meanwhile he had stirred up a hornets' nest in Valparaiso. The *Kreuzergeschwader*'s arrival provoked immediate protests by the British Consul, Allan Maclean, who claimed that, as the Germans had already anchored at Easter Island, they could not legally enter another Chilean port for three months. The Chileans ignored him, more concerned with the warships on their doorstep than an irate diplomat with no guns to back him up. Maclean then telegraphed the first report of the calamity to London, based on the German accounts that were flying around Valparaiso.

At the Admiralty Churchill and the newly reappointed Fisher were struggling to catch up. Just after 03:00 on 3 November they had been passed a series of vague sightings obtained from Chilean merchant ships, which seemed to confirm that the *Kreuzergeschwader* was in the area. Consequently Churchill signalled Stoddart to release *Defence* at 18.20. Fifteen minutes later he signalled Cradock that the powerful reinforcement he so desperately needed was finally on its way, but by now, as Churchill dramatically wrote years later, 'we were already talking to the void'.[8] At 07:00 on 4 November the First Lord opened his despatch boxes and found Maclean's report. The diplomat's terse note brought an end to hope:

> German admiral states that on Sunday at sunset, in thick and wicked weather, his ships met *Good Hope*, *Glasgow*, *Otranto* and *Monmouth*. Action was joined and *Monmouth* turned over and sank after about an hour's fighting. *Good Hope*, *Glasgow* and *Otranto* drew off into darkness. *Good Hope* was on fire, an explosion was heard and she is believed to have sunk.[9]

It has been claimed, with some justification, that the Admiralty had left Cradock poorly informed, outnumbered and, to quote one of the more outspoken critics, 'bombarded ... with signals which cramped [his] initiative and misdirected [his] efforts'.[10] Churchill, in a lengthy and arguably rather tasteless attempt to bat away this criticism, responded that he had repeatedly instructed Cradock to keep his force, including *Canopus*, concentrated, and that it was impossible to reinforce him until von Spee had been located.[11] Cradock, he claimed, 'was an experienced and fearless officer' who had deliberately sacrificed himself and his command, and the Admiralty bore 'no responsibility' for his decision.[12] Although Churchill's account appears loaded with self-interest, some truth underlies it. Certainly Cradock was aware of where his duty lay, one young diplomat in the service of Governor Sir William Allardyce at the Falkland Islands recalling how 'the Admiral ... knew he was going to almost certain death in fighting these people in these new and powerful ships and it seemed quite all right as far as he was concerned'.[13] He also wrote to his friend Admiral Hedworth Meux that 'I will take care I do not suffer the fate of poor Troubridge.'[14] Perhaps, as Churchill implied, he had indeed concluded that the chance of damaging the German squadron and depleting their ammunition was worth taking, and death was better than dishonour. One thing is certain: the destruction of Cradock's squadron left the Admiralty with some questions to answer. Where would von Spee go next? Were the German ships damaged? And where were the three surviving British ships?

In fact, the latter were heading south into the teeth of a strengthening gale. With the advantage of a head start, *Otranto* was well on her way to safety, but *Canopus* and *Glasgow* were still perilously close to the battle area. Even the broad-beamed *Canopus* found the going heavy, her blunt bow rearing up over the looming wave crests before plunging down deep into the troughs. The strain proved too much for the hawsers securing the forward 12-inch turret, which parted, causing the huge weapons to swing slowly from side to side as the ship rolled. By noon on 2 November the fourteen-year-old battleship was taking on water badly, and Captain Grant was forced to reduce speed. The following day he made the courageous decision to take a shortcut through a series of narrow inland waterways: 'Never before had anyone taken a heavy ship through these poorly charted and treacherous waters,' one of his junior officers recalled, 'which ended in a desolate inlet appropriately called "Last Hope Inlet" where we came to anchor at midnight.'[15] Grant's men had been at action stations for two days and three nights without respite, and he had rightly concluded that they needed rest. If he had to fight, he would prefer to do so in confined waters, rather than on the open sea, where the German advantages of speed and numbers would be more pronounced. The Germans never came, and Grant left at dawn on the 5th, threading his way through the Straits of Magellan to Punta Arenas, where he met the battered *Glasgow* the next day. Both ships finally dropped anchor at the Falkland Islands on the morning of 8 November.

Glasgow's journey had been just as nightmarish, the men patching up battle damage in the teeth of a vicious gale, all the while bracing themselves for another action. Edward Pullen was assigned to a damage control party repairing a hole in the side of his own smoke-filled mess deck, his home for the last two years. Ears ringing with the terrified screeches of his two pet parrots, he worked up to his waist in water, improvising a patch from hammocks, kitbags, a capstan bar and a plank. Later he was ordered below to stop more flooding in *Glasgow*'s filthy, dark coal bunkers. The work was exhausting and terrifying: 'I was covered with dust,' he recalled. 'I was in darkness, I was tearing my hair out down there.'[16] The damage control parties worked all night and throughout the following day, without food or water, while Luce conned his ship through the treacherous waters of the Straits of Magellan.

Glasgow needed a dockyard, and Luce left the Falklands for Montevideo after taking on coal. *Canopus* accompanied him but was ordered back to the Falklands on 10 November. Nobody knew where von Spee was and Captain Grant's old battleship was the colony's only defence. Midshipman Young recalled,

> I think it was about this time that we got one of those cheerful signals from the Admiralty to the effect that Their Lordships were confident that should the *Canopus* meet the enemy she would act in the highest traditions of the service ... a polite way of saying 'have a crack at him if you get the chance and we shan't blame you if you're sunk'.[17]

Grant's preparations were thorough. First, he sent out *Canopus*'s picket boat, armed with a 3-pounder gun and two torpedoes, to patrol the harbour mouth. He despatched look-outs and signallers to the summit of nearby Sapper Hill, and a gunnery observation team to another peak, which would allow her to fire 'blind', protected from enemy fire by the hills. Armed parties of sailors and Royal Marines defended possible landing beaches, assisted by the Falkland Islands Volunteers, an enthusiastic if ill-prepared militia drawn from the local fishermen and sheep farmers. These grim preparations did not go unnoticed by local residents, who started burying their valuables and carrying their furniture out into the 'camp', as the Falkland Islanders named their wilderness.

Grant moored *Canopus* in shallow water, from where her guns could cover most approaches to Port Stanley, the capital. Ten anchors ensured the ship maintained an even keel and was unable to swing out of position, and her double bottom was flooded so that she rested on the sea bed. Her topmasts and yards were lowered and her funnels and upper works painted in camouflage paint. Batteries of 12-pounder quick-firing guns were also set up ashore.

'I think our 12-pounder battery was about our best effort,' recalled Midshipman Young:

> We had to improvise gun emplacements with baulks of timber to form the base plates. The guns and mountings were then put into ship's boats and towed round to the battery where they had to be hauled up a steep hill, almost a cliff, and then bolted down ... this sort of entertainment during a Falklands Island December called for a good deal of endurance ...[18]

Finally, Grant's torpedo officer improvised 'do-it-yourself mines' from empty oil drums and 'guncotton' (the cellulose nitrate propellant from the ship's main guns), which were moored in a line across the harbour and then connected to a concealed firing point ashore.[19] *Canopus* was ready for action. But where was the enemy?

Von Spee followed up the most significant victory of the Imperial German Navy's brief history by doing nothing for weeks, possibly because he was waiting to see whether he was going to be reinforced by the powerful battle-cruisers *Moltke* and *Seydlitz*, which were believed to be making their way into the Atlantic, laden with ammunition.[20] The armoured cruisers and *Nürnberg* returned to Isla Más Afuera from Valparaiso on 6 November, to find *Leipzig* with two laden colliers and a French prize, also carrying coal. Haun was finally able to confirm that *Good Hope* had sunk, as he had steamed through wreckage and bodies at the end of the battle.[21] Over the next two days they were joined by the AMC *Prinz Eitel Friedrich*, two more colliers and the Norwegian barque *Helicon*, another prize full of coal. The *Kreuzergeschwader* remained at anchor for nine days, before finally putting back to sea on 15 November, news of the loss of *Emden* and the fall of Tsingtao doubtless increasing the men's sense of isolation.

On 21 November, in thick fog, the squadron anchored again in the Gulf of Penas on the Chilean coast, where they rendezvoused with two more colliers and stopped for another five days, coaling and taking on supplies. On the 26th von Spee made notional medal awards for Coronel, although his men would have to wait to receive the actual decorations, before returning to sea. Although von Spee had telegraphed his intentions to Berlin on 19 November, the *Vizeadmiral* kept them from his men for days, resulting in a bewildering string of contradictory 'rumours and conjectures' circulating around the mess decks of the cruisers, ranging from 'a voyage northward by way of South Georgia' to 'a cruise to South Africa, and a continuation of cruiser warfare in the Indian Ocean'.[22] Finally, he ended the speculation, announcing that the *Kreuzergeschwader* was going around Cape Horn into the Atlantic, where the

Etappen at New York and La Plata had been instructed to arrange 20,000 tons of coal and provisions for 2,000 men for three months – enough to get home.[23] The AMC *Prinz Eitel Friedrich* would remain in the Pacific, broadcasting decoy wireless signals to conceal their departure for as long as possible.

The weather was filthy again when the squadron weighed on 27 November, one of *Gneisenau's* officers recording 30-metre high waves in his diary: 'Impossible to lay the tables. Broken up furniture thrown overboard. All crockery was smashed. In the ship and in the mess there were water leaks everywhere. Impossible to be on deck. Necessary to secure oneself with ropes.'[24] They rounded Cape Horn at midnight on 1 December, the great, rugged peak clearly visible through the driving hail, and shortly afterwards *Gneisenau's* look-outs sighted the first icebergs. The following day one of the light cruisers captured the British sailing vessel *Dunmuir*, laden with another welcome 2,800 tons of coal.

On 3 December the squadron anchored in remote Picton Sound at the eastern entrance to the Beagle Channel, to strip *Dunmuir* of her cargo. A few officers went ashore, although the region was bare and wild, with no signs of life beyond a solitary sealion.[25] Finally, at a captains' conference on 6 December, von Spee announced his intention to carry out one last operation before making for home. Overruling the objections of several of his officers, notably Maerker of *Gneisenau*, he proposed to make for the Falkland Islands, where he would destroy the wireless station and the colony's limited port facilities, burn the coal stocks and abduct Governor Allardyce.[26] No opposition was expected. Only a few shepherds witnessed the *Kreuzergeschwader* depart on what would turn out to be its final voyage, leaving the hapless *Dunmuir*, her bottom blown out by a scuttling party from *Gneisenau*, slowly sinking behind them.

Back in Britain, across the Empire and around the world the news of Coronel broke like a thunderclap. By the morning of 6 November even Australia's *Northern Times* was proclaiming the 'Chilean Naval Disaster'.[27] The London *Times* found solace in the theory that Cradock could only have been deceived into a trap.[28] Neutral commentators seemed to take malicious pleasure in the humiliation of a superpower, the *New York Times* unhesitatingly taking the German line that Cradock's 'fleet' had been 'wiped out'. That the loss of two old cruisers on the other side of the globe did not fundamentally affect Britain's overwhelming superiority at sea, nor do much to improve von Spee's essentially poor strategic situation, did not matter; nobody was in the mood for perspective in the face of the Royal Navy's first defeat since the Battle of Lake Champlain during the war of 1812 against the United States. Britannia ruled the waves, and Britons were simply not prepared for defeat at sea. The country was already reeling from the loss of three cruisers to a single U-boat in the North Sea at the end of September, but this was worse; in a fair fight in open water a British squadron had been beaten. The nation and the navy needed vengeance. Joseph Murray was an 18-year-old recruit who had arrived at Devonport Barracks at the end of October, just days before the battle. Even with less than a month in the service, his anger and shame at the defeat was visceral: 'I was out for blood. I swore blind that I'd kill every so-and-so that I could and I did! ... That were me, out for revenge ... taught to hate.'[29]

There was already a substantial force to deal with von Spee. Stoddart, in the western Atlantic, now had the armoured cruisers *Defence*, *Carnarvon* and *Cornwall*, and the light cruiser *Bristol*, as well as the Coronel survivors; he was ordered to concentrate at Montevideo and await further instructions. Captain John Allen was ordered to abandon his search for the elusive *Karlsruhe* and join him in his cruiser *Kent*. But this was still not enough. The Royal Navy's already overstretched responsibilities were about to be extended following the formal entry of Turkey into the war on 5 November. Everything seemed to be unravelling, with 'every vulnerable point all over the world ... exposed to a telling blow from Admiral von Spee'. The *Kreuzergeschwader* had to be dealt with quickly, and comprehensively, in a single, overwhelming blow.[30]

An hour after receiving news of Coronel, Churchill drafted a memorandum outlining the various options available if the Admiralty wished to concentrate against von Spee. Among them was an almost tentative suggestion that the battlecruiser *Invincible* be detached from the Grand Fleet at Scapa Flow and sent to the South Atlantic. Interestingly, it was not Churchill but Fisher, the advocate of concentrating naval force in home waters and the arch-enemy of overseas distractions, who proved the greater gambler:

> I found Lord Fisher in a bolder mood. He would take two battlecruisers from the Grand Fleet for the South American station. More than that, and much more questionable, he would take a third – the *Princess Royal* – for Halifax and later for the West Indies in case von Spee came through the Panama Canal.[31]

At 12:40 on 4 November the battlecruisers *Invincible* and *Inflexible* were ordered to coal immediately and head south from the Cromarty Firth, as they were 'urgently needed for foreign service'.[32] By 14:00 on 8 November both ships were in dry dock in Devonport, undergoing a hasty refit and filling up with stores. When the cautious admiral in command at Devonport hinted that the ships might not be ready to sail until 13 November, Churchill drafted a peremptory signal: 'Ships are to sail Wednesday 11th. They are needed for war service and dockyard arrangements must be made to conform ... you are held responsible for the speedy despatch of these ships in an efficient condition. Acknowledge. Signed W.S.C.'[33]

Invincible and *Inflexible* were the oldest of the Royal Navy's battlecruisers, but this kind of operation was exactly what Jackie Fisher had in mind when he had proposed this new class of ship. With eight 12-inch guns mounted in four double turrets, sixteen 4-inch guns and speeds in excess of 25 knots, they were more than a match for von Spee's worn-out cruisers; if they could find the *Kreuzergeschwader*, victory was almost inevitable. Nevertheless, denuding the Grand Fleet of three battlecruisers was a bold decision. While the threat posed by von Spee was grave, it was the battleships of the Kaiser's High Seas Fleet, lurking in their North Sea bases, which had the real power to affect the naval balance of power and thus the outcome of the war. The British priority since hostilities began had been to maintain superiority over this formidable force, the creation of which had been instrumental in bringing Britain into the war in the first place. The Commander-in-Chief of Britain's Grand Fleet, Admiral Sir John Jellicoe, had just lost the brand-new dreadnought battleship *Audacious* to a mine on 28 October; replacements were still building or working up, and he was painfully aware that the situation was handing the Germans the best opportunity they were ever likely to have to fight, and win, a decisive action in the North Sea. 'I will of course do the best I can with the force at my disposal,' he wrote with dignity to Fisher on 11 November, 'but ... I hope I shall not be held responsible if the force is unequal to the task devolving upon it ... the annihilation of the High Seas Fleet.'[34]

Churchill and Fisher had rolled the dice. The outcome was now in the hands of the two ships heading south, and their commander-in-chief. Protocol dictated that two battlecruisers required a vice-admiral in command, which ruled out Stoddart, even though he was on the spot and understood the situation. Instead, Churchill used a major crisis to solve a minor one, and appointed his chief-of-staff, 55-year-old Vice-Admiral Frederick Doveton Sturdee. Sturdee had fallen foul of Fisher some ten years before, when he had been Beresford's chief-of-staff in the Mediterranean. Fisher, as First Sea Lord, had essentially asked Sturdee to spy on his boss but Sturdee, outraged, had refused to do anything so ungentlemanly, and Fisher had pathologically loathed him ever since. When Fisher returned to the Admiralty, he blamed Sturdee for the Coronel debacle, and Churchill needed to move him out of harm's way as soon as possible.[35] The new role of Commander-in-Chief, South Atlantic and Pacific, seemed an ideal solution; whether Sturdee was the best qualified man for the job does not seem to have entered into the equation. Clean-shaven, with a jutting jaw and a prominent nose, Sturdee had a reputation for being rigid and obstinate; Fisher called him a 'pedantic ass', and in a letter to his wife dated 16 November 1914 Vice-Admiral David Beatty, the charismatic commander-in-chief of the Grand Fleet's battle-cruisers, called him 'one of the curses of the Navy'.[36] Originally a gunnery specialist, like many senior Royal Navy officers of the period, in his favour he was also calm and methodical, qualities that would stand him in good stead in the South Atlantic.

Sturdee joined *Invincible* on 8 November, and the two ships sailed three days later. *Inflexible* had been in the Mediterranean since the start of the war and was efficient and battle-ready, but *Invincible* was a different story. Her experimental electrically powered turrets had only recently been converted back to the more conventional hydraulic power, and she left Devonport carrying a 'boffin' named Lance Levison and a contingent of Vickers employees, who were installing a new fire control system.[37] Her crew had been hastily assembled from the Royal Yacht *Victoria & Albert* and the Admiralty Yacht *Enchantress*, both paid off for the duration of the war, and although fine seamen with high standards of deportment and presentation, few had much recent experience in a 'fighting' warship; according to *Invincible*'s gunnery officer, Lieutenant-Commander Hubert Dannreuther, the four turret officers who commanded the turrets had not been inside one since they were midshipmen.[38]

Although the mission was secret, Sturdee and other senior officers knew where they were bound, and according to Dannreuther, 'everyone in the Dockyard seemed to know where we were going'.[39] Some of the more perceptive members of the ships' companies could make an educated guess. 'Putting two and two together,' Sub-Lieutenant Robert Stewart wrote in his diary, 'we came to the conclusion that we were obviously going out to "settle things".'[40] Others had absolutely no idea. 'We learned we were going on a big mission somewhere,' recalled 22-year-old seaman George Miller:

> We loaded up to the top ... with coal, munitions, food and everything else. And of course there were all kind of buzzes around the ship about what we were going to do but nobody knew, nobody could tell you. Anyhow by about ten o'clock at night the ropes were cast off and like a thief in the night we made our way out to sea. Sunday morning came, divisions for church, and still no story where we were going.[41]

Inflexible's men were no better informed but *Inflexible*'s 50-year-old captain, Richard Fortescue Phillimore, an experienced veteran from an old naval family, with combat experience ashore in China and Somaliland, sensibly decided to kill the bewildering swirl of lower deck 'buzzes' as soon as he could, clearing lower deck on the first full day at sea:

He said, 'No doubt you've been hearing all these rumours and buzzes going around and I'm going to tell you … what we're going to do … We've had instructions that the *Good Hope* and *Monmouth* were sunk off Valparaiso but we don't know for certain. In any case we're going out to find these German ships and we're going to sink them, whether we go round the world once or whether we go round the world twice.'[42]

Two days later Sturdee carried out the same exercise on board *Invincible*, reading out his orders from Churchill to the assembled ship's company, orders that were later pithily summarised by the young seaman George Miller as 'this bloody man's got to be caught!'[43] 'We congratulated ourselves unreservedly,' recalled Lieutenant-Commander Barry Bingham of *Invincible*, 'in that Nemesis had chosen us as two of her instruments.'[44]

On 17 November the battlecruisers arrived at St Vincent in the Cape Verde Islands, which at the time were controlled by Portugal, Britain's oldest ally. *Invincible*'s Engineer Lieutenant Commander, Fraser Shaw, visiting the islands for the first time, recalled them as 'spiky and dry and barren', although the surrounding water was 'beautifully clear and … a brilliant blue'.[45] Here they took on coal, no joke in the searing tropical heat. 'We arrived about 4.30pm,' Shaw recalled, 'my men had been steaming the ship all the time of course, and so had done a fair day's work, but by 8.00pm we had started coaling and we didn't stop till 2.00pm the following day.'[46] In the course of this gruelling work *Inflexible* sustained her first fatality: a young boy telegraphist from Norwich named Percy Stuart, who had only been in the ship a few weeks. Inexperienced and doubtless exhausted, he had foolishly curled up for a nap against the cable reel of one of *Inflexible*'s winches, which he was supposed to be watching. In a ghastly tragedy the 17-year-old Stuart was dragged around the drum and died almost instantaneously. He was buried at sea the following day, when the battlecruisers left the Cape Verdes.

Early twentieth-century warships were not well ventilated at the best of times – air conditioning still lay many years in the future – and the heat was stifling; the situation was made far worse by the need to 'darken ship' by shutting the scuttles (portholes) and sealing them with a steel deadlight. Fraser Shaw described sitting in his cabin when off-watch 'with absolutely nothing on, with a fan blowing down on me', and spending his off-duty hours desperately trying to improve conditions in the wardroom by constructing an ice chest.[47] Despite the discomfort, the two ships' companies still found time to observe the traditional ceremonies when they crossed the Equator on the 19th. On board *Invincible*, the order was given to clear the lower deck at 10:00, and the men swarmed on to the upper decks, perching like starlings on the battlecruiser's guns, turrets, mast and yards to watch the arrival of 'King

re slaughter, more misery and more ruin than has ever before been borne within the compass of
ip': *Goeben* (centre left) and *Breslau* (centre right) at anchor near Constantinople, 1914.
M, HU 110858)

Vizeadmiral Maximilian Graf von Spee, commanding officer of Germany's *Kreuzergeschwader Ostasien*. (*Mary Evans Picture Library*)

Korvettenkapitän Karl Friedrich Max von Müller, SMS *Emden*. (IWM, Q 45324)

Fregattenkapitän Max Looff, SMS *Königsberg*.

Fregattenkapitän Erich Köhler, SMS *Karlsruhe*.

Fregattenkapitän Fritz Lüdecke, SMS *Dresden*.

Rear Admiral Sir Christoph 'Kit' Cradock. (*IWM, Q 69171*)

Commander Richard Denny Townsend, HMS *Invincible*. (IWM, *Department of Documents, TownsendRHD 4480_1*)

The dapper, determined Captain Sidney Drury-Lowe of HMS *Chatham*. (IWM, Q 69045)

Dogged, resourceful and inspiring: Captain John All of HMS *Kent*. (IWM, HU 1108

Vizeadmiral Wilhelm Souchon (front row, third from left), with Colonel Holland, the British Chief of Staff of the Turkish Naval College in Istanbul, Kemal Pasha, the Turkish Navy Minister, and Turkish officers, 1910. (*IWM, Q 81526*)

Vice Admiral Sir Frederick Doveton Sturdee and his staff take a relaxed stroll on East Falkland, December 1914. (*IWM, Department of Documents, TownsendRHD 4480_2*)

'A lithe and graceful representative of the shipbuilder's art.' SMS *Karlsruhe* in 1914. (IWM, HU 1108.

Raider at work. Photographed from *Kabinga*, her first 'rubbish dump', *Em* approaches the coll Killin, 12 September 1914. (*IWM, HU 57273*

Shocked, half-naked *Zhemchug* survivors help a badly wounded comrade on the waterfront at Penang, 28 October 1914. (*IWM, HU 110855*)

Eastern Telegraph Company
employee and members of von
Mücke's landing party watch Emden's
last battle from the roof of the cable
relay station, 9 November 1914.
(IWM, HU 110863)

'She was a total wreck ... her sides
perforated with gaping holes, her
upper deck a mass of twisted steel.'
Emden after the battle. (IWM, HU 110864)

HMS *Glasgow*, veteran of
Coronel, the Falklands, and
Dresden action. *Gloucester*,
Bristol, *Chatham* and other
Town Class light cruisers we
similar ships. (*IWM, HU 110871*

'The peerless ruthlessness
which helped the Royal Nav
to win Britain's wars for
centuries': Captain John Luc
(centre) and his officers aboa
HMS *Glasgow*. (*IWM, HU 11087*

'Enemy Armoured Cruisers
Sight': *Glasgow* sights the
Kreuzergeschwader, 1 Novemb
1914. (*IWM, HU 110868*)

icers of HMS *Good Hope* at Port Stanley, October 1914. None of these men would survive Coronel,
rt from the photographer, Mate Robert Roe, who went ashore to set up an observation post
ore the battle. (*IWM, Q 36422*)

ely visible in the centre of the crowd, von Spee arrives in Valparaiso, 2 November 1914.
M, Q 61345)

The massive armoured bulk of *Scharnhorst*, taking on coal and supplies at Valparaiso after Coronel *Gneisenau* was an identical ship. *(IWM, HU 110859)*

Scharnhorst, *Gneisenau*, and *Nürnberg* (L–R, background) leave Valparaiso after Coronel, November 1914. The Chilean warships are the cruisers *Esmeralda*, *O'Higgins* and *Blanco Encalda* and the battleship *Capitan Prat*. *(IWM, Q 51051)*

e big ships buried their
ns in their wakes as
y dashed onwards.'
4S *Invincible* in pursuit
he *Kreuzergeschwader*,
otographed from
narvon, 8 December
4. (*IWM, HU 110862*)

ost of the watching British sailors had never seen a ship sunk in battle before.' Curious crowds
her on *Invincible*'s upper deck at the end of the battlecruiser action, 8 December 1914.
M, *HU 72107*)

ere were heaps of men in the water clinging to pieces of wreckage.' *Inflexible* sends out her cutters
escue *Gneisenau*'s survivors, photographed by Arthur Duckworth, 8 December 1914. (*IWM, Q 20898*)

'I was knee-deep in these charges, with a roaring fire ju[st] four feet away!' The sinister hole next to HMS *Kent*'s starboard 6-inch casemate which nearly spelled disaster (*IWM, Q 45916*)

'"Stripey" used his loaf!' Roy[al] Marine Sergeant Charles May (second from left), who turne[d] a hose on burning charges an[d] probably saved his ship, on *Kent*'s battered upper deck after the battle. He was later awarded the Conspicuous Gallantry Medal. (*IWM, Q 4592*[...])

1914 each captain's
vements were dictated by
next opportunity to top up
coal bunkers. Here,
MS *Kent*'s crew get stuck in
th their shovels. Note the
hy decks, littered with coal
st and sacks, and the men's
ry coaling rig.
M, HU 110860)

len tried every trick he knew
extract every knot from his
ship.' Breaking up
MS *Kent*'s decks for fuel
ring the pursuit of *Dresden*,
larch 1915. (IWM, HU 110861)

White flags fluttering at h
foremast, *Dresden* lies
anchored in Cumberland
Bay under the towering
peak of El Yunque, Isla M
a Tierra. (*IWM, Q 46021*)

Nearly a hundred years later:
an unexploded British 6-inch
shell embedded in the cliff face
at Más a Tierra. (*Courtesy of
Professor Andrew Lambert*)

Dresden after the so-called
'Battle of Más a Tierra', almost
deserted with smoke rising
from her decks, photographed
from the boat carrying across
Lieutenant Commander
Wilfred Thompson and
Surgeon Robert Gilmour.
(*IWM, HU 110870*)

'Bathed every day and on Sundays wears an Iron Cross around his neck': Tirpitz the Pig and an admirer. *(IWM, HU 110867)*

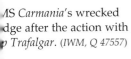

IS Carmania's wrecked
dge after the action with
p *Trafalgar*. *(IWM, Q 47557)*

Kronprinz Wilhelm after her epic cruise, her sides filthy and dented from ramming prizes and repeated coaling at sea. (*IWM, Q 50996*)

SMS *Königsberg* navigates the Suez Canal on her way out to East Africa, June 1914. (*IWM, HU 110856*)

The remains of HMS *Pegasus*: 'by midday she had rolled over and sunk, only her masts marking the site of the one-sided Battle of Zanzibar'. (*IWM, HU 110865*)

man trenches along the Rufiji, May 1915. (*IWM, Q 46269*)

m 700 feet, Flight Lieutenant John Cull captures *Königsberg* in her lair, awnings spread and
ke rising from her after funnel, 25 April 1915. *Severn* and *Mersey* shelled her across the trees in
right foreground. (*IWM, HU 58507*)

'Ugly, unseaworthy and capable of only 4 knots in open water': HMS *Severn* illustrates her low freeboard and poor seakeeping qualities alongside HMS *Trent*, July 1915. (*IWM, Q 46246*)

End of the last pirate: *Königsberg* rests on the Rufiji river bed, riddled with splinter holes, her midd funnel lying on her deck. In the foreground is the mass grave, inscribed 'Here lie the fallen of SMS *Königsberg* II.VII.15'. (*IWM, HU 42477*)

Neptune' (William Hunt, the ship's senior commissioned gunner) and his
outlandishly costumed heralds and courtiers:

> His train must have been at least twenty strong, two Barbers, two
> Doctors, several Devils, and many Bears and a good number of Police-
> men ... The Bears were woolly people as far as their waists anyway, they
> were covered with Oakum [tarred hemp] ... the whole troop drew up
> before the Admiral, and there was greeting from one to the other.
> Neptune then ... proceeded to invest the Admiral with an enormous
> Brass Star, which he hung around his neck with red ribbon (the Admiral
> kneeling the while). Then he gave Iron Crosses to the Commander No. 1
> and one of the other Lieutenants, then the Admiral made a very lengthy
> reply, in which he told Neptune about what rank outsiders the Germans
> were ... then we adjourned to the bath.[48]

Neptune's 'initiates' – those who had never 'crossed the line' before – were
allowed to change into something more appropriate, in Fraser Shaw's case
football shorts and a vest, before being speedily dunked in a canvas bath of salt
water.

> Hanging over the bath were two revolving boxes on which one sat to be
> shaved, and from which one was violently ejected into the bath below ...
> all except some half dozen of the officers had to go through, some of the
> youngsters getting a good ducking from all the Bears and Devils in the
> retinue ... they had passed some 240 victims through before dinner, so
> that the water for the afternoon performance was getting somewhat
> thick.[49]

The festivities ended with the anointing of the smallest ship's boy, 'a tiny little
brat', as a 'Knight of the Bloater', 'the jewel of the order being a very sad
looking one of its species which had been hanging from Neptune's trident all
day'.[50] In total, 650 men and 28 officers were 'initiated'. Despite the urgency
of his mission, Sturdee understood full well the importance of such rituals for
the morale and cohesion of his relatively untried crews, and it is telling that
nearly all of the German cruiser captains also made time for the ceremonies
when they could: 'Crossing the Line' was a truly international phenomenon.
Certainly Fraser Shaw appreciated the gesture: 'It really was a very good
show,' he wrote in his diary, 'and was an utter change for the men, it being
really the first bit of relaxation we have had since commissioning.'[51]

As the battlecruisers resumed their journey south, the atmosphere reverted
to the discomfort and strain of constant 'action stations' and 'darkened ship'.
The fug on the lower mess decks was so stifling that the men were allowed
to open their scuttles, the trade-off being that no lights could be shown,

forcing them to grope around their meagre accommodation like blind men. Finally, at dawn on 26 November, the battlecruisers crept into Britain's secret coaling base off the Brazilian coast, Abrolhos Rocks, and dropped anchor, having steamed nearly 5,000 miles since leaving Devonport. Sturdee's poor operational security almost defied belief: his ships had regularly investigated suspicious merchantmen, revealing themselves in the process by making regular wireless transmissions as they did so, and the squadron's composition, voyage and mission were being openly discussed in bars and clubs from Plymouth to Rio de Janeiro. Despite this, their luck had held: von Spee had no idea they were there.

Abrolhos was a horseshoe-shaped group of five stark, pinnacled islets, surrounded by vicious coral reefs which made them tricky to navigate but easy to defend; the main island was 'desolate [and] ... populated chiefly by lizards', according to Sturdee's most junior clerk, 18-year-old Arthur Duckworth. 'Here,' he went on, 'we joined up with various oddments of the British Fleet that had been in different parts of the world when war was declared.'[52] The ships so dismissively described by the teenaged Duckworth were the component parts of Rear Admiral Stoddart's reinforced squadron: the armoured cruisers *Defence*, *Kent*, *Carnarvon* and *Cornwall*, the light cruisers *Glasgow* and *Bristol*, the AMC *Orama* and nine colliers. The overwhelming concentration of force desired by Fisher and Churchill had been successfully assembled. In fact, with the arrival of the battlecruisers, the Admiralty decided that *Defence* could now be released, after her powerful Poulson wireless equipment had been transferred to *Invincible*.[53] In what must have seemed a ghastly irony to those aboard, the ship that had been belatedly despatched to Cradock's aid would be denied the chance to avenge him. 'We all felt we had been done out of our own particular scrap,' recalled her captain's clerk as the cruiser prepared to cross the Atlantic yet again, bound for South Africa and the Cape Station, 'we are certainly a most unlucky ship.'[54]

Stoddart had endured a long weary wait, constantly on the alert for a surprise attack. Although he enjoyed a small numerical advantage over the *Kreuzergeschwader*, the fate of Cradock's older ships at Coronel must have made him painfully aware that his older armoured cruisers in particular were no match for *Scharnhorst* and *Gneisenau*, and each new arrival served marginally to increase his sense of security. The last had been John Luce's battered *Glasgow*, which dropped anchor at Abrolhos just three days before the battlecruisers, after spending five days pushing the laws of neutrality to the limit by having her action damage repaired in a neutral Brazilian floating dock until the light cruiser was 'dished up as good as new ... all our holes properly mended ... [and] our bottom cleaned and painted'.[55]

For Stoddart's men the battlecruisers meant mail, stores and welcome news from home. For Sturdee, Abrolhos meant coal. The back-breaking work of coaling and storing took two days, and was challenging in the primitive environment of Abrolhos, which lacked even the most rudimentary base facilities. Barry Bingham recalled:

> We had to contend with a heavy swell due to the geographical position of the rendezvous – a few rocks – which provide only an indifferent lee. Coaling was therefore an extremely awkward business ... it was difficult enough for the Admiralty colliers to come alongside, and then when they were, both ships began to grind against one another in an alarming manner. Unless carefully watched, hawsers here will snap like threads of cotton.[56]

Almost as soon as Sturdee anchored, he was accosted by a deeply frustrated and persistent John Luce, who had personally witnessed the desperate vulnerability of the Falklands. Sturdee had rarely succumbed to any undignified sense of urgency during his journey south; besides the regular delays to investigate merchant ships and carry out gunnery drills, he had kept his speed down to a stately 10 knots to conserve coal. Now he intended to delay for a further three days before proceeding to the Falklands, until Luce insisted that time was of the essence and an early departure might be wise. 'Dammit, Luce,' replied Sturdee, 'We're sailing the day after tomorrow. Isn't that good enough for you?' But the departure date was brought forward.[57] Sturdee set off for the Falklands on 28 November, his ships spread 12 miles apart to maximise the chances of sighting the enemy. On the other side of South America von Spee was still anchored in the Gulf of Penas, working up his plan to head east. The cast was assembling for the final act.

Sturdee, typically, was still in no hurry, steaming at no more than 11 knots to conserve coal. He could not be sure that von Spee would attack the Falklands, or how soon he might arrive if he decided to do so. Once there, he meant to coal and head around Cape Horn to search for the *Kreuzergeschwader* in the Pacific, if the enemy did not deign to come to him. On the afternoon of 30 November Sturdee ordered main armament gunnery practice in all his ships, forcibly bringing home to the men under his command that battle almost inevitably awaited them in the bitterly cold South Atlantic. The two battlecruisers worked together, each towing targets for the other, the big 12-inch guns booming across the grey waters at a range of 12,000 yards until at 19:15 *Invincible* suffered an irritating mishap, later recounted by the battlecruiser's 37-year-old first lieutenant, Commander Dick Townsend, in a letter to his wife: 'A silly ass let some of the towing wire get foul of one of the screws and we had to stop in mid-ocean and send divers down, a difficult job as there was a long swell and it was hard for them to work.'[58]

To the frustration of Luce and some of Sturdee's other more zealous subordinates, the methodical, careful (or pedantic) Sturdee ordered the entire squadron to heave to in mid-ocean for almost eight hours while the flagship's divers laboured in vain to clear it. Although frustrating at the time, this unsought delay, along with another brought about by the sighting of a suspicious ship on the horizon, was ultimately to have the most extraordinary consequences.

Other battle preparations, more mundane but just as vital, took place as the squadron approached the Falklands. Layers of paint, applied for years by sweating matelots under the direction of zealous officers anxious to make their ships as 'tiddly' as possible, were painstakingly chipped off as it constituted a serious fire hazard – in fact it was rumoured that 'most of *Good Hope* and *Monmouth*'s misfortunes were due to fires which were caused by paint'.[59] Like coaling, chipping paint was something that everyone took part in: rank provided no immunity, especially for the officer with a more enlightened and inspirational leadership style. Dick Townsend even encountered Sturdee hard at work on a 'beastly raw and foggy' morning, chipping paint off a gun turret.[60]

On the night of the 4th *Invincible*'s wireless operators intercepted a message from a Montevideo station to the Governor of the Falklands, indicating that the *Kreuzergeschwader* had been in the Straits of Magellan two days earlier. But the reports were vague, and nobody gave them much credence, not even Sturdee. Hubert Dannreuther was in the admiral's day cabin, now pressed into service as a makeshift operations room, on 6 December, when the admiral came in, proclaiming that 'he did not think we would get any definite information about the whereabouts of the enemy till we got round to the west coast of South America'.[61] The following day, 7 December 1914, the squadron made landfall at the Falklands, the forbidding peaks and moors emerging through the rain squalls early in the forenoon watch.

Gradually the topography became more distinct, revealing what Dick Townsend called 'a weird-looking place not unlike Scotland'.[62] Finally the squadron sighted the Cape Pembroke lighthouse, followed by East Falkland's great natural harbour and the tiny timber and corrugated-iron capital, Port Stanley. 'Great was the relief of one and all,' Barry Bingham vividly recalled, 'as [the Falklanders] watched a powerful squadron of eight British warships majestically entering the harbour and bringing just that kind of assistance which they sorely needed. It must have seemed as if the deliverance was directly inspired by heaven.'[63] As the squadron approached, a tiny pilot launch appeared from around a point, its fluttering Union flag serving as a reminder that this desolate, windswept archipelago was still an outpost of the most powerful empire in the world. The pilot boarded the flagship, and the squadron slipped quietly in to anchor at 10:00, the light cruisers *Glasgow* and *Bristol* passing into the inner harbour of Port Stanley itself, the larger ships remaining in the deeper, outer anchorage, Port William. The splash of anchors into the water completed a 27-day, 7,000-mile odyssey for the men in the battlecruisers. Town and garrison lay tranquil and unmolested, *Canopus* maintaining her dignified watch like an elderly but determined night watchman, her steel bottom clinging to the mud and her guns elevated to the sky.

Port Stanley had plenty of coal, some 35,000 tons in total, but its facilities were far too primitive for large warships to come alongside; instead, Sturdee's ships would have to transfer it from colliers lashed alongside. Only three colliers were available, which meant that only half his warships could do this simultaneously. Although Sturdee had no intention of staying long, it was therefore inevitable that he would not be able to depart until the next day. Accordingly, ships not coaling immediately were instructed to stand down and rest their crews after the long voyage, and some even doused their boiler fires to carry out essential repairs. The usual night precautions were relaxed, and no guards were posted. One ship would be kept on patrol outside the harbour as guard ship during this time of maximum vulnerability; first up for this onerous but vital duty was the AMC *Macedonia*, to be relieved by HMS *Kent* as soon as the latter vessel finished coaling the following morning. Sturdee held a brief captains' conference in his flagship, after which the battlecruisers' officers were granted five hours' shore leave to take advantage of the limited diversions Port Stanley had to offer. Some took the opportunity to shoot hares and geese, which, with locally supplied fresh mutton, provided a welcome addition to the otherwise monotonous wardroom fare. Others, with a more enlightened attitude to the local fauna, took the opportunity to study the penguin rookeries that surrounded the harbour: 'It was the breeding season,' one officer recalled, 'and on approaching them hundreds would stand up and waddle forward in a threatening attitude, making a terrible din.'[64] The holiday atmosphere seems to have extended to Sturdee; one contemporary photograph shows the admiral relaxed, in full uniform, with walking-stick in hand, tramping across the bleak foreshore accompanied by his flag lieutenant, Reginald Blake, and his secretary, Cyril Johnson. The image, it must be said, manages to convey a quite striking lack of urgency.

As night fell, the men aboard *Glasgow*, *Bristol* and *Carnarvon* continued coaling, the quiet harbour echoing to a chorus of grunts and curses, accompanied by the scrape of shovels and the rattle of winches. On board the other ships the men gratefully turned into their hammocks, no doubt painfully aware that their turn would come in the morning.

The squadron made an early start on the morning of 8 December. *Invincible* and *Inflexible* began coaling at 05:00, with the other ships following soon afterwards. After hours of laborious work the hands went to breakfast; the time varied from ship to ship, but by 07:30 most men had gratefully downed tools. At this point Mrs Felton, the wife of a sheep farmer living near Port Pleasant, entered the story. This redoubtable lady had sent her maid and her 'house-boy' to the top of a nearby ridge, under strict instructions to report anything they saw. Mrs Felton would then relay the information by telephone to the nearest signal station on Sapper Hill. Shortly after 07:30 the house-boy came careering down the hill to the house, and Mrs Felton telephoned Sapper Hill to report a suspicious cloud of smoke to the south-east, which soon turned into von Spee's colliers, *Baden*, *Santa Isabel* and *Seydlitz*. As the Sapper Hill look-outs began frantic attempts to signal the squadron, the rest of the *Kreuzergeschwader* came into sight, led by *Gneisenau* and *Nürnberg*.[65]

Von Spee had arrived, and the British squadron could not have been less prepared. In *Cornwall* most of the officers were in civilian clothes, preparing for a day's shooting. One of the ship's engines had been stripped down and the cruiser was at six hours' notice for steam. *Carnarvon* had coal sacks strewn across her decks. *Bristol* also had an engine in pieces, stripped down to repair a burst boiler tube. Neither of the battlecruisers had completed coaling, and *Kent*, *Cornwall*, *Bristol* and *Macedonia* had not even begun.

The sighting report from Sapper Hill took nearly twenty minutes to pass around the squadron. First to receive it was *Canopus*, which passed the message to *Glasgow*. John Luce, to his immense frustration, could not attract the attention of the flagship, which was surrounded by a haze of coal dust and with most of the ship's company already dismissed below to eat. Eventually he fired a gun and shone a powerful searchlight directly at the battlecruiser's bridge. It was 07:56 before the report reached Sturdee, who was shaving in his cabin. In the wardroom Barry Bingham had reached 'the third cup-of-coffee-and-marmalade stage', when an excited signalman burst in, still black from coaling, to report, 'with praiseworthy efforts to preserve his official calm', that the enemy was in sight.[66] The Battle of the Falklands was about to begin.

Chapter 7

In the Old Style: the Battle of the Falklands

'It was not a Victory – it was Annihilation!'

Jackie Fisher, writing on 22 August 1917

The morning of 8 December 1914 dawned bitterly cold but unnaturally bright, clear and calm for the South Atlantic in winter. Von Spee's attack was to follow the well-tried pattern evolved by the *Kreuzergeschwader* in the Pacific. At 05:00 he detached *Gneisenau* and *Nürnberg*, ordering Maerker and von Schönberg to sweep down upon the islands and enter the outer harbour, preceded by their boats as a precaution against mines. Maerker was then supposed to anchor *Gneisenau* and bully the local authorities into handing over Governor Allardyce, along with a 'war levy' of supplies and cash, while von Schönberg entered the inner harbour to bombard the port facilities and the wireless station. If the two cruisers encountered any British warships, they were to turn back and rejoin the squadron at a previously agreed rendezvous, well over the horizon, where von Spee could consider his next move.[1] As a precaution, he instructed the rest of the squadron to clear for action and raise steam for 18 knots.

Von Spee anticipated finding British warships at Port Stanley; according to two *Gneisenau* survivors, just after he left Picton Island a Dutch merchant ship had warned him to expect *Glasgow*, *Canopus* and perhaps one or two of Stoddart's cruisers.[2] But had Sturdee been possessed of any greater sense of urgency, the islands would have been almost undefended, as the British warships would surely have coaled and left for Cape Horn by the time the Germans arrived. The Battle of the Falklands was as much a consequence of *Invincible*'s fouled propeller on 30 November as it was down to what Hubert Dannreuther emphatically called 'a fine example of good strategy to be at the RIGHT PLACE at the RIGHT TIME with the maximum STRIKING FORCE' (original emphasis).[3]

The two German ships approached from the south, which meant that a range of low hills and dunes stretching east from the British observation post on Sapper Hill screened the harbour and the ships within it. It was thus some time after the initial British sighting at 07:30 before the approaching Germans began to understand that not all was as it should be. However, the delay in getting the sighting report to Sturdee meant that this potential advantage was largely negated.

Just before 08:00 look-outs aboard *Gneisenau* observed thick columns of black smoke rising from inside the harbour, which were assumed to be the British burning their coal stocks. Shortly afterwards, *Gneisenau*'s senior gunnery officer, *Korvettenkapitän* Johann Busche, reported sighting the distinctive tripod masts of a Royal Navy capital ship through a gap in the hills. An animated debate on the bridge ended with Maerker concluding that the ominous structures belonged to nothing more threatening than colliers, and the German ships continued to advance. The sight of HMS *Kent* lumbering from the harbour entrance did not deter them either; Maerker hoisted his battle ensigns, increased speed and turned to the north-east, hoping to catch her as she came out. With the sentimental objectivity of hindsight, one observer in *Kent* recalled how the German cruisers 'made a perfect picture, closing to 14,500 yards, the crews going to action stations and the guns training round as they turned'.[4]

As the vulnerable AMC *Macedonia* steamed back past him for the safety of the harbour, Captain John Allen brought *Kent* to a stop at 08:54, just outside the harbour mouth, from where he could observe the enemy and pass reports to the flagship. For those aboard, the excitement of impending battle sat uneasily alongside a painful awareness of how exposed their obsolescent ship was. One anonymous diarist later tried to explain this peculiar mix of emotions: 'impatience that *Invincible* and *Inflexible* were not under way ... an exhilarating feeling that we were to have a taste of fire. Then I thought of my home – my dear wife and child – and dear people there. Friends, too, in all my thoughts – but little time to stop and think – there was work on hand.'[5]

Back in the harbour the British warships were casting off from colliers and raising steam, filling the clear winter air above the harbour with dense clouds of acrid smoke. At about 09:20 the first shots were fired. Captain Heathcote Grant had planned some long-overdue gunnery practice for his grounded battleship *Canopus*. The crew of the pre-dreadnought's forward 12-inch turret had crept from their mess decks during the preceding night and stealthily loaded the guns, ensuring a decisive advantage over their rivals in the after turret. With no time to unload, the two practice rounds had to be fired to get them out of the way. The range was some 15,000 metres, well beyond the theoretical maximum for the battleship's old guns, but unlike high explosive shells, which exploded on impact with water, the two solid shots ricocheted and, according to one eye-witness, 'by a piece of luck defying all the probabilities, they landed a hit on the *Gneisenau*'.[6] *Canopus* discharged four rounds in all, the other three falling well short.

Maerker turned away when the first 12-inch shells screamed across the water, but once it became apparent that no more heavy calibre projectiles were coming his way, he resumed his previous course, reporting first two, then four and then six warships inside the harbour, until von Spee signalled him to rejoin the *Kreuzergeschwader*. According to one junior officer in *Canopus*, *Gneisenau* and *Nürnberg* 'legged it as hard as they could', leaving some aboard the old battleship convinced that they had single-handedly sent the enemy packing.[7]

The two battlecruisers appeared at the harbour mouth shortly after 10:00, the smaller cruisers straggling behind them, and Sturdee ordered his signallers to hoist the vividly Nelsonic signal for 'General Chase'; according to Dannreuther, this was 'the only known occasion in both world wars that this signal was hoisted'.[8] From a standing start, with her fires out, boilers opened and one tube removed altogether, *Invincible* was steaming at 25 knots just two and half hours later, a tribute to the efforts of her engineering staff: 'the men smacked about splendidly,' recalled Engineer Lieutenant-Commander Fraser Shaw, 'and things fairly hummed'.[9] As the battlecruiser gathered speed, she cut remorselessly through *Cornwall*'s sailing pinnace, which had been abandoned laden with mutton and flour, although the cruiser's junior officers had found time to save the wardroom beer before casting it adrift.[10]

As they gained speed, Sturdee's squadron shook out into a loose line, *Invincible* in the lead with five battle ensigns fluttering at her mastheads, followed by *Inflexible*, *Glasgow* and the elderly *Kent*: 'I nearly had a fit', wrote 'Fred', one of the flagship's stokers, 'when I saw her plodding away.'[11] Further back were the other two armoured cruisers, *Carnarvon* and *Cornwall*. *Macedonia* remained in harbour with *Bristol*, whose engineers were frantically reassembling her engine. Lieutenant-Commander Henry Spencer-Cooper of HMS *Cornwall* vividly recalled the scene:

Imagine a calm, smooth sea, the sun shining and not a cloud in the sky, the ship steaming at something over 23 knots, and the men crowded on the turrets and in every available corner, tier upon tier, for all the world as if looking at a cup tie at the Crystal Palace ... it was a wonderful sight. The big ships buried their sterns in their wakes as they dashed onwards.[12]

Luck was with Sturdee. Had von Spee realised that the British ships were anchored with colliers alongside, fires out and machinery in pieces, he might have entered the harbour and raked them at close range before making off into the Atlantic, leaving the British humiliated and none the wiser about his location. But by 11:00 this window of opportunity had closed, and von Spee had identified the two mystery warships as battlecruisers. Now his only hope lay in outrunning his formidable foe and finding shelter in darkness, fog or heavy weather. Von Spee turned to the south-east and cracked on the best speed his weary ships could make, a miserable 22 knots, as the sun shone brightly, the indifferent sky remained frustratingly clear and the sea calm.

Sturdee set off in pursuit, confident that his superior speed ensured the long stern chase would only end in despair for the Germans. In the meantime the British prepared for battle. Aboard *Inflexible*, the ship's company cleaned the ship before going below to wash and change. 'Then we had early dinner,' recalled Captain Phillimore, '11.30 instead of noon, and were all ready to begin.'[13] In *Cornwall* an intense game of chess began behind the wireless office.[14] These distractions were not just *sang-froid*. The long pursuit, watching an enemy draw slowly near whose gunfire might bring death or, worse, mutilation, was as hard on Sturdee's men as it was on the Germans, and domestic routine was a vital distraction, as the seconds ticked away and the German cruisers loomed larger in watching lenses. The technique had been tested in battle for hundreds of years, and it worked; Royal Marines Captain Robert Sinclair recalled with unselfconscious enthusiasm in a letter to his sister Lucy how, when Phillimore finally announced that *Inflexible* was about to engage the enemy, his words were 'accompanied by a storm of cheers (contrary to all regulations) and the men rushed to their stations laughing and joking with their eyes sparkling with joy'.[15]

The German ships were steaming in roughly line abreast, with *Nürnberg* and *Leipzig* slightly to the rear. According to Dick Townsend, it was *Invincible* that opened fire first, at 12:50, targeting *Leipzig* at extreme range, *Inflexible* following at 12:57. Seeing little *Leipzig* vanishing among filthy columns of ravaged, contaminated water, von Spee signalled Haun to leave the line. Shortly afterwards, recognising the futility of keeping light cruisers in the line against such powerful opponents, he made his famously chivalrous signal: '*Gneisenau* [and *Scharnhorst*] will accept action, light cruisers act independently', giving all his smaller consorts a chance to escape. At 13:20 they sheered away, engines straining to provide every possible knot, everyone aboard knowing that von Spee was steaming to his doom: 'Each one of us knew he probably would never see his brave comrades again.'[16]

Sturdee had prepared for this development at Abrolhos, and *Kent*, *Cornwall* and *Glasgow* altered course in pursuit of the now-fleeing *Leipzig*, *Nürnberg* and *Dresden*. Stoddart's sluggish flagship *Carnarvon*, 10 miles adrift with no realistic chance of catching up, trailed in the battlecruisers' wake as they closed *Scharnhorst* and *Gneisenau*. At this point the battle splintered into several elements.

The Battlecruiser Action

Von Spee had only one, very slim, chance of success: to bring his ships close to the British leviathans and bring his cruisers' secondary 150mm guns into action. This might in part redress Sturdee's shockingly superior weight of metal: *Invincible* and *Inflexible* each fired a main armament broadside of 5,100lb (2,313kg), as against the 1,957lb (887kg) of *Scharnhorst* and *Gneisenau*.[17] A little nearer, and von Spee might be able to use his torpedoes. If he could slow one or both of the pursuing battlecruisers with a torpedo hit, he might, just, be able to escape. Accordingly, as his fleeing light cruisers scattered over the horizon, von Spee turned *Scharnhorst* and *Gneisenau*, trying to close the enemy as quickly as possible, bring all his guns to bear and keep the prevailing gentle breeze on to his engaged side, blowing the smoke from his guns and funnels back across the ship and preventing it from interfering with his gunnery. The British shifted their fire, *Invincible* engaging *Gneisenau* and *Inflexible* the German flagship.

Von Spee's ships lacked firepower but the superior skill and training of his gunners was marked. Although the British enjoyed nearly half an hour of uninterrupted shooting, as the four ships closed steadily to a range of around 10,000 metres it was the Germans who obtained the first straddles, plumes of filthy water erupting around Sturdee's ships. 'I expected it would be over in an hour,' recalled *Invincible*'s Lieutenant-Commander Edward Smyth-Osbourne, 'but to my surprise we did not seem to be hitting her [*Gneisenau*] at all, and she straddled us at once and kept it up practically all the time, firing beautifully controlled salvoes.'[18] *Scharnhorst*, too, distinguished herself by the quality of her gunnery, one observer aboard *Inflexible* commenting on her 'good salvoes, spreading some 200 yards and fired frequently'.[19]

At 13:45 *Invincible* was hit for the first time, before the British could turn and open up the range. *Gneisenau*'s shells could not penetrate the thick armoured belt that protected the battlecruiser's engines and magazines, and with the sea so calm the chance of striking a telling blow 'below the belt' when the ship rolled was small. But for the men working five decks down to keep *Invincible*'s four mighty turbines turning, the first hammer blow must have been terrifying; Fraser Shaw recalled how the 20,000-ton ship 'quivered from end to end' when she was struck, and every so often a sinister rattle of steel fragments against the side could be clearly heard.[20]

In the great 12-inch turrets, and the handling rooms below, men worked like automatons, feeding ammunition to the great guns as they belched fury at the enemy. For all the technological advances of the industrial era, naval warfare in 1914 was still a crude, physical business, lubricated in the main by human sweat. The experience of gunnery ratings like *Invincible*'s George Miller might not have been entirely alien to Nelson's cursing seamen, heaving at HMS *Victory*'s cannon more than a hundred years before:

> The shell goes ... in to the gun ... you put the cordite roll in behind it ... in big long tubes in like cellophane bags. And of course when the gunners fire, it sends fire to the cordite and that causes the explosion on the shell and away it goes, this present to von Spee or whoever you're firing at. The sky is absolutely stifled with the smell of cordite, yellow fumes ... and the ship itself after you've been struck a time or two, everything is knocked over, the mess deck is anything but a sitting room![21]

After ten minutes *Scharnhorst* drew ahead of her consort, and the British battlecruisers switched targets. British gunnery remained poor, in part due to the prevailing wind, which drove thick clouds of funnel and gun smoke out in front of the guns. *Invincible* was further hindered by her recently replaced fire control equipment, her new turret mechanisms and her inexperienced crew, but even the more experienced *Inflexible* was not immune to error, as Lieutenant-Commander Rudolph Verner, high in her spotting top, was painfully aware:

> I hardly felt in a position to remind anyone that we still held the Battle Practice Cup ... at one period, having found and then lost the target, I gave an order of 'down 200' and was delighted to see a good straddle, and for some time ... watched with much satisfaction a regular deluge of water falling round and about the enemy; when suddenly into the right-hand field of my glasses there crept the stem of another ship and I realised that I had been an admiring spectator of *Invincible*'s shooting, during which time our own shots had remained unspotted on the *Gneisenau*.[22]

Equipment failures added to the British difficulties; Sub-Lieutenant Robert Stewart recalled problems with the fuse caps on the lyddite shells, a lack of spares and appalling ventilation, which caused the turrets to fill with choking cordite fumes.[23] Midshipman Rupert Montagu, sealed into the stifling steel box that was *Invincible*'s A-turret, remembered 'great difficulty with the right gun, the breech having closed on the shot guide and jammed, [and] the lock in the latter part of the action was continually causing misfires'.[24]

The battlecruisers expended over 200 12-inch shells during the first phase, but scored just three hits on *Gneisenau* and one on *Scharnhorst*. However, just one 12-inch lyddite shell could cause catastrophic damage. Two exploded on *Gneisenau*'s upper deck, bursting against the cruiser's third funnel, smashing her boats to matchwood and wrecking her wardroom. But the third sliced through *Gneisenau*'s armoured belt, pierced the armoured deck and entered a magazine, starting a fire. A quick-thinking gunner's mate named Lange flooded the magazine, preventing what could have been a serious explosion.[25] The three hits killed or wounded nearly fifty men; the British battlecruisers had sustained no serious casualties at all. This was a battle von Spee could not win.

At 13:45 Sturdee turned to open out the range, trying to find the elusive ideal distance from where the British could hit without being hit back. Von Spee saw an opportunity and just after 14:00 he made a sudden attempt to escape, turning hard to starboard. Sturdee followed, periodically altering course fractionally to try to bring his ships out of their own smoke. The result was another stern chase and a brief lull in the action, as both sides jockeyed for position. In *Scharnhorst* and *Gneisenau* damage control parties took the opportunity to patch up the wounded cruisers, while medical teams patched up the wounded men, and carried off the dead. In *Gneisenau* a meal appeared, miraculously conjured up by the ship's cooks. The German cruisers were not yet out of the fight: their guns, engines, boilers and steering gear were still in good working order. On the British side *Invincible* sported a large, smoking hole in her side. Another German shell had severed one of the struts of the foremast, and the flagship's once-pristine decks were a chaotic litter of broken derricks, ladders and other impedimenta, but both battlecruisers were essentially unscathed. As the embattled ships drew apart, each side peered intently at the other across miles of smoke-shrouded ocean, looking hopefully for signs of damage and finding scant comfort in what little they could see.

The interlude ended at 14:45, when Sturdee opened fire again at just under 14,000m range. Confident in his superior firepower, and aware that the Germans must have fired a significant proportion of their ammunition at Coronel, the British admiral set caution to one side and allowed the range to fall, the two squadrons steaming on almost parallel but gradually converging courses. At this juncture, both sides must have been startled to watch a ghostly new player step gracefully on to the stage: 'A full-rigged sailing ship appeared ... she was painted white, and her sails were shining as if bleached in the bright sunlight; with stunsails and every stitch of canvas spread she sailed majestically along, looking a perfect picture.'[26] The interloper was the Norwegian barque *Fairport*, homeward-bound from Tocapilla. She passed slowly along the port beam of the British squadron and out of sight. History has not recorded the feelings of her crew at finding themselves in the middle of a brutal naval action, but one suspects that it may not have been the 'thrilling and dramatic moment' suggested by HMS *Cornwall*'s Henry Spencer-Cooper.

At just over 11,000m the sharper crack of von Spee's secondary armament became distinguishable, but Sturdee maintained his course. Shell after shell plunged into *Invincible*, ravaging the flagship's upper decks. Her damaged mast was wobbling dangerously, and the wardroom had taken a direct hit which reduced most of the furniture to matchwood, put a 4-foot hole in the deck and wrecked the piano; Sturdee's 18-year-old clerk Arthur Duckworth later described the bulkheads as 'riddled with shot holes like a nutmeg grater'.[27] The sick bay and canteen were smashed, along with several cabins, and a German shell had blown off the muzzle of a 4-inch gun. But most of the damage constituted little more than an inconvenience. Not one man had been killed, and wounds were largely superficial, as all non-essential personnel had been sent below before the action. One minor casualty was Dick Townsend, who in the course of making rounds to assess damage, had discovered that the Paymaster's cabin had taken a direct hit, which had wrecked the safe and left the deck 'strewn with gold and postal orders'. Townsend gathered the loot into a sea-boot and hid it in his cabin, safe from the attention of any opportunistic matelot, but as he returned a second shell added him to the casualty list, to his considerable embarrassment:

> I was scouting around for signs of a fire after we had got a biff forward … when piff! Smash! And I was knocked flying … I felt my left foot was numb but that otherwise I was fit as a flea … I am not in the <u>least wounded</u> [original emphasis], only got a big bruise on my left heel and I will be up and about in about a week.

Sturdee suggested he be reported as 'slightly wounded' to enhance his promotion prospects, but Townsend demurred, writing that it would have been like a soldier being 'shot through the breeches'.[28]

Invincible's only truly dangerous moment came when one shell, diving in at an impossible angle, penetrated the ship's side under the armoured belt. Passing straight through a coal bunker, it came to rest against the side of one of *Invincible*'s magazines, but failed to explode. According to Hubert Dannreuther, 'if it had exploded it might well have ignited P Magazine and blown up the ship … if [it] had entered the ship's side a few feet further forward it would have flooded the hydraulic room and all power to the turrets would have ceased and the ship would have been completely out of action'. The German shell was missing its base fuse. According to Dannreuther, German fuses had a right-hand thread, which meant they turned in the same direction as the shell in flight, and unless the fuse was perfectly tight it could come undone as the shell spun. British fuses had left-hand threads, so if they were not fitted properly – an obvious risk during the stress of battle – they would turn against the spin of the shell and tighten themselves in flight. *Invincible* had been saved by a naval version of the 'horseshoe nail'.[29]

Von Spee could not know how close he had come to salvation. Across the water the British battlecruisers looked indestructible, ploughing through the waves, their guns repeatedly flashing, fractions of a second before the watching Germans heard the accompanying roar. By 15:15 *Gneisenau* was listing, and five minutes later *Scharnhorst* was severely hit amidships. When the smoke cleared, she was on fire and her third funnel had disappeared, a dismal cloud of vapour spreading outwards from the shattered stump.[30] Sturdee took the opportunity to reverse course in one last attempt to overcome the irritating distraction of the wind, turning his ships together in a manoeuvre which placed *Inflexible* in the lead for the first time. Von Spee mirrored his move, but turned his ships in succession, determined to keep his flagship in front. As a result, for a full five minutes the battered *Scharnhorst* was bows-on to the British ships, and exposed to the full weight of their broadsides. By 15:30 she was a wreck, 'her upper-works … seemed to be but a shambles of torn and twisted steel and iron, and through the holes in her side … could be seen dull red glows as the flames gradually gained the mastery between decks'.[31] A splinter cut von Spee's personal flag, prompting Maerker to signal, asking if the admiral was dead. 'I am all right so far,' replied von Spee. 'Have you hit anything?' His last signal read 'You were right after all' – a typically generous acknowledgement that Maerker had been correct to express reservations about the Falklands raid two days earlier.[32]

The course reversal allowed Captain Schultz, if he was still alive, to bring the undamaged guns on his previously disengaged starboard side into action, and for a while *Scharnhorst*'s gunfire increased in ferocity, but the end was near. At 15:45 von Spee signalled Maerker, ordering him to escape under cover of a torpedo attack by the dying flagship. It was a gallant but futile gesture. Eyewitnesses on board *Gneisenau* believed that *Scharnhorst*'s torpedoes had already exploded, tearing a mortal wound in the ship's hull: 'the ship was considerably down by the head with her propellers revolving in the air, and she looked a complete wreck … her leak party was working with the strength of desperation, but could make no headway against the volume of water that forced its way into the ship.'[33]

The German flagship began her death throes at 16:00, just as Stoddart's flagship *Carnarvon* finally wheezed into range, an elderly foxhound trying to keep up with the hunt. As the old cruiser fired for the first time, *Scharnhorst*'s bows sank deeper into the water, her surviving crew assembled on her twisted decks, clutching hammocks and singing patriotic songs.[34] Seventeen minutes later, with terrifying suddenness, she lurched over on to her side, her stern rose into the air like a macabre memorial to the dead and dying men entombed inside her, and she plunged to the bottom with her battle ensigns flying. Preoccupied with the continuing battle, as von Spee had been at Coronel, no British ship stopped to rescue survivors, and von Spee, Schultz and all 860 officers and men went down with her.

Gneisenau was left to face the full fury of the British alone. Against the odds, Maerker fought his ship for another hour and a half. British 12-inch shells carved through *Gneisenau*'s armour with monotonous regularity and she was repeatedly hit below the waterline. *Kapitänleutnant* Ancker, at the cruiser's forward starboard 208mm battery, experienced the full, drawn-out horror of the battle's last phase:

> A shell struck us just above the gun ... the gun was completely put out of action, and the whole gun's crew blown to pieces. The violent air-blast burst open the splinter-door, disabled the port gun, and killed most of the gun's crew. Sub-Lieutenant Pfülf and I escaped death by a miracle, although we were both standing close to the gun in the casemate that was hit. Pfülf was merely flung aside; I received several burns and splinter wounds. The survivors of the port gun's crew at once hurried up with their fire hoses, and the Sub-Lieutenant with their help dragged me out from under the dead bodies, and put out my burning clothes.[35]

Gneisenau continued to hit back for another fifteen minutes, although she had used up her armour-piercing ammunition and was resorting to low-explosive 'common shell' and even practice rounds. She scored three hits, which caused little damage but prompted grudging admiration from her adversaries: 'What the devil can we do?' rhetorically enquired Rudolph Verner of his rate operator, high in *Inflexible*'s spotting top, watching as the tortured *Gneisenau*, immersed in shell splashes, perforated and burning, somehow returned fire:

> Through the spray of our short shots one could see the twinkles of her gun discharges and she continued to fire the most perfect salvoes. Rapid independent (P turret had three shells in the air at one time), though apparently accurate, seemed to have no effect. [The rate operator's] answer, though brief, was neither to the point nor repeatable.[36]

It could not last. At 16:50 Captain Phillimore took *Inflexible* in a wide curve astern of the embattled *Gneisenau*, trying to steam clear of the thick smoke surrounding his consorts to give his gunners a better view; the German cruiser was now under fire from both sides. Just before 17:00 her steering jammed and she began to make a long, slow turn to starboard, mercilessly mirrored by the three British ships. One at a time *Gneisenau*'s remaining guns were put out of action; one shell from *Inflexible*, crashing through the deck with terrible force, exploded behind one of her 208mm casemates, blowing gun, crew and several tons of armour out of the side of the ship. Internal communications broke down and fire control was no longer possible; disciplined salvoes were replaced by ragged, despairing shots loosed off by the few battle-crazed gunners left alive. By 17:28 *Gneisenau* was clearly in terrible distress, wallowing uncontrollably. As the weather deteriorated into low cloud, rising winds and drizzle, the British ships ceased fire and men surreptitiously drifted out on deck to watch the end. This was premature; a few minutes later *Gneisenau* opened fire again from her dented and blackened forward turret – the only undamaged gun that would still bear. The sporadic shots provoked a six-minute storm of return fire, followed by another silence. Surely it was over? In *Gneisenau* Maerker asked *Korvettenkapitän* Busche why he had ceased fire. The senior gunnery officer replied, 'I cannot speak to the guns.' Maerker asked him to walk around the ship and physically check each gun, but this was impossible owing to the severity of the damage. 'All the guns are disabled or have no men,' continued Busche. 'The fore turret is all right, but has only one round; there is ammunition below but it cannot come up.'[37]

And so one last shell screamed across the narrowing strip of water that separated the ships, scattering a group of curious sailors who had gathered on the roof of *Inflexible*'s after turret. The battlecruiser pumped another ten shells into *Gneisenau*, until the guns fell silent for the last time. Inside *Gneisenau*'s battered hull, explosive charges were set off and the torpedo tubes opened to the sea, establishing a German naval tradition of scuttling before surrender which would last through two world wars. Slowly, she rolled over onto her beam ends and slipped under the surface, her grave marked by a haze of steam and smoke. It was 17:48.

Most of the watching British sailors had never seen a ship sunk in battle before, and had been below decks when *Scharnhorst* went down. Hundreds contrived to be on the upper decks of *Invincible*, *Inflexible* and *Carnarvon* when *Gneisenau* went to the bottom. For 18-year-old Arthur Duckworth it was 'a truly terrible sight, and one I hope never to see again. All around the ship there floated bodies, some on hammocks, some on spars, others struggling by themselves, others again drowning before one's very eyes'.[38]

Aboard *Inflexible*, Captain Phillimore forestalled his excited men making an undignified rush to the forecastle by piping the 'alert'; discipline triumphed and the entire ship's company stood in silence at attention as *Gneisenau* sank: 'a terrible and awful sight ... so different from looking at a picture', remembered his young clerk, C.F. Laborde.[39]

Even in the late arriving *Carnarvon*, cheated of a share in the victory by her aged engines, there was little sense of triumph. Lieutenant-Commander Arthur Leslie wrote to his father, confessing that 'I was very depressed and have not once felt any feeling of exultation on the action, but only one of pity that such fine fellows, after putting up such a splendid fight, should have to perish so miserably.'[40]

The British sailors turned to with a will to rescue as many of their erstwhile opponents as they could. 'There were heaps of men in the water clinging to pieces of wreckage,' recalled *Invincible*'s Sub-Lieutenant Ross Stewart, 'and they appeared to make a noise just like the bleating of lambs as they called out to their rescuers ... I saw a good many sink.' As a young 'Snottie', or Midshipman, Stewart had served on the China Station before the war and had known the officers of the *Kreuzergeschwader Ostasien* well:

> Some of the officers which we rescued from the South Atlantic were officers who less than six months before I'd been dining with on board their own German ship ... these officers had been my friends and my reaction was that although it had been my duty to engage them, or engage their ships, there was a feeling of satisfaction that we had been able to save some of their lives.[41]

Stewart's generosity of spirit is all the more remarkable when one considers that the ship in which he had served in China was HMS *Good Hope*, and he had gone on to serve in HMS *Monmouth*. Ties between the British and German fleets before the war had been strong, and such coincidences were by no means uncommon; one half-drowned *Gneisenau* officer scrambled aboard *Carnarvon* and announced that he had a cousin in one of the British ships. It turned out to be Archibald Stoddart, the man whose flagship had just rescued him.[42]

Most of the boats had been filled with water before the battle, and many were pitted with splinter holes. Instead, the sailors threw out anything that would help the men struggling in the water to float, or swung out cumbersome anti-torpedo booms until they projected from the side of the ship like monstrous oars, a welcome handhold for a sodden, exhausted man to cling to. Lieutenant Hugh Begbie distinguished himself by repeatedly jumping into the icy water to secure lines around choking, half-dead Germans; 'all were moaning and suffering from shock and exposure ... several had bad scalds and were pitted with powder marks,' Dick Townsend wrote later to his wife.[43]

Invincible picked up 108 survivors and *Inflexible* sixty-two. *Carnarvon* saved twenty. They included *Gneisenau*'s executive officer, *Fregattenkapitän* Hans Pochhammer, and fifteen other officers. Some 592 men died. British casualties in the battlecruiser action numbered just four, all from *Inflexible*, rather strangely, since she had taken far fewer hits than the flagship. Only one was a fatality, 35-year-old Able Seaman Neil Livingstone of Glen Lean, Argyllshire. As Jackie Fisher wrote exultantly to a friend, 'it was not a Victory – it was Annihilation!'[44] But at this stage, nobody could be sure. The remainder of the *Kreuzergeschwader* was still unaccounted for.

Dresden and the Colliers

The humdrum but necessary task of rounding up the German colliers had fallen to Captain Basil Fanshawe's cruiser *Bristol* and the AMC *Macedonia*, commanded by Captain Bertram Evans. Fanshawe's ship had left Port Stanley last, his crew having reassembled an engine in record time, but she was a thoroughbred and caught up with the squadron in time to see the first shots fired, before backtracking to overhaul *Macedonia*. By 16:00 Fanshawe and Evans had caught the colliers *Baden* and *Santa Isabel*, as an able seaman from *Bristol* described:

> When we were about 5 miles away, we fired our foremost 6-inch gun and the shell fell just alongside the second ship and she stopped at once and turned showing us she had no guns. We gained a couple of miles on the other one and she did the same before we could fire. Then we made a signal, 'Hoist your ensigns and we will allow you twenty minutes to take to your boats and come on board here.' Then we started to sink them.[45]

Fanshawe sank the auxiliaries in the mistaken belief that they were transporting military equipment and landing parties; a mistake, as it turned out, as the coal and stores they carried would have been invaluable. After holing both colliers below the waterline, he left the disconsolate survivors to *Macedonia*, taking *Bristol* back to the Falklands at high speed. Petty Officer C.A. Bourne RNR, aboard the AMC, watched the two ships go down: 'What a sight it is to see ships sink ... they went down stern first and you see the bow come out of the water like a whale, it slides down out of the way and it's gone.'[46]

Von Spee's third auxiliary, *Seydlitz*, was faster and was only a smudge of smoke on the horizon when *Macedonia* and *Bristol* arrived. Skirting the battle, she finally found safety and internment in San Antonio on 18 December.

Fregattenkapitän Fritz Lüdecke's *Dresden* was another escapee. When Sturdee instructed *Kent*, *Glasgow* and *Cornwall* to pursue the German light cruisers, Captain Walter Ellerton of *Cornwall* had suggested he take *Leipzig*, *Kent* take *Nürnberg* and *Glasgow* take *Dresden*. But at the time *Glasgow* was steaming with the battlecruisers, 4 miles ahead of the pack, and was already engaged in a sporadic duel with *Leipzig*, just under 11,000m off his starboard quarter. Luce, senior of the three captains and perhaps mindful of unfinished business from Coronel, therefore decided to hold *Leipzig* until *Cornwall* could come up, instead of going after *Dresden* straight away. *Dresden* was the fastest of the German ships, and by the time Ellerton arrived to tackle *Leipzig*, Lüdecke was 16 miles away and out of *Glasgow*'s reach, vanishing into the gathering mist and drizzle. Some in the fleet criticized Luce for this decision;

certainly, *Cornwall*'s Lieutenant Kenneth Millar was still furious more than two weeks later, writing to his mother that

> we are all very bitter with the *Glasgow*. I can't make out why she did not go on after the *Dresden*. As a matter of fact, I don't think she was very keen on meeting her. She didn't seem to like the fire from the *Leipzig* and ... hid in our smoke, where she really did more harm than good.[47]

There was, however, never any question of a formal reprimand.

Leipzig

While *Cornwall* and *Kent*, identical sisters of the lost *Monmouth*, raced through the water almost neck-and-neck, their engines straining to produce every possible knot of speed, Luce began to exchange blows with Haun at extreme range. Although *Glasgow* was nominally a 6-inch cruiser, she had only two such guns, only one of which would actually bear, and *Leipzig*'s smaller 105s comfortably outranged her 4-inch secondary weapons – German guns consistently outranged British weapons of equal or even heavier calibre, as their mounts allowed them to be elevated much higher. Every time Luce closed the range to fire, Haun turned to expose his starboard broadside, and his well-drilled gunners surrounded *Glasgow* with perfect straddles. One direct hit killed 26-year-old Stoker Petty Officer Edwin Martell and injured five other men; one Royal Marine bugler had a narrow escape when he was hit in the centre of his cap badge by a splinter 'which shaved his hair from his head and came out again through the top of his cap without injuring him at all'.[48] *Leipzig*'s formidable gunnery forced Luce to pull away, but time was not on Haun's side. His tired little ship was long overdue a refit, her engines only capable of 23 knots at best, and every time he turned to ward off *Glasgow* he lost precious time, allowing *Kent* and *Cornwall* to close the range.

At 15:02 Captain Ellerton ordered *Cornwall* to action stations, 'and at the sound of the bugle a great cheer went up from the ship's company'.[49] Eight minutes later he signalled Captain Allen, suggesting *Kent* alter course and go after *Nürnberg*. Minute by minute the running fight increased in ferocity as the range decreased. *Leipzig* was hit for the first time at exactly 16:00. *Torpedo Maschinist* Paul Siebert recalled,

> When the armoured deck was struck it was if the ship had received a blow from below. She seemed to leap up, and the propellers and rivet heads quivered in the same manner ... the sound of the projectile striking and exploding was of a quite peculiar nature: a short, clear, singing note.[50]

The shell exploded in the warrant officers' galley, splinters tearing through bulkheads, killing the gunnery order transmitter and damaging the gunnery voice-pipe. More splinters damaged the ventilation trunking, causing a loss of steam pressure. Soon afterwards a second shell smashed down the foretopmast, destroying the range-finder and killing the gunnery officer. *Leipzig*'s flawless gunnery was becoming harder to sustain. The cruiser's broken mast hung drunkenly downwards for the rest of the action, its attached battle ensign fluttering upside down in a ghastly parody of the international signal for distress.[51]

Soon afterwards the two armoured cruisers drew within range, *Kent* opening fire with her forward guns at 18:15 and *Cornwall* two minutes later, before the former peeled off in pursuit of *Nürnberg*. Several 6-inch shells crashed into *Leipzig*'s thin plating aft, one bursting in the clothing store and drying room and starting a fire that the crew were unable to bring fully under control. Stung, Haun altered course and turned *Leipzig*'s broadside on *Cornwall*, while *Glasgow* ducked and weaved in and out of range like an irritable terrier. As the three ships aggressively manoeuvred, their targets swung in and out of sight, bringing about opportunities for repairs during brief lulls in the firing, but *Leipzig*'s steam pressure continued to fall, and her weary engines were labouring.

At 17:00 *Leipzig* passed across *Cornwall*'s bows, all guns blazing as she pummelled the British cruiser on her previously unengaged port side. Although *Cornwall*'s armour was proof against any serious damage, her upperworks were pockmarked with splinter holes. Below, in the casemate batteries that bulged from the ship's side, near-misses drenched the gunners with freezing water. Between 17:35 and 17:40 *Cornwall* was hit nine times without achieving any tangible results in exchange; by now the weather was deteriorating into a dreary blend of mist and rain, making spotting difficult and forcing Ellerton to switch from controlled broadsides to the random disorder of 'independent firing'.[52] At the same time he adopted similar tactics to *Glasgow*, racing in to fire his forward guns then darting back as soon as *Leipzig* found the range – a challenging manoeuvre for a cumbersome old lady like *Cornwall*. Ellerton later paid glowing tribute to his engineering department:

> Too much credit cannot be given to the engine room staff of this ship ... we were steaming at an average of 146 revolutions and for half an hour we crept up to 147 ... the ship would never have got into action but for the splendid cooperation of the entire engine room staff and ... Engineer Lieutenant [George] Campbell.[53]

At 17:46 Ellerton checked fire briefly and brought his ship in closer, her guns pulsing in slow, rhythmic broadsides once more. At 18:15 *Cornwall* switched to the dreadful lyddite. 'The result was stupendous,' one eyewitness recalled, 'we could see the dark smoke and flash of these projectiles as they hit, and shortly afterwards saw the enemy was on fire. Her fire began to slacken visibly ... we continued to close her ... and at 7,125 yards turned our port broadside and let her have it.'[54]

Below decks in the torpedo flat Paul Siebert felt *Leipzig* quiver like a wounded animal as she was hit repeatedly. Filthy clouds of smoke seeped down from the upper deck, causing terrible, racking coughs and prompting panicky rumours of poison gas. By 18:30 *Leipzig* had run out of ammunition; in a last despairing attempt to hit back, Haun ordered Siebert and his comrades to fire torpedoes, even though *Cornwall* was far outside effective range. Calmly, the filthy, suffering men loaded and fired three torpedoes, before abandoning the compartment for the upper deck.

Sometime after 19:00 Siebert climbed into an inferno: *Leipzig* was ablaze from stem to stern. Only the forecastle remained clear of fire, although the compartments below were ablaze, tongues of flame licking from the wounds in her deck. Through the smoke, Siebert could dimly make out the figures of men searching for anything that would float. The topmasts had been shot away, along with the forward funnel and half of the centre one. One battle ensign still fluttered bravely from the mainmast, until it swayed drunkenly and suddenly crashed over the side. Low down on the starboard side there was 'a hole in the ship's side that a carriage could have driven through'. And everywhere the appalled *Torpedo Maschinist* looked, were 'fragments of bodies', and the dead and dying, their skin tinted a macabre yellow by the British lyddite shells.[55]

Roughly half of *Leipzig*'s crew dragged themselves to the forecastle, where they assembled to abandon ship: 'one had lost his right leg up to the thigh, and the stump protruded from his bound trouser leg and was not even bound up. The left arm of another had been shattered and splinters of bone were sticking through his sleeve.' *Fregattenkapitän* Johann-Siegfried Haun walked calmly about, smiling and talking to his maimed sailors, shaking hands and passing out cigarettes. Pointing to his favourite old cane chair, which had been brought down from the shattered bridge, he laughed that he would take it into the water with him, so he would have something to sit on.[56] Then he led what remained of his crew in three cheers for the Kaiser. Haun's first lieutenant, *Korvettenkapitän* Ulrich Kretschmar, responded with three cheers for Haun and a chorus of the unofficial German naval anthem '*Stolz weht die Flagge Schwarz-Weiß-Rot*', the 'Song of the Flag'. Then, quietly, the disciplined crew transformed into survivors, breaking into small groups and exchanging last messages with tears in their eyes. Haun had ordered the sea cocks opened and *Leipzig* was settling. One torn ensign still flew above the flames. Haun gesticulated to it, telling his men that if any man cared to take it down, they could do so; one man apparently tried, but collapsed, burning, before he could reach it.[57]

Leipzig's tormentors circled warily, surveying the battered cruiser through the rain and smoke. She was stationary, ablaze and obviously sinking. Visibility was poor and it was impossible to determine much detail, but that shredded ensign still flew. *Leipzig* had stopped firing but, as far as Luce and Ellerton were aware, she still had torpedoes. Luce signalled her, demanding she surrender; receiving no reply, he fell back on the peerless ruthlessness that had helped the Royal Navy to win Britain's wars for centuries. At 19:25 a new storm of lyddite shells tore into the huddled mass of humanity on *Leipzig*'s forecastle, killing or maiming more than half of them. Shocked, Haun ordered his terrified, bewildered men to abandon ship, and as the British shells continued to rain down, they staggered cursing to the side, clutching hammocks. Someone had the presence of mind to fire off two green distress flares, and the British guns fell silent for the last time.

Very few men made it to the dubious safety of the water. Although unwounded, Haun was not one of them; he never even tried. *Leipzig*'s captain was last seen making his way back along the warped, smouldering deck, smoking. Many of the survivors must have been wounded; all would have been exhausted and clinically shocked. By the time the British cruisers had lowered their boats, it was nearly 21:00 and dark. As the boats pulled towards *Leipzig*, the listing, blazing cruiser finally gave up the fight. Clinging to a piece of timber, Paul Siebert was among the few from her crew who remained alive to witness her end: 'I looked round for *Leipzig* and just saw her as she lay over on her side with both propellers exposed. She lay thus for a moment and then plunged into the depths bow-first, with a bubbling, hissing noise.'[58]

Only seven officers and eleven men were rescued, most of them by *Glasgow*, the high proportion of officers a consequence of the whistles with which they were issued.[59] *Leipzig* took 315 men down with her. On the British side PO Martell remained the only fatality, and damage to both ships was light, although *Cornwall* was hit below the waterline, returning to the Falklands with two coal bunkers flooded and a heavy list. The grim reality of this one-sided naval battle shocked many British sailors. One young midshipman in *Cornwall* wrote 'I don't want another action for some time to come. It was beastly.'[60] Even among *Glasgow*'s hard-bitten Coronel veterans, 'nobody could help feeling sorry for the exhausted wrecks of men that were helped out of our boats'.[61] Captain Ellerton's report provided a fitting epitaph for *Leipzig*, and her commanding officer:

> I cannot refrain from expressing the intense admiration felt by myself, my officers and ship's company for the gallant manner in which our opponents fought their ship ... they continued firing until all their

ammunition was finished, and then sat on the deck and sang their national songs and smoked, waiting for the end. The captain went about among his men encouraging them and the survivors speak most warmly of his splendid example. I only regret that so gallant an officer was not saved. [His] spirit is recorded in history.[62]

Nürnberg

At first it seemed as if von Schönberg might get away. *Nürnberg* was five years newer than HMS *Kent*, her pursuer, and her top speed when she was built was over 25 knots; *Kent* had been designed for 23, but had rarely reached those dizzy speeds during the latter stages of her career. Known to her crew with exasperated affection as 'the lame duck of the county class', she had steamed 10,000 miles in the last two months and her worn-out engines were long overdue an overhaul.[63] Like *Monmouth*, *Kent* was another reserve fleet ship, hauled out of retirement and given a hastily assembled crew of reservists, many of them Scottish fishermen.[64] But it seems that in just sixty-seven days Captain John Allen had managed to instil the most extraordinary *esprit de corps* among his raw crew. As the chase developed during the day, the hands had gathered on the forecastle, watching the German squadron on the horizon, Lieutenant Victor Danckwerts recalling that he had 'never seen such a general air of happiness' in his life. On the bridge the officers laughed and joked, photographing one another like tourists on a cruise. When the battlecruisers opened fire, cheers and applause echoed through the ship.[65]

When *Kent* sheered away at 16:15 in pursuit of *Nürnberg*, it was clear that Allen's engine room staff would have to pull out all the stops if they were to overhaul their quarry. Deep in the bowels of the old cruiser, cursing, sweating stokers shovelled coal, while engineers made minute adjustments to her old machinery, mentally crossing their fingers. *Kent* had not coaled and supplies were low, so as the chase wore on every piece of spare timber was taken below to feed the roaring furnaces, from the cruiser's smaller boats and their oars, to capstan bars, targets, hatch covers, furniture and even the officers' sea chests.

Eventually, the extraordinary efforts made by Engineer Commander George Andrew and his men started to pay off, and *Kent* started to overhaul her newer opponent; according to one account, the 'lame duck' reached nearly 30 knots. It seems unlikely that von Schönberg would have been surprised; although technically faster, *Nürnberg* had not refitted for three years and had steamed thousands of miles since the war began. At 17:00 the German cruiser opened fire with her stern guns, startled observers in *Kent* watching *Nürnberg*'s first salvoes fly overhead, and learning the now-familiar lesson that larger calibre guns were absolutely no guarantee of superior range. It was nine long minutes before *Kent* could return fire, and even then the poor light made spotting the fall of shot almost impossible. In the meantime a steady stream of 105mm projectiles fell on and around *Kent*, each shriek and crash making her untried crew involuntarily flinch. Splinters perforated the cruiser's funnels, and one direct hit ripped through her forecastle, 'crumpling and tearing steel plating as though it were paper'.[66] Another shell burst outside the armoured conning tower, three splinters punching through the steel just six inches from the head of Petty Officer H.S. Welch: '[I] never dreamed that death was so near.' he wrote after the action.[67] *Kent*'s most dangerous moment came when a shell ripped through the ship's starboard side and exploded inside a 6-inch casemate, igniting a stack of cordite charges and incinerating most of the crew almost instantaneously. Two survivors, Able Seaman William Austin and Royal Marine Sergeant Charles Mayes, were still alive inside the compartment, but quick action was essential to prevent fire reaching the magazine and destroying the ship:

> I was knee-deep in these charges, with a roaring fire just four feet away! The watertight steel door at the side of me was slammed shut to stop the fire reaching the magazine. A Sergeant of Marines and myself were on the wrong side of that door and there was no other way of escape. Well, 'Stripey' used his loaf, for luckily there was a hosepipe close by ... so he turned the water on to the explosives and on to me, with a drop for himself. I then got my brains going and I spied a horizontal sliding door resting on a track, with a big wheel above my head to operate it. Using all my energy I managed to close the door and so shut off the fire from the gun compartment. I don't remember being frightened – there was not enough time for that.[68]

Austin and Mayes were not freed for another hour; Mayes was later awarded the Conspicuous Gallantry Medal for his actions. As the action wore on and shell after shell plunged into and around *Kent*, it must surely have seemed at times that the action was going against the British cruiser.

This was far from the case. Shortly after the action began, von Schönberg's ailing engines gave up the fight, two or possibly three of her boilers bursting in protest at the demands being placed upon them. *Nürnberg*'s speed dropped to 19 knots, and at 17:45 von Schönberg reluctantly turned to fight his older but more powerful pursuer. Steadily *Kent*'s heavier weight of shell began to tell. When Allen ordered his gun crews to switch to the fearsome lyddite, he brought the unequal battle to an end in twenty minutes. Up in *Kent*'s armoured conning tower, Petty Officer Welch watched it unfold:

> Her foretopmast was shot clean off at two minutes to six and four minutes later she caught fire between decks, just between the foremost

funnel and the foremast ... several of her guns were smashed up and she seemed to be badly holed and fearfully knocked about. Nine of our guns were firing simultaneously with each salvo ... and nearly every shell found its mark. It must have been a horrible slaughter aboard there.[69]

By 18:30 *Nürnberg* had ceased firing and the ship was a mass of flame, although her colours still flapped bravely from what remained of her masts. The German cruiser's funnels were so riddled with splinter holes that watchers in *Kent* mistook the twisted metal for men climbing away from the fires.[70] Six minutes later Captain Allen ordered his gunners to cease fire, and signalled *Nürnberg*, requesting she surrender. In a dismal echo of the *Leipzig* affair, he received no response and at 18:52 he reluctantly opened fire again, a five-minute bombardment wreaking havoc among the surviving *Nürnberg* men who were lining her side waiting for the order to abandon ship. William Austin emerged from his shattered casemate to see them hanging from the ship's rails 'like a lot of washing'.[71]

At 18:57 von Schönberg ordered his colours hauled down. As his command began to list to starboard, he assembled the survivors amidships and thanked them before leading them in three cheers for the Kaiser and Fatherland. To his men's dismay, von Schönberg then quietly asked one of his officers to make sure Germany heard the tale of *Nürnberg*'s last fight, before disappearing back into the cruiser's shot-torn conning tower.[72] He was never seen again; as he disappeared out of sight, *Nürnberg* heeled over on to her side, tipping the survivors into the bitterly cold water, before rolling over completely and slipping out of sight, 'as peacefully and gracefully as would a cup in a basin of water'.[73] As she went down, a small group of men clung to her stern, led by a signaller who slowly waved an ensign until he vanished out of sight. Although she was the last of the *Kreuzergeschwader* to be brought to action, *Nürnberg* was not the last to sink; miles away across the grey Atlantic the agony of Johannes Haun's *Leipzig* lasted for another forty minutes.

Rescue work was hindered by poor light, worsening seas and a lack of boats: most had been burned as fuel or damaged in the battle, and only two were in a fit state to put in the water. The appalled crews were guided towards the survivors by albatrosses, which swooped to attack the helpless Germans as they slowly expired. Von Schönberg and 327 of his men were killed in action or drowned; just twelve were rescued, of whom five later died. *Kent* was hit thirty-seven times and her upperworks were a shambles, but the old armoured cruiser sustained only sixteen casualties, of whom four were killed. Ten of these casualties were in William Austin's 6-inch casemate: 'Awful War!' he wrote at the end of his graphic account of the battle. 'God grant that it might soon end. Oh! That the Kaiser had been here, what tortures he should have had.'[74]

One shell had smashed *Kent*'s wireless transmitter, preventing Allen from reporting his success, so for hours the rest of the squadron were unsure whether *Kent* was still afloat. As she laboured back to the Falklands, a monotonous stream of increasingly concerned transmissions blared from her still-intact receiver: '*Kent, Kent, Kent,* where are you? *Kent, Kent, Kent.*' When she arrived at Port Stanley the following morning, most of the squadron had given her up for lost, and she was greeted with a wave of delighted cheering that spread from ship to ship. Sturdee was not there, as he had taken some of his ships to look for *Kent*'s survivors.

The Battle of the Falklands was fought 'in the old style' – the last action between surface ships fought without the aid of aircraft, airships, radar or submarines. When it was over, the *Kreuzergeschwader Ostasien* was no more, and over 2,000 Germans had died, including von Spee, his two sons, Heinrich and Otto, junior officers in *Gneisenau* and *Nürnberg* respectively, and all four captains whose ships were engaged. British fatalities numbered ten in total. It was a crushing victory, and Sturdee's brother officers heaped praise upon him, one writing that he had won 'the greatest sea victory the British Navy has known since Trafalgar', unwittingly exposing the shadow which that long-ago battle still cast over the dreadnought navy.[75] But *Dresden* remained at large. Back in London the men who directed British naval operations picked over the consequences and planned their next moves.

Chapter 8

Fugitive: the Pursuit of *Dresden*

'We hunted for her in and out of these channels, with glaciers and snow-covered mountains on either side of us, never knowing when we should run into her.'

Engineer Commander Percy Shrubsole, HMS *Glasgow*

At the start of the war *Fregattenkapitän* Fritz Lüdecke had operated against Allied trade in the South Atlantic, but although the *Etappen* kept him well provided with colliers and he had repeatedly crossed the great trade route which ran up the South American coast for two months, he had enjoyed little success. On 6 August he released the first British ships he met, *Drumcliffe*, *Lynton Grange* and *Hostilius*. In accordance with the Prize Code he tried to force the captains to sign an undertaking that they would not 'do any service in the British Navy or Army, and will not give any assistance to the British government against Germany during the present war', but when the captain of *Hostilius* refused, Lüdecke released him anyway.[1] Such behaviour speaks volumes for Lüdecke's qualities as a human being, but is rather less convincing evidence for his possessing the requisite ruthlessness for commerce raiding.

In fact, Lüdecke intercepted and sank just two ships before he came under von Spee's command on 12 October: the British & South American Steam Navigation Company steamer *Hyades* on 15 August off Pernambuco, and the North Wales Shipping Company collier *Holmwood* on 26 August off Cape Santa Maria Grande. Both were well off the main South American shipping lanes and, to add insult to injury, *Hyades* was carrying a German cargo of corn, prompting the British Consul at Buenos Aires to describe her loss as 'not an unmixed evil'. John Morrison, her captain, described *Dresden*'s gunnery as very poor, remarking that it took the cruiser forty minutes to sink his ship.[2] A third ship, *Katharine Park*, was caught and released, as she was carrying an American cargo.

Lüdecke's record did not improve on passing around Cape Horn into the Pacific. On 18 September he met Captain Douglas Kinneir's Pacific Steam Navigation Company steamer *Ortega* to the west of the Straits of Magellan

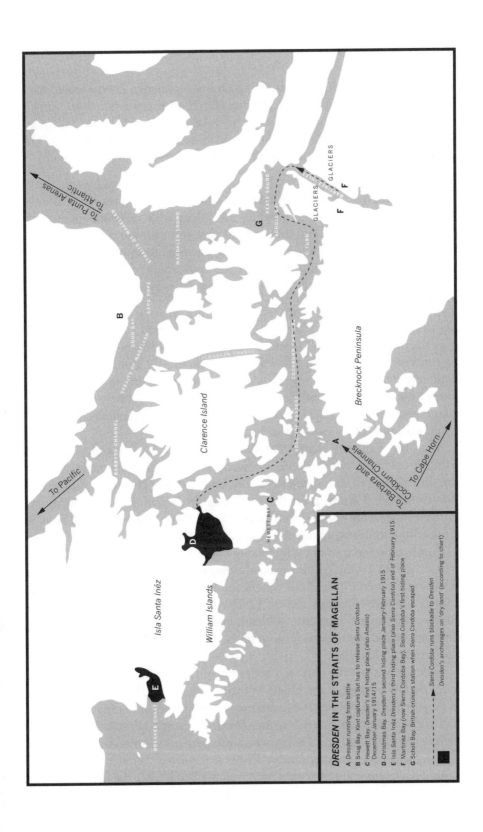

DRESDEN IN THE STRAITS OF MAGELLAN

A *Dresden* running from battle

B Snug Bay. *Kent* captures but has to release *Sierra Cordoba*

C Hewett Bay. *Dresden*'s first hiding place (also *Amasis*)
   December–January 1914/15

D Christmas Bay. *Dresden*'s second hiding place January–February 1915

E Isla Santa Inéz *Dresden*'s third hiding place (also *Sierra Cordoba*) end of February 1915

F Martinez Bay (now Sierra Cordoba Bay). *Sierra Cordoba*'s first hiding place

G Scholl Bay. British cruisers station when *Sierra Cordoba* escaped

- - - - - - - *Sierra Cordoba* runs blockade to *Dresden*

     Dresden's anchorages on 'dry land' (according to chart)

and pursued her for three hours, firing on her repeatedly. *Ortega* would have been a rich prize as she was carrying 300 French reservists, but Kinneir apparently called for volunteers to help stoke, ran his old ship at full speed straight into the uncharted and dangerous Nelson Strait, and got away. The British Consul at Buenos Aires sent a report eulogising his achievement:

> It must be remembered that Nelson's Strait is entirely uncharted, and that the narrow, tortuous passage in question constitutes a veritable nightmare for navigators, bristling as it does with reefs and pinnacle rocks, swept by fierce currents and tiderips, and with the cliffs on either side sheer-to, without any anchorage. I can speak from personal experience as to the terrifying nature of the navigation of Nelson's Strait, having once passed safely through it many years ago in a small sealing schooner.[3]

Dresden was at Isla Más Afuera when von Spee ordered Lüdecke to join the *Kreuzergeschwader* at Easter Island, and he made the 1,500-mile trip under tow to conserve coal, the collier *Baden* hauling the cruiser along at 9 knots and completing the journey in seven days.[4] The rendezvous on the 12th ended the first phase of what can really only be described as a singularly unpromising solo career, although Lüdecke did take another prize while under von Spee's command, the collier *North Wales* on 16 November.

After the Falklands battle *Dresden* ran west at high speed, Lüdecke's wireless operators relating a demoralising litany of British signals detailing the dismal scale of von Spee's defeat. Rounding Cape Horn, she passed into the Cockburn Channel, finally anchoring in Scholl Bay at midday on 10 December with just 150 tons of coal left.[5] Here Lüdecke set his crew to work felling timber to augment *Dresden*'s fuel supplies until the evening of the 11th, when he was moved on by the big Chilean destroyer *Almirante Condell*, whose captain reminded him robustly that under international law *Dresden* could only remain in Chilean waters for twenty-four hours. Without coal, Lüdecke had few options and on 12 December he headed north for Punta Arenas, the Chilean port city, goldrush boom town and former penal colony nestling on the north-eastern shore of the Brunswick Peninsula, overlooking the Straits of Magellan.

Lüdecke was not the only one under pressure. The British had expended a great deal of treasure, if not blood, in fruitless hunts for *Dresden* and *Karlsruhe* in August and September 1914, and now one of these infuriating, elusive foes had slipped through the net again. *Dresden*'s escape tainted the Falklands victory for Churchill and Fisher, who were perhaps haunted by the fear that she might become another *Emden*. Fisher was furious, believing that Sturdee should have sent a ship to Punta Arenas immediately after the battle to report the victory, where he could have cornered *Dresden* as a bonus. In vain, Sturdee argued that he had sent his report by the quickest route (by wireless from the Falkland Islands via Montevideo), and under international law any ship at Punta Arenas would have had to leave after twenty-four hours, long before *Dresden* arrived. Fisher, in no mood for excuses and doubtless influenced by his long-standing antipathy towards Sturdee, described *Dresden*'s escape as 'criminal ineptitude', and blasted off a series of peremptory signals at the Vice Admiral, demanding an explanation.[6] Sturdee replied with dignity that 'Their Lordships selected me as commander-in-chief to destroy the two hostile armoured cruisers and I endeavoured to the best of my ability to carry out their orders. I submit', he went on, 'that my being called upon in three separate telegrams to give reasons for my subsequent action was unexpected.' 'Unexpected' was a fairly tame word given the circumstances, but Fisher would not be defied: 'Your telegram ... is improper', he replied, 'and such observations must not be repeated.'[7] Fisher's spite knew no bounds. Aware that the battlecruisers must return as soon as possible, he tried to insist that Sturdee transfer to the insultingly archaic *Carnarvon* and remain in South American waters until *Dresden* was caught. He was overruled by Churchill, the shrewd politician, who realised that whatever its shortcomings, the Falklands victory had removed the stain of Coronel, and lifted the spirits of the country and the navy. To punish the successful commander so publicly would bewilder everyone. Exile in *Carnarvon*, Churchill later wrote, was 'scarcely suited to his rank and standing, and woefully out of harmony with his recent achievement. I was obliged to veto this proposal.' He went on tactfully to record that his irascible mentor was 'for some time much vexed at my decision', although he did his best to smooth the waters, writing to his old friend that 'this was your show and your luck ... your flair was quite true'.[8]

So had Sturdee been guilty of 'criminal ineptitude'? After the battle his squadron was desperately short of fuel, as only *Glasgow* and *Carnarvon* had completed coaling before von Spee arrived. Colliers were on their way, escorted by the AMC *Orama*, but while this provided a solution to one problem, it posed another: *Dresden* might attack the convoy, supported by *Nürnberg*, which was then presumed still afloat, and one or more of the German AMCs that were still at large. Some of Sturdee's ships were damaged and carrying their own or German wounded. *Kent*, missing and possibly sunk, remained Sturdee's greatest concern, as the weather was deteriorating badly. Intelligence from prisoners suggested that Cape Horn was *Dresden*'s likely destination, and the admiral made his dispositions accordingly. *Cornwall* and *Glasgow* were supposed to cover the Straits of Magellan but as the former had just 250 tons of coal left and the latter almost no ammunition, both ships were forced to return to Port Stanley. *Carnarvon* went north to bring in the collier convoy. The battlecruisers remained at sea with *Bristol* for as long as possible, at first sweeping for *Kent* and then, after learning of her return, moving westwards towards Tierra del Fuego, before a shortage of coal drove them back to the Falklands on the morning of the 11th.

Sturdee's dispositions were not random, nor ill considered. The problem was that Punta Arenas was only an obvious destination with hindsight: Lüdecke might instead choose to cruise out in the vast Atlantic, to hide in a secluded inlet in West Falkland, or to tuck himself away in some lonely bay in the Straits of Magellan. Sturdee did not have enough ships to search everywhere and, as he signalled the Admiralty, 'I therefore selected what, from the information to hand on 8 December, appeared to be the most likely place in which to find the enemy.'[9] It was a necessary judgment call which ultimately proved wrong, much to Fisher's fury. The First Sea Lord's secondary complaint, about the battlecruisers' poor gunnery and enormous expenditure of ammunition, was more justifiable; ultimately, it was put down to funnel smoke, an excuse which masked serious failings in British gunnery.[10]

After Sturdee returned on the 11th, the wounded were brought ashore to Port Stanley's tiny hospital and the prisoners transferred off the warships. (Dick Townsend was not sorry to see them go, writing to his wife that 'I hate their guttural mutterings outside my cabin'.[11]) Sturdee, Governor Allardyce and a contingent of sailors and islanders attended a short funeral service at Port Stanley's Christ Church Cathedral, where the seven British fatalities were interred. *Glasgow*'s Lieutenant Harold Hickling attended: 'the strains of the funeral march of Beethoven ringing out with pathetic sadness in the still summer air ... so we leave them sleeping for a while after having done their best and very best to uphold "England's home and beauty".'[12]

Lüdecke was permitted to stay at Punta Arenas for fifty-one hours – the exact length of time previously granted to the British AMC *Otranto*. Gratefully, he set his men to filling the ship's bunkers with poor-quality coal briquettes from the collier *Turpin*, the only available supply, while he went ashore to meet the German Consul.[13] Apparently resigned to life on the run, he declined the consul's suggestion that he submit to internment; the decision was left to Lüdecke, who was at least spared the distraction of having his every move micromanaged from home. This was not the case for his British opponents.

For two days Sturdee received a stream of conflicting orders from Whitehall. On 11 December he was ordered to send *Kent* and *Orama* into the Pacific to cooperate with the various Anglo-Japanese formations operating off the Chilean coast. *Carnarvon*, *Glasgow* and the other two AMCs were to remain at the Falklands under Stoddart, and Sturdee himself was to move north. These orders stood for less than a day; on the 12th Fisher and Churchill decided that

Sturdee and the battlecruisers must return home, leaving the rest of the squadron under Stoddart to search for *Dresden*. One hour after these orders were dispatched, at 16:45 on the 13th, the British Consul in Punta Arenas, a retired sea captain named Charles Milward, notified London that *Dresden* was in town. This prompted yet another change, giving Sturdee discretion to take the battlecruisers to Punta Arenas if this meant he could bring *Dresden* to action. Four hours later, when Milward confirmed that the German cruiser was coaling, this discretionary suggestion was amended to a direct order.[14]

It was perhaps inevitable that Fisher could not resist micromanaging an officer whom he loathed and whom he believed had failed him, but this stream of contradictory instructions must have been intensely irritating to Sturdee, thousands of miles away in a different time zone. The news that *Dresden* was at Punta Arenas took thirty-six hours to reach him and he could not have been worse prepared. His ships had returned, but only *Bristol* was ready for sea: the remainder were repairing battle damage and coaling.

Punta Arenas was a frontier town, swarming with migrants seeking their fortunes from mining, hunting, trapping or farming. One of these adventurers was Albert Pagels, a seal trapper and former bosun's mate in the German Navy, and 'a herculean, steadfast, red-bearded mariner of unalterable fidelity', who had lost most of one hand on active service during the Boxer Rebellion in China in 1900.[15] Learning that the British battlecruisers had been at Montevideo, Pagels had taken his fishing boat *Elfreda* to sea in a gale to warn von Spee. He had tried to reach the German liner *Amasis*, which was hidden in Hewett Bay, an obscure cove 130 miles from Punta Arenas, hoping to use the liner's powerful transmitter, but the dreadful weather meant he did not get there until the day after the battle; in fact, he passed the fleeing *Dresden* on the way but failed to understand the implications of the sighting. Repeated transmissions produced no reply and the downhearted Pagels returned to Punta Arenas, taking *Amasis* with him; almost out of coal, her captain had chosen internment. Hearing that *Dresden* had coaled and left, the determined old sailor rested for a day before making the gruelling trip again, this time to find Lüdecke and offer help.[16]

Lüdecke had not gone far. In fact, he had threaded his way in the opposite direction by a different route and anchored in Hewett Bay, whence Pagels had just departed. Recognising that the seal trapper's local knowledge could mean the difference between life and death, Lüdecke gratefully accepted his offer. In an age when everyone has military-grade satellite technology at their fingertips, it is perhaps hard to convey how much real wilderness there was in 1914. Much of the Straits of Magellan were uncharted, a labyrinth of rocky channels and tiny islands, surrounded by towering peaks and majestic glaciers. There was no shortage of hiding places for *Dresden*, if the right guide was available; indeed, Pagels helped Lüdecke find several anchorages that according to the chart were on dry land.[17]

The British cruisers *Glasgow* and *Bristol* arrived at Punta Arenas on the afternoon of 14 December to discover that their bird had flown the day before, much to Fisher's fury. The best opportunity to catch *Dresden* had passed, and for three months Lüdecke played a miserable game of hide and seek among the myriad bays and islands of Tierra del Fuego, against a dwindling and increasingly frustrated band of British cruiser captains.

For twelve days he remained at Hewett Bay, Pagels visiting three times to deliver supplies and intelligence. This hiding place was blown on 26 December, when the grubby motor cutter *Galileo* chugged into the cove. Lüdecke sent away a boat, and the crew tried in vain to persuade the visitors, a Frenchman and a Russian, that they were not German, but the strangers pointed to the gothic tattoos on their arms and motored away again, laughing.[18] Arriving later that day, Pagels was suspicious; he knew the cutter and its crew, and believed they had been chartered by the British to search for *Dresden*. He warned Lüdecke that 'no such rarities as neutrals had their being in Magellan; even a German might betray him for a consideration', and the next day Lüdecke relocated to the appropriately named Christmas Bay, another remote and, according to the chart, landlocked cove some 40 miles away.[19] *Dresden* crept into the narrow inlet with her propellers barely turning over, creeping behind a steam pinnace where a freezing and miserable sailor huddled in the bows, 'swinging the lead' to sound the depth of this obscure and unsurveyed bay. Here, with nothing but coal dust, timber and the almost useless briquettes in his bunkers, Lüdecke would have to stay.

A plan was already in motion to resolve Lüdecke's supply crisis. *Kapitän* Heinrich Schaeffer's Norddeutscher–Lloyd liner *Sierra Cordoba* was lying at Montevideo, nearly 2,000 miles away, loaded with supplies and coal for the AMC *Kronprinz Wilhelm*, but Berlin signalled the local *Etappe* with new orders that sent her scurrying south. Schaeffer, unfamiliar with the waters and piloting a ship that was twice the size of *Dresden*, rode his luck all the way, avoiding the watching British cruisers outside Punta Arenas by choosing, either by accident or design, channels that were supposed to be unnavigable. One contemporary observer recalled how, armoured by ignorance, Schaeffer drove *Sierra Cordoba* unscathed over one notorious patch of shallows, the Orange Bank, 'contemptuous of buoys or any refinement of present-day navigation [and] in blissful ignorance that he had achieved the miraculous', and going on to note that 'This is the first occasion that a vessel of any size has sailed over the Orange Bank, and it is likely to be the last.'[20]

At Punta Arenas Schaeffer was told where to find *Dresden*, and immediately took his ship to sea again. Shortly afterwards Stoddart's flagship *Carnarvon* arrived, and the German Consul sent a local German national named Harry Rothemburg out in a tug to warn Schaeffer, Pagels' fishing boat *Elfreda* having cracked a cylinder. In the meantime Captain Harry Skipwith turned *Carnarvon* and thundered back out of the harbour in hot pursuit. The bizarre three horse race ended two hours later when *Kent* overhauled *Sierra Cordoba*, the tug puffing up behind. Resigned to capture, Schaeffer threw his log and codebooks overboard and stopped *Sierra Cordoba* near Snug Bay, but before *Carnarvon's* boarding party could climb up the side, the Chilean destroyer *Lynch* arrived and ordered Skipwith to take his aggressive behaviour out of Chilean waters. Skipwith reluctantly complied and Schaeffer continued his odyssey, taking Rothemburg to help him navigate the treacherous waters. He finally slipped into Martinez Inlet, a narrow slash of water flanked by the gleaming splendour of the Sarmiento glaciers, just 100 miles from *Dresden*. With no accurate charts, and having exceeded the limits of Rothemburg's local knowledge and courage, which was diminishing by the minute, Schaeffer had run out of options.[21]

He reckoned without Pagels. Back in Punta Arenas the red-bearded skipper had repaired his cracked cylinder with gum, silenced it with a perforated paraffin tin and set off with fresh codebooks. Passing Scholl Bay at 02:00 he was alarmed to see *Carnarvon* and *Bristol* lying close inshore, but steamed boldly past, surreptitiously dumping the new codebooks while blazing away at imaginary waterfowl. With quite extraordinary composure, he then anchored between the two warships and threw out nets, remaining there 'fishing' until the British left five hours later. Aware that attempting to reach *Sierra Cordoba* might now blow the liner's cover, he instead made for *Dresden*, retrieving the sunken codebooks on the way. He reached the cruiser after dark after narrowly missing HMS *Glasgow* on the way.[22]

The following morning Pagels was on his way back. Lüdecke had decided that as the waters were teeming with British cruisers, *Sierra Cordoba* would have to come to him; other colliers could always be found, but there was only one *Dresden*, and she did not have enough coal to fight a battle. Schaeffer agreed to run the blockade on the first available dirty night, and although apparently 'outraged to the point of convulsions' at the thought of handing over his ship to such a 'disreputable-looking ruffian', he also reluctantly consented temporarily to place his ship under Pagels' command. This was the last straw for Rothemburg: the pilot, fearful of execution 'from a British yardarm', demanded to be returned to Punta Arenas, a task which fell, inevitably, to Pagels and further delayed *Sierra Cordoba's* escape.[23]

Finally, on the evening of 3 January, Pagels returned to *Sierra Cordoba* in suitably foul weather: 'a continuous hurricane' which came close to swamping the little *Elfreda* and left Pagels and his mate 'exhausted and all but dead from exposure'. At 20:00 *Elfreda* was hoisted aboard *Sierra Cordoba* and the liner weighed anchor, 'her boiler pressure at its highest and her smoke stack shrouded in wire gauze to avoid betrayal by sparks'. Under Pagels' command, she made her way to *Dresden*, steaming perilously close to the precipitous shore in pitch darkness and a howling gale, as Pagels vividly recalled years later:

> The entrance to Christmas Bay ... might well have spelt disaster ... This passage is a snaky S-shaped narrow, at most a hundred yards wide, banked by lowering, lofty cliffs, a most hazardous pass for any bark of greater tonnage than a canoe ... *Sierra Cordoba* braved it on a strong outflowing tide, a roaring current, and this gave the ship, with her twin screws and powerful engines, good steerage-way. The last danger-point was successfully negotiated and soon *Sierra Cordoba* ... dropped anchor 400 yards from *Dresden*.[24]

Lüdecke had his coal. The exhausted Pagels collapsed in a cabin; he continued to support *Dresden* over the next two months, and was later awarded the Iron Cross. After the war German officers from warships calling at Punta Arenas would always pay him a respectful visit.[25]

While the Germans executed this remarkable clandestine operation, the British were reorganising their forces. *Canopus*, freed from her muddy bed, fired up her wheezy old engines for the first time in months and Captain Grant took her north to Abrolhos Rocks and then home, where his engineer commander was invalided out of the service. Sturdee left in *Invincible* on 15 December. Much to Fisher's disgust, he was rewarded with the first hereditary peerage awarded to a Royal Navy officer since Trafalgar, and given command of the Grand Fleet's prestigious 4th Battle Squadron.[26] *Inflexible* left for the Dardanelles on 19 December and *Cornwall* for Saint Helena on 3 January.

The relentless, weary search of the Straits of Magellan was left to *Kent*, *Bristol*, *Carnarvon* and *Glasgow*, supported by the AMCs *Orama* and *Otranto*, the whole force under Stoddart's command. For weeks the cruisers crept around an endless succession of islands or thrust their salt-stained bows into bay after bay, sending in boats if the waters appeared too treacherous. In theory it was summer in these southerly latitudes, but this was summer in one of the wildest regions on earth and the weather could still be diabolical. The smallest diversions relieved the monotony. Percy Shrubsole of *Glasgow* recalled 'canoes of Indians stark naked in the bitter cold who were frightened out of their lives as a rule and who could speak no language but their own'.[27] William Austin of *Kent* remembered a bleak bay nicknamed 'Icy Sound', where a local family eked out an existence in a primitive houseboat, 'a hollowed-out tree trunk with a makeshift cabin of driftwood boards. A family lived in that canoe: two men and two women and a small child of little more than a year old, who seemed to have been trained to bale constantly with the aid of tin can.'[28] Diary entries for the period become noticeably shorter and more sporadic; there was simply nothing to say, and even the undeniably spectacular scenery began to lose its attraction fairly quickly. 'We are sick to death of playing hide and seek down here,' wrote one disillusioned officer in *Glasgow*. 'I think this must be the nastiest place in the world.'[29]

Christmas Day was dismal. *Bristol* spent it in Vallens Roads, one sailor recalling a chicken dinner with beans, and 'a bit of a sing-song'. 'A pretty good dinner under circs', he went on, 'but there were a few too many sarcastic Merry Xmas's.'[30] In *Kent* the officers went around each mess deck sampling cake and plum pudding, after which 'each officer had to undergo the punishment of being carried round the deck ... on the shoulders of two or three men'. This doubtless morale-boosting process began with Captain Allen himself, and ended with what one sailor called a 'hurrah-party' with tin whistles and mouth organs.[31]

The captains were aware of the risks inherent in repeatedly taking their ships into such confined, treacherous and uncharted waters. As 1914 turned to 1915 with still no progress, Captain Allen fitted *Kent*'s picket boat with a wireless, two torpedoes, a Maxim gun and, rather marvellously, cutlasses; she was formally commissioned as HMS *Gillingham* and, commanded by Lieutenant-Commander Eric Wharton, was used to enter bays and inlets that were too narrow or shallow for the cruiser. *Glasgow*'s John Luce apparently chartered a Punta Arenas-based tug named *Eduardo*. He put aboard a local expatriate farmer, Robert Ridell, and three of his own officers thinly disguised as 'prospectors', and sent her on fruitless patrols up and down the Barbara Channel; she passed within yards of *Dresden*'s hiding place without sighting the cruiser.[32]

Resupply was a nightmare; with every captain reluctant to leave the search area, the crews became generous at helping each other out and adept at scrounging. When *Bristol* picked up the steamer *Colorado* in the Straits of Magellan, Captain Fanshawe gratefully accepted a gift of twenty live sheep, which were somehow transferred across by boat in a very rough sea.[33]

The occasional false alarm inevitably ended in disappointment. *Bristol* went to action stations in response to some spurious *Dresden* alert almost every day between 24 January and the end of February. Each time the cruiser nosed into some desolate bay behind her pinnace, the weather foul and visibility poor, every man tense and ready for battle – and each time she found nothing. The constant strain and exhaustion perhaps accounts for the death of Able Seaman Charles Halligan during a coaling accident on 4 February.[34]

The most reliable information tended to be ignored. Consul Charles Milward in Punta Arenas knew of Pagels' frequent nocturnal trips to the south, and was sure that other vessels were being chartered to take supplies to the fugitive cruiser. He repeatedly warned the Admiralty that he was sure *Dresden* was still nearby, but London and Stoddart ignored him, suspecting a trap to lure British ships into uncharted waters where they might run aground. Instead, Stoddart took *Carnarvon*, *Bristol* and *Otranto* miles away up the east coast back to Abrolhos Rocks, where, ironically, his flagship did run aground, and nearly sank, on 22 February. Morale among the pursuers was at an all-time low.[35]

It was worse for Lüdecke, cut off in one of the most hostile regions on earth. Although he still clung to the notion of carrying out cruiser warfare, he needed coal to do it, and he expected Berlin to solve that problem for him. *Sierra Cordoba* had restored his mobility, but he needed far more for raiding. The *Etappen* organised colliers to find him, but all ran into difficulties. The crew of one, *Gladstone*, mutinied at Pernambuco, and several others were interned by increasingly unsympathetic Latin American governments, which, after von Spee's defeat, were beginning to understand that there was only one maritime power worth ingratiating themselves with. *Josephina* was captured by *Carnarvon* outside the Straits of Magellan, and *Eleonore Woermann* was sunk by the battlecruiser *Australia*.[36] Recognising that it was impossible to provide Lüdecke with the resources he needed, the *Admiralstab* suggested he return home by the old sailing ship route that ran due north up the middle of the Atlantic. Lüdecke rejected the suggestion outright: *Dresden* could neither find nor carry the thousands of tons of coal necessary, and her engines were not up to the journey. Instead, he proposed to leave the Straits of Magellan from the west and enter the Pacific, apparently with the aim of commerce raiding in *Emden*'s old hunting grounds in the Indian Ocean.[37]

Shortly afterwards another local hunter discovered *Dresden* in Christmas Bay. Lüdecke had learned his lesson and, although the newcomer was German, he was detained until the German captain could shift his berth. On 4 February he moved *Dresden* and *Sierra Cordoba* to a new refuge at Isla Santa Inés, near the Pacific entrance to the Gonzalez Channel. Here he bade farewell to Pagels, who was 'heart-broken' at Lüdecke's decision. 'If you venture into the Pacific, it must indeed be goodbye, *Herr Kapitän*' he is said to have told Lüdecke, before offering to scuttle *Elfreda* and come with him.[38]

Lüdecke declined the offer, telling Pagels that he could best help by ostentatiously keeping up the pretence that *Dresden* was in the Straits of Magellan for as long as possible. Pagels and his network began to spread rumours that *Dresden* had moved to the near-impenetrable Last Hope Inlet. The deception exceeded expectations, as the Admiralty ordered *Kent* and *Orama* back east to join *Bristol* and *Glasgow* in a concentrated search. *Bristol* ran aground in the confined and poorly charted waters on 23 February, starting a series of leaks, smashing her propellers and rudder, and effectively putting herself out of the hunt.[39] In the meantime Consul Milward, now convinced that *Dresden* was in Christmas Bay, chartered the nondescript motor cutter *Galileo* himself and visited at the beginning of March. Although Milward found the evidence he needed, in the form of cut trees and crude water chutes, he was two weeks too late; on 14 February Lüdecke had taken the elusive *Dresden* out into the Pacific.

Cautious as ever, he kept 300 miles out to sea, far from the main shipping lanes, and sent *Sierra Cordoba* ahead as a scout. He steamed steadily northwards until 19 February, and then stopped in open water for three days, before continuing north to a position just south of Isla Más Afuera, where on 25 February he coaled for the last time from *Sierra Cordoba* and sent the almost-empty liner into Valparaiso to replenish. Although she was technically a naval auxiliary, the Chileans allowed Schaeffer to load 1,200 tons of coal and leave, but by the time he returned to sea, it was too late; *Dresden* had been sighted.[40]

Lüdecke remained south of Isla Más Afuera, where he sank the sailing barque *Conway Castle* on 27 February. Desperately short of coal, he then remained stationary until 8 March, wallowing in the swell, occasionally turning over his engines to maintain position. Back in open water with no Pagels to pass messages, Lüdecke had to fall back on the Achilles heel of all the pirates: he had to use his wireless to summon a collier. As soon as messages began to fly across the ether, his fate was sealed.

On 4 March the Admiralty learned that on the following day the collier *Gotha* would rendezvous with Lüdecke at latitude 37° south, longitude 80° west. The collier had been ordered to remain at that location for a month, and so HMS *Kent* was urgently ordered north to intercept her. Allen took the most direct route, a near impassable channel known as Shag Narrows, 3km long and just 73m wide, with a 45 degree bend in the middle and strong tidal flows. *Kent*'s beam was some 20m and Allen made the passage at speed; one contemporary account describes the experience as 'intensely interesting'.[41] But it saved Allen a full day. Once out in open water, he turned north and pushed his veteran cruiser up to a steady 17 knots. He reached the rendezvous at daylight on 7 March and settled down to wait, all that day and through the following night. The following morning, 8 March, brought low cloud and a steady, wearying drizzle, with visibility down to about a mile. Allen knew that he could only stay for one more day before he would have to make for Coronel for coal. Finally, at 15:50, his patience was rewarded. The cloud lifted momentarily and Leading Signalman Hill spotted a three-funnelled cruiser 12 miles away on the starboard beam. For the first time since fleeing the Battle of the Falklands, *Dresden* had been sighted by a British warship.[42]

Allen ordered full speed ahead and water began to foam under *Kent*'s old-fashioned, raked stem; slowly the old cruiser began to creep closer to *Dresden*, which did not appear to have spotted her. *Kent* closed to within 15,000 metres before *Dresden* sprang to life, writer H.S. Welch recalling how she 'turned tail and scooted', turning sharply to the west and increasing speed.[43] The chase was on.

Allen tried every trick he knew to extract every knot from his old ship. As at the Falklands, he burned all the spare wood he could find, removed *Kent*'s canvas screens to reduce wind resistance and even assembled any unoccupied men on the quarterdeck to help trim the ship down by the stern, raising her bow and forcing her propellers to bite deep in the water.[44] Once again the 'lame duck' exceeded the records set at her trials eleven years before, flames and showers of burning ashes streaking from her red-hot funnels in the gathering darkness as her old engines shuddered and roared and cursing stokers shovelled coal for all they were worth.[45] But this time it was no use. *Dresden* had turbines and, for all her trials and tribulations, her boilers were not going to burst like *Nürnberg*'s. And *Kent*'s bottom was foul with weed after three fruitless months in Tierra del Fuego. Slowly but surely Allen watched *Dresden* draw away until she was, according to William Austin, just 'a silhouette against the rays of the setting sun away to the west, about 12 miles distant; a real picture against a brilliant sunset ... She wanted none of us.'[46]

Down to his last coal after a five-hour, high-speed chase, Allen made for Coronel, bitterly disappointed and worried that the German cruiser might vanish again for months on end. Just one hope remained. *Dresden* had been high in the water, indicating that she too was low on coal, and the high-speed chase would have left her with even less. *Kent* had intercepted several coded signals, presumably Lüdecke calling for replenishment, and Allen passed them on, hoping that someone might be able to read them.

It took more than four days, but late on 12 March Lieutenant Charles Stuart, *Glasgow*'s signals officer, finally cracked the German code. The desperate messages, intended for *Gotha* and *Sierra Cordoba*, indicated that Lüdecke meant to make for Cumberland Bay on Isla Más a Tierra, the largest of the Juan Fernandez Islands and the remote island chain's centre of government. The last act would take place at Robinson Crusoe's Island, a densely wooded, rugged speck in the Pacific.

Dresden reached Cumberland Bay at 08:00 on 9 March, her coal exhausted and her engines failing. The Chilean governor, who doubled as the local lighthouse keeper, forcefully insisted he leave within twenty-four hours or be interned.[47] Lüdecke protested that he could not leave until his engines had been repaired, as under international law he could not be forced back out to sea in an unseaworthy ship. The governor, aware perhaps that his retinue of four policemen might not prove adequate against *Dresden*'s 300 or more sailors and 105mm guns, retired to await the arrival of a Chilean warship, beginning an uneasy stand-off that lasted for five days. On the first night Lüdecke received a short signal, which read simply 'His Majesty the Kaiser sets you free to lay yourself up', but the fugitive pirate was not ready to throw in his cards.[48] While he stalled the Chilean authorities, his men worked around the clock to repair the engines. Outside the mouth of the bay, *Dresden*'s pinnace patrolled back and forth, the crew warily scanning the horizon for any approaching ship, hoping desperately for a friendly collier.

At 08:30 on 14 March the pinnace came in sight, rushing back to *Dresden*, its crew frantically signalling. Behind it, steaming into view around the headland, were HM ships *Glasgow* and *Orama*, followed ten minutes later by the inevitable, archaic silhouette of HMS *Kent*. As soon as Stuart had decoded the German signals, Luce and Allen had arranged to meet at Isla Más a Tierra, and both captains were delighted to discover that this time the bird had not flown. It was, however, an interesting dilemma. *Dresden* was anchored in Chilean territorial waters, but she had not been interned, as her ensigns were still flying. Lüdecke had repeatedly flouted Chilean neutrality for three months and for John Luce, the senior officer present, there was only one thing to do: shoot first, and argue about international law afterwards. His belligerent superiors at the Admiralty concurred, signalling that 'objective is destruction not internment'.[49] Even so, Luce waited for twenty minutes to see if Lüdecke would surrender.

To Lüdecke's immense credit, he did not immediately do so, even though he was outnumbered, his ship was anchored with half her guns facing inland, all but one of her boilers out, and she was trapped in a bay. The one-sided exchange of fire that has occasionally been given the overblown title of 'The Battle of Más a Tierra' lasted less than five minutes. Luce, Allen and Captain John Segrave of *Orama* ran up their battle ensigns at 08:50 and opened 'a lively salvo fire', *Dresden* replying with a few desultory rounds before lyddite shells set her on fire aft. The fire spread, forcing Lüdecke to flood his after magazine. Soon afterwards the British ships moved outside the arcs of *Dresden*'s forward guns, and methodically knocked out the remaining weapons on the starboard side.[50] Lüdecke apparently ordered his pinnace to try to pull the ship around to bring her port guns to bear, but the current was too strong and the attempt was abandoned after just a few minutes; reluctantly, the German captain ordered his colours hauled down and a white flag hoisted.[51] The unequal contest was over before it had begun. No British ships were hit, and no British casualties were sustained; in *Dresden* eight men were killed and thirty wounded.

As the guns fell silent, *Dresden*'s crew abandoned ship, some in boats, others swimming for their lives: 'the water being fairly warm and sharks few, most of them reached [safety]'.[52] As they did so, scuttling parties were busy below decks, opening the cruiser's sea cocks and placing charges. Buying time for them to complete their work, Lüdecke sent his intelligence officer across to *Glasgow* to negotiate: a young *Oberleutnant zur See* named Wilhelm Canaris, who later achieved notoriety as Adolf Hitler's chief of military intelligence.[53] As Canaris drew alongside *Glasgow*, Luce's first lieutenant, Lieutenant-Commander Wilfred Thompson, was heading in the opposite direction with *Glasgow*'s surgeon, Robert Gilmour.

The 'negotiations' did not last long. Canaris protested that *Dresden* had been fired on in neutral waters. Luce, staring implacably, demanded the German cruiser's unconditional surrender. Canaris turned around and headed back. Across the water, Thompson and Gilmour were nearing the battered and almost-deserted *Dresden*, peering up at her crazily angled guns and the wisps of smoke rising from her decks. According to William Hawkes, one of the boat's crew, Thompson asked Lüdecke for his word of honour that he would not attempt to blow up his ship, and Lüdecke agreed.[54] But as the two officers returned to *Glasgow*, the German battle ensign broke out at *Dresden*'s masthead again, and 'a fearful explosion' ripped through the cruiser's forepart; the vows Lüdecke had made as a German naval officer far outweighed any promises made to his enemies.[55] The charges blew out the bottom of the ship. Although little damage was visible above the waterline, *Dresden* began to settle by the bows; in less than half an hour she rolled over and sank, her battle ensign and white flag still flapping in uneasy juxtaposition. Ashore, her ship's company assembled on a nearby hill, where they came to attention and cheered their ship, before Lüdecke led them in a chorus of '*Deutschland über Alles*'.

Luce, Allen and Segrave now had time for chivalry, and the three ships sent surgeons ashore to tend the German wounded, *Dresden*'s own surgeon being among the injured. Sydney Welham was one of *Orama*'s surgeons, and this was his first battle. As he stepped ashore, one of Lüdecke's officers directed him to a small house near the beach:

> They had got a lot of wounded laid out in a sort of back garden. I shall never forget the sight of that back garden if I live to be a hundred. The wounded, lying around in the sunlight, groaning and moaning – one had just arrived as I arrived, all twisted up in agony ... the first case I did was the German first lieutenant – I took his leg off halfway up the thigh – he had his knee and lower part of the thigh absolutely pulped by a piece of

shell. One man had six separate injuries, including a hole in his skull down to the brain.[56]

Once the worst cases had been stabilised, they were taken aboard *Orama* and transported to Valparaiso the same evening, Luce having gallantly assured Lüdecke that they would not be treated as prisoners-of-war. While Luce roamed the island with a bag of sovereigns, paying off locals whose property had been damaged, his men and Allen's relaxed for the first time in months, rowing around retrieving souvenirs and scooping up hundreds of fish that had been stunned by the exploding shells. Midshipman George Barker retrieved an officer's cap and badge, and *Kent*'s H.S. Welch recalled salvaging 'a nice little skiff, quite undamaged', as well as, oddly, a chair.[57] But the prize belonged to *Glasgow*. 'We were all fishing,' recalled Engineer Lieutenant-Commander Percy Shrubsole, 'when we saw something making a lot of fuss in the water. It turned out to be a pig from the *Dresden*, which had managed to keep afloat. A couple of men dived overboard and brought it on board.' *Glasgow*'s crew adopted the pig. Nicknamed 'Tirpitz', he was 'bathed every day and on Sundays wears an Iron Cross around his neck'.[58]

Chile formally protested the Royal Navy's violation of its neutrality, but the gesture was a mere formality and a perfunctory British apology was accepted without comment; the days of the *Etappen* system and the generally benign indulgence of the pirates by neutrals were numbered. *Dresden*'s destruction ended the long, sometimes tragic and often frustrating struggle against von Spee's *Kreuzergeschwader Ostasien*. Lüdecke had not scored the spectacular successes of von Müller or Köhler, sinking just four ships totalling 12,960 tons, and has been described as having 'none of the aggressiveness or audacity necessary to become a legendary captain'.[59] Another author implies rather cruelly that he deserves no place alongside von Schönberg, Haun, Maerker and the others.[60] This is unfair; unlike von Müller, who had the advantage of surprise and an unprepared enemy at the start of his campaign, after the Falklands Lüdecke was a fugitive, who had already fought two battles. His ship had been in continuous operation for months and overseas for a year. He was also short of supplies and was being hunted by one of the greatest concentrations of British sea power outside home waters. Simply by refusing to be interned, he posed a continuing threat to British trade, tied up a greatly superior force, kept badly needed ships from other duties and caused the Admiralty a great deal of frustration. We should, perhaps, refrain from passing judgement until we have ourselves lived under such tremendous strain; the fact that his beleaguered crew apparently retained their patriotism and cohesion to the end is a tribute to the leadership qualities of this humane and rather unassuming man.

As to his record before joining von Spee, Lüdecke did not have 'pirate' in his job description. He was a career naval officer who had performed well enough to be granted an independent command, but he had never been tested in battle. The *Admiralstab* did not select men with a predisposition for commerce raiding for these appointments; indeed, it is arguably impossible to identify this particular gift in peacetime, and it was sheer luck that in August 1914 some of them possessed it. Lüdecke did his duty, his courage was perhaps of a different kind, but it was certainly not lacking. Interned with his men on Quiriquana Island, north of Coronel, until the war ended, he was repatriated in 1919 and died in 1931.[61]

By the time he was defeated, on 14 March 1915, just two pirates remained at large.

Chapter 9

Part-time Pirates:
the Armed Liners

'Forty-two fast German merchant cruisers needed only a breathing
space to get loose and to arm upon the seas.'

Winston Churchill, in *The World Crisis*

Before the war the Admiralty was concerned about the threat posed by
Germany's fast modern liners. The Royal Navy armed thirty-nine liners
within a few days of war breaking out, and there was every reason to assume
the *Admiralstab* would do the same. The British estimated that forty-two
German liners could be converted, most of them large modern ships built to
carry migrants to the Americas.

In fact there were fifty-nine possible candidates, and the *Admiralstab*
certainly intended to arm them, but, although pre-war planning aimed to
ensure that armed liners would proceed to sea when the fleet mobilised,
around twenty were still in German ports when war broke out.[1] Each poorly
armed, unarmoured, improvised warship would thus have to run the gauntlet
of the British blockade before they could begin operations. Surmising, rightly
as subsequent events showed, that even the oldest warship would be more
than a match for an AMC, the *Admiralstab* decided not to take the risk, and
only three AMCs successfully ran the blockade. The Hamburg–Amerika ferry
Königin Luise was fitted out as a minelayer, but was found and sunk by Royal
Navy destroyers in the Thames Estuary on 5 August. The Norddeutscher–
Lloyd liner *Kaiser Wilhelm der Grosse* made a clean break; her fate will be
related below. Norddeutscher–Lloyd's *Berlin* sortied on 21 September,
returned home a day later, left again on 16 October and was interned in
Norway in November, although the mines she laid sank the new British
dreadnought *Audacious* on 28 October.

The remaining ships were either on open water or in foreign ports, mostly
in North America; on 7 August the *New York Times* reported twelve
Hamburg–Amerika and six Norddeutscher–Lloyd liners in New York, and
two in Boston.[2] Formidable obstacles prevented them being armed and

equipped as commerce raiders. The British had control of the sea, and could simply bring their liners home, where they could be turned into AMCs quickly and efficiently. German liners could not get home, and had not plied their trade with guns and ammunition stored in their holds, although lurid rumours to that effect circulated freely around less well informed British clubs and smoking rooms, and even embassies; on 5 August the British Embassy in Buenos Aires reported to London that the Hamburg–Sudamerika liner *Cap Trafalgar* 'has on board, besides guns with which to assist her own conversion into a cruiser, spare guns which she is gradually transferring to other German merchantmen in the port under cover of night'.[3]

In fact *Cap Trafalgar*, like Germany's other liners, had no guns and nowhere to obtain them from in a neutral port. Arming them meant getting them to sea and trying to arrange a rendezvous with a German warship. This imme- diately limited the number of available guns; certainly, there were never enough to turn all the remaining ships into cruisers. It was also by no means certain that they would be allowed to sail; if the local authorities enforced neutrality laws, naval auxiliaries were subject to internment.

Even if an enterprising liner skipper managed to get to sea, and obtained guns, he still faced considerable challenges. Transatlantic liners were designed for speed not economy, and consumed coal at an alarming rate of around a ton per nautical mile, that figure almost doubling if they dared to approach maximum revolutions.[4] Worse, their bunkers were small, as they were only designed to travel around 3,000 miles – a typical ocean crossing – before refuelling and most of their internal space consisted of passenger accommodation. Liners thus tended to run out of coal after a few days. They also had no armour or fire control equipment. Even the British, whose AMCs enjoyed ready access to coal and dockyard facilities and were unlikely to run into enemy warships, gradually decommissioned them or converted them into troopships once the initial crisis was over. The Germans only managed to get five to sea; their careers illustrate almost every limitation inherent in an inferior naval power without sea control or access to bases using armed liners as commerce raiders.

Kaiser Wilhelm der Grosse, the only liner to break out according to the *Admiralstab* plan, had been something of a celebrity in her day; in 1898 she had become the first German liner to be awarded the Blue Riband prize for the fastest transatlantic crossing. But by 1914 she was past her prime, sup- planted by newer, faster ships, and Norddeutscher–Lloyd must have raised few objections when she was requisitioned for war service. Still commanded by her peacetime skipper, 42-year-old *Fregattenkapitän* Max Reymann, she left Bremen on 4 August, crept north along the Norwegian coast and then ran fast into the Atlantic before the British blockade could be properly established. *Kaiser Wilhelm der Grosse* was armed with six 105mm guns and two 37mm quick-firers, and carried 5,000 tons of coal – enough to steam 5,000 miles if Reymann kept to an economical 12 knots.[5]

The cruise began promisingly, *Kaiser Wilhelm* overhauling the Grimsby trawler *Tubal Cain* near Iceland on 7 August. Reymann shelled her after taking off the crew, although according to her skipper, Charles Smith, it took forty-eight shots to sink her, the embarrassed German gunnery officer apparently explaining that 'being British, [she] took a lot of sinking'![6]

Heading south to the Canary Islands, Reymann caught the Union Castle liner *Galician*, homeward-bound from South Africa, on 15 August. However, when the raider's boarding parties reported that she was carrying passengers, Reymann let her go after first destroying her radios: another example of how the 1914–1915 'pirates' tended to observe the rules of war. 'On account of your women and children I will not sink the ship,' Reymann signalled *Galician*'s relieved Captain Makepeace on the morning of 16 August, concluding with a courteous 'You are released. Bon Voyage.'[7]

Later the same day *Kaiser Wilhelm* captured and sank the eleven-year-old New Zealand-registered *Kaipara*, carrying frozen meat from South America and unencumbered with inconvenient passengers. The next day he caught the Royal Mail Steam Packet Company's *Arlanza*, another passenger ship, releasing her after signalling 'you are dismissed on account of your having women and children on board', and on the 18th he sank the Elder Dempster liner *Nyanga*.[8] By now two weeks of fairly low-intensity steaming had exhausted *Kaiser Wilhelm*'s coal supply, and Reymann headed for a remote anchorage on the coast of Rio de Oro, in the Spanish Sahara, where the *Etappen* had arranged a rendezvous with three colliers.

In the meantime *Arlanza* made for Las Palmas in the Canary Islands, rigging up her auxiliary wireless and warning the cruiser *Cornwall*, the only warship in the area, on the way. The Admiralty transferred three AMCs and three old cruisers from other stations to reinforce *Cornwall* and within a few days a search had begun that almost immediately netted the German auxiliaries *Werner Vinnen* and *Professor Woermann*.

In the event it was the old cruiser *Highflyer*, on loan from Admiral John de Robeck's 9th Cruiser Squadron, that scooped the prize. Before the war *Highflyer* had been a cadet training ship, a familiar sight in many ports, immaculate and well drilled with a crew of fresh-faced youngsters lining her rails, but in August 1914 she had been commissioned for war service under Captain Henry Buller. Buller had already scored one notable success, intercepting the Dutch liner *Tubantia*, which was homeward-bound carrying German reservists and gold. Now, on 24 August, Buller received a signal from

Las Palmas indicating that *Kaiser Wilhelm* was coaling at Rio de Oro in defiance of Spanish neutrality.

At 13:30 on 26 August *Kaiser Wilhelm*'s look-outs sighted *Highflyer*'s distinctive silhouette on the horizon. The raider was outgunned, with her fires out and a collier along each side, so Buller signalled Reymann to surrender. 'German warships do not surrender,' the German replied. 'I request you to observe Spanish neutrality' – ignoring the obvious contradiction that he was himself violating it.[9] In the meantime he prepared for action, ordering his prisoners across to the collier *Arucas* and instructing both colliers to cast off. Buller ordered Reymann to surrender again, and after receiving another refusal, signalled that he would give *Kaiser Wilhelm* an hour and a half to strike her colours or leave neutral waters. At 15:10 *Highflyer* opened fire.

Among the British prisoners was a British army officer who had been taken from the *Galician*. Rushed across to the *Arucas*, he watched the unequal action from her decks, as Buller manoeuvred his ship to bring his full broadside to bear:

> The cruiser was lying about four miles off when she opened fire, and the collier was still held by a hawser on the port side ... the shells were falling all the time and the *Arucas* was under fire ten minutes before she got out of range ... the cannonade from both ships lasted about forty minutes. All the *Kaiser*'s shots appeared to be falling short.[10]

Reymann's colliers scattered like a shoal of fish, the skipper of *Magdeburg*, which was carrying dynamite, given a particularly powerful incentive when a wild shell from *Highflyer* smashed into his ship's forecastle.[11] By 16:45 *Kaiser Wilhelm* had fired all her ammunition and was burning furiously. As Buller ordered his gun crews to cease fire and tried again to get Reymann to surrender to avoid further bloodshed, the German skipper ordered his crew to abandon ship, possibly after first firing explosive charges in *Kaiser Wilhelm*'s holds. While the German sailors rowed ashore and established themselves 'in a menacing position behind the sand-hills', the liner heeled over and sank on her side in shallow water.[12] Her great slab sides remained visible as a rusty, disintegrating island off the West African coast until she was eventually scrapped in 1952. Reymann, 24 officers and 503 men were interned by the Spanish authorities and later handed over to the British. The British prisoners were taken to Las Palmas aboard *Arucas* and released.

Highflyer sustained ten minor hits, losing one man killed and five wounded. Captain Buller's despatch was suitably laconic: 'We opened fire at 3:10 o'clock,' he wrote, 'and finished at 4:25. The *Kaiser Wilhelm* sank at 5:10. Our lyddite shells soon settled things. Our ship was struck ten times.'[13] Back in London, Churchill was more effusive, signalling Buller, 'Bravo! You have rendered a service not only to Great Britain but to the peaceful commerce of the world.'[14] The one-sided 'Battle of Rio de Oro' proved that even the most obsolete cruiser could take care of an AMC.

In fact, sometimes it did not even take a cruiser. On the other side of the Atlantic *Cap Trafalgar* left Buenos Aires on 18 August and headed downriver to Montevideo, where coal supplies were waiting. The liner was still commanded by the Hamburg–Sudamerika Line's Fritz Langerhannsz, a bulky, jolly-looking and spectacularly bearded officer whose distinctly festive appearance belied both his determination and his education: he was a graduate, fluent in several languages, with a passion for architecture, polo and sailing.[15] He was also, bizarrely and ironically, given the name of his command, a Nelson enthusiast who had personally translated Robert Southey's *Life of Nelson* into German, and had decorated his ship with memorabilia relating to the great admiral and his last battle.[16]

The brand-new *Cap Trafalgar* had been formally requisitioned as an auxiliary cruiser by the local naval attaché a few days earlier, but her changed status meant nothing in practical terms. With no guns and no gunners, Langerhannsz was in no condition to take on Captain John Luce's cruiser *Glasgow*, the Royal Navy's sole representative on the South American Station, whose sinister silhouette could be seen from time to time, prowling along the horizon just outside Uruguayan waters. Langerhannsz only managed to slip out on 22 August, after Luce was ordered away north to look for Fritz Lüdecke's *Dresden*; the ocean was very big, and the Royal Navy simply did not have enough ships to be strong everywhere in August 1914.[17]

Free at last, but unarmed and vulnerable, Langerhannsz headed north-west to remote Trindade, nearly 1,200 kilometres off the Brazilian coast, where he had been instructed to wait for further orders. Oddly enough, as Luce had steamed north, Lüdecke had steamed south, and the tiny volcanic island was also where *Dresden* was hiding, with four colliers and the gunboat *Eber*, commanded by 38-year-old *Korvettenkapitän* Julius Wirth. Wirth had left Luderitz in German South West Africa on 3 August and, with the old collier *Steiermark* tagging along, had embarked on an epic voyage across the Atlantic in his tiny, unseaworthy craft. When he arrived on 15 August, Lüdecke had ordered Wirth to transfer his guns, ammunition and crew to *Cap Trafalgar* when she arrived, then take command of her as the Kaiser's latest commerce raider. Wirth waited patiently for nearly three weeks, doing his best to tidy his ship, and sending his men aboard *Dresden* to bathe and use the laundry. A serious-looking man with a youthful, round face and an immaculate centre parting, he impressed Lüdecke, who described him as 'a very remarkable young officer'. The statement speaks volumes about the personalities of both men, as Wirth was only three years younger than Lüdecke.[18]

Cap Trafalgar arrived on 28 August. On the way Langerhannsz had prepared his ship for her new role as best he could, cutting down one funnel and altering her silhouette to resemble a British liner. After due consideration, the vessel he opted for as his disguise was the nine-year-old Cunard liner *Carmania*.

Once alongside *Eber*, work began to transfer the gunboat's two 105mm guns and six 37mm quick-firers, a painstaking task, as although the liner had been built with gun rings set into her decks for this very eventuality, they had been constructed for modern naval guns, not *Eber's* ancient weapons. In the meantime the two captains arranged an amicable exchange of command. Langerhannsz remained in the liner until Wirth was familiar with the ship and those personnel remaining aboard as she embarked on her new career, then left *Cap Trafalgar* to take command of the colliers and the look-out post and rudimentary base infrastructure at Trindade. It was a startling transition from the gunboat's limited accommodation, especially for Otto Steffan, *Eber's* wireless officer, who was still getting over a severe case of malaria and blood poisoning contracted in Africa: 'We had to get used to the silk sheets and the cabins still smelling of the perfume of the last passengers to leave this luxury liner – memories of peacetime!'[19] On 4 September *Cap Trafalgar* put to sea for her first operational cruise. As she steamed away from Trindade, her off-duty watch lined the rail and stared, no doubt a little wistfully, as a skeleton crew took the now demilitarised *Eber* away to eventual internment in Brazil.

Wirth steamed around for ten days but sighted nothing; troubled by nearby wireless transmissions from British warships, he returned to Trindade on 13 September to coal from the colliers *Berwind* and *Pontos*, sending a third tender, *Eleonore Woermann*, out on picket duty in case a marauding British warship caught *Cap Trafalgar* at her time of maximum vulnerability. According to one account, *Eleonore Woermann* was armed with a vintage muzzle-loading mortar, salvaged, refurbished and manned by the redoubtable Langerhannsz.[20] By dawn on the 14th the AMC's crew were hard at work:

> Soon coal and coal dust had permeated the ship. It was everywhere. We couldn't get away from it. We were up to our necks in coal! As the sun rose, we were engaged not only in this task but in alterations around the gun emplacements, with hammers and acetylene torches, burning away obstructions to the line of fire. There was so much complaining and swearing over the difficulties involved![21]

At 07:00 *Cap Trafalgar's* duty wireless operator reported to Steffan that he was picking up strong signals, indicating an approaching ship. The transmissions were Marconi, not Telefunken, which meant the intruder was British, not

German. Steffan reported to Wirth on the bridge, who flicked an uneasy glance around his filthy, cluttered and immobile ship, and asked his subordinate for his opinion. He was, perhaps, betraying his inexperience, but it was a very big leap indeed from commanding a colonial gunboat to responsibility for a lone raider operating against the world's most powerful navy. But although Steffan's response was to 'get out of here as fast as we can raise anchor', Wirth stayed put and continued coaling until his bunkers were full.[22] Just after 11:00 *Cap Trafalgar*'s masthead look-out signalled an ominous cloud of smoke on the horizon, and 'a shrill whistle brought coaling to a halt. Shovels were thrown aside. Crewmen crawled out of the bunkers. The anchor was hauled in … alarms shrilled. Buglers sounded battle stations! Clear the ship for action!'[23]

The enemy ship was another AMC, a large, high-sided grey steamship with two funnels, flying the White Ensign of the Royal Navy. More perceptive observers in *Cap Trafalgar* realised that, superficially, she looked much like their own ship, which was hardly surprising as in a bizarre twist of fate, she was their alter ego, the former Cunarder *Carmania*.

Carmania had been requisitioned by the Royal Navy in Liverpool on the morning of 7 August and returned to sea as a warship a week later, after a contingent of naval reservists and Royal Marines had trooped on board and she had been hastily equipped with eight 4.7-inch guns, a Barr & Stroud range-finder and two searchlights. Her commanding officer was 45-year-old Captain Noel Grant, an officer with a reputation for discipline and efficiency, but who suffered from poor health and had never seen active service, had never commanded anything as big as *Carmania* and had run a ship aground earlier in his career. It is perhaps due to this mixed record that *Carmania*'s 60-year-old captain, James Barr, had been hastily appointed a lieutenant commander in the Royal Naval Reserve and was asked to remain in the ship as Grant's adviser.[24] The relationship was not easy, and at one point the two officers were barely speaking, although the situation had improved somewhat by the time the AMC reached Trindade. They had, perhaps, found common grounds for shared resentment when *Carmania*'s first Admiralty orders assigned them an undignified 'mission' to haul coal and provisions to Cradock's squadron in the South Atlantic. It was only after they had delivered these mundane essentials that Cradock released *Carmania* to reconnoitre Trindade, which was suspected of being a possible German base.

Grant was approaching from the other side of Trindade, but his look-outs had sighted masts above the low-lying island and he had sent his men to action stations at 10:45. Although he had not identified *Cap Trafalgar*, Grant knew no British ships were anywhere near and assumed the strange vessel was hostile. This impression was reinforced when *Cap Trafalgar* came into view, raising steam and clearing away her colliers alongside as fast as she could, before accelerating away from *Carmania*.

At 12:30 Grant ordered his gunners to fire a shot across *Cap Trafalgar*'s bows, just as Wirth turned back towards *Carmania*, running up his colours. As it exploded 50 metres ahead, Wirth's gunners replied, slamming a brace of 105mm shells across the 4,500-metre gap which separated *Cap Trafalgar* from her enemy. His last doubts dispelled, Grant yelled 'Let him have it', an unusual departure from the rule book (which stipulated the word 'Commence' for opening fire) for this most orthodox of captains, and the first-ever action between ocean liners was on.[25]

Wirth was outgunned at long range, and knew that his only chance of evening the odds was to close the range as fast as he could and bring his quick-firers into action. In the meantime his gunners laid down accurate salvoes as fast as they could. Almost immediately, a German shell smashed into a winch on *Carmania*'s starboard side, shattering it into vicious fragments that killed most of a gun's crew. Shortly afterwards Wirth ordered his gunners to concentrate on *Carmania*'s bridge, setting it alight. In the meantime *Carmania*'s gunners were punishing *Cap Trafalgar*. The first British shell ricocheted off the foremast before exploding on the deck, blowing off the head of a seaman named Schneider, *Cap Trafalgar*'s first fatality. Soon the British weight of shell began to tell, and the once-luxurious Hamburg–Sudamerika liner slowly started to disintegrate:

> Enemy shells and shrapnel tore to bits the flowers in our elegant Winter-garten. Marble was peeled from the walls. Rubble was heaped on other rubble ... our fire-fighting parties worked bravely to extinguish the many fires about the ship ... their task was made the more difficult since the water and steam lines were all shot with holes.[26]

By now Wirth had brought his quick-firers into action and, realising the danger, Grant altered course to open the range and bring his starboard guns to bear; by this point the barrels of the port guns were red hot and the paint was blistering. As the two ships drew apart, observers in *Carmania* noticed that their opponent was noticeably listing to starboard, and Grant ordered his gunners to concentrate on *Cap Trafalgar*'s waterline. It was almost impossible to miss the German liner's towering sides, and shell after shell tore into her hull, worsening her list. It was now a race against time. Although *Carmania* clearly had the upper hand, the Cunarder was also badly wounded. Her aerials, boats, ventilators and rigging had been shot to ribbons, and the fire on her foredeck was blazing out of control, as the fire mains had been shot through, making firefighting impossible. Grant had been forced to abandon the bridge and the liner was being steered from an emergency control position aft. Below decks, Engineer Lieutenant Harold Kendall recalled the dreadful conditions in the forward boiler room, where he was in charge:

> Instead of getting air down the ventilators we were getting down clouds of smoke from the wood, rope and paint, from all around the burning bridge, and every shell that hit the ship bringing down choking clouds of soot and dust ... I saw [the stokers] on their bellies on the stokehold plates gasping for air and then up again and at their fires.[27]

Grant was faced with a difficult decision. *Cap Trafalgar* was clearly in a terrible state. Some 5 miles away, she was listing badly and enveloped in smoke, steaming painfully back towards Trindade. But she was not yet finished and was still firing rapidly and accurately. If Grant kept steering his present course, he would be forced to leave the battle, but if he turned *Carmania* towards *Cap Trafalgar*, the wind would fan the flames on his bridge and spread them aft along the ship. Ultimately the decision was taken out of his hands. As Grant and Barr watched, *Cap Trafalgar* ceased firing and her crew began launching boats as fast as they could. As they pulled away, the German AMC heeled over on to her side, her funnels lying on the water, before making her final plunge: 'Suddenly she tilted to a greater angle, her stern came right out of the water, and she dived down, the last part to disappear being the main trunk with the German ensign still streaming from it in the breeze ... as she disappeared a cheer was raised, as much for the defeated enemy as for the *Carmania*.'[28]

Casualties for both sides were remarkably low. Nine British sailors died. On *Cap Trafalgar* only two men were killed in action, but another eighteen died in the water or later from their wounds. One was Julius Wirth, who had fought his first and only fight; a splinter pierced his armpit, cutting off the blood supply to his heart, and he suffered a fatal heart attack in the water.

As *Cap Trafalgar* shuddered in her death throes, Otto Steffan's wireless operators had begun rhythmically tapping out a distress signal. Across the water another raider, the former Norddeutscher–Lloyd liner *Kronprinz Wilhelm*, heard the cry for help and altered course to assist. Although she was far too late to change the outcome, according to some accounts *Carmania*'s look-outs briefly sighted her four funnels on the horizon before she turned away, perhaps fortunately for Captain Grant's badly wounded ship. *Kronprinz Wilhelm* had slipped quietly from her berth in Hoboken, New York, at 20:45 on 3 August, blacked-out with her holds jammed with supplies and coal. Rumours flew around New York that she had been carrying a concealed gun, hidden beneath a curious cruciform packing case on her foredeck, and her escape for what seemed to be a military mission infuriated the US authorities, one embarrassed official conceding that 'the Government at Washington is not accustomed to this business'.[29] Shortly afterwards the US government posted the powerful dreadnought USS *Florida* outside the harbour to prevent any future unauthorised departures, by force if necessary.

In the meantime *Kronprinz Wilhelm*, now repainted a dull camouflage grey, collected her guns from *Karlsruhe* on 6 August at the rendezvous that was so rudely interrupted by Admiral Cradock in HMS *Suffolk*, before beginning her new career as a raider under the command of *Kapitänleutnant* Paul Thierfelder.[30] Her subsequent cruise was the longest and most successful of all the AMCs, and is also the best documented, as one of her junior officers, the minor Polish aristocrat and adventurer Count Alfred von Niezychowski, wrote a somewhat sensational book about it.[31] Apart from its dramatic beginning and tense end, however, it was also quite startlingly uneventful, only the occasional capture breaking up the monotony of long weeks of open-water cruising.

There was no doubt that the *Suffolk* encounter made Thierfelder painfully aware of his new command's limitations as a warship, and as the liner sped west he ordered further precautions to make her as battle ready as he could. The two 88mm guns were securely mounted on the forecastle, and crews were recruited from among the liner's naval reservists, directed by ex-*Karlsruhe* men. Mattresses and carpets from the passenger cabins were nailed up around the ship as splinter matting, or were used to create protected nests for sharpshooters on the upper decks. In addition to the guns, which were nicknamed 'White Arrow' and 'Bass Drum', Köhler also provided *Kronprinz Wilhelm* with fifty rifles, and a Maxim machine gun whose staccato rattle earned it the nickname 'The Riveter'. The liner's cosy smoking room was converted into a sick bay, and the grand saloon, formerly 'a chamber of palatial magnificence', was brutally ripped apart and converted into an extra coal bunker.[32]

The new raider's commanding officer was as improvised as his ship. Thierfelder was a quiet, understated man, just 30 years old. Considerably younger than the other pirates, his courage was never in doubt and he was clearly a competent navigating officer, but he was, perhaps, rather inexperienced for the responsibility of independent command, particularly when that command was a poorly armed, improvised warship operating in very hostile waters. Nevertheless, he appears to have been a popular commanding officer, who enjoyed the respect of his men.[33]

It was 18 August before *Kronprinz Wilhelm* met another ship, the German collier *Walhalla*, which had been sent out to meet her; after just a few days at sea the liner was already low on coal. Coaling at sea was no easy task for a ship the size of *Kronprinz Wilhelm*, which loomed over her supply ships and prizes and was designed to do the job in a well-equipped harbour, not lashed alongside some rusty old tub, rolling and pitching on the high seas. Thierfelder had done what he could to make the task easier, ordering large, circular holes to be cut in *Kronprinz Wilhelm*'s decks and inserting ingenious tubes improvised from the liner's ventilators, so that coal could simply be shovelled directly from the decks rather than being hauled below in sacks. Temporary derricks had also been installed so that coal could be transferred from ship to ship in mid-air.[34] Nevertheless, it was still a back-breaking task that took three days and was terribly hard on both men and ship: *Kronprinz Wilhelm*'s flimsy sides took a terrible battering every time the liner coaled, and by the end of her cruise the resulting damage is clearly visible in contemporary photographs.

Kronprinz Wilhelm parted from *Walhalla* on 21 August, with 2,500 tons of coal, a female fox terrier named Nelka and a 15-year-old stowaway named Karl Sturm. In exchange, Thierfelder had offloaded anyone too old for military service. A week later he intercepted his first prize, the Russian sailing schooner *Pittan*. However, according to Niezychowski, when the grim-faced boarding party explained what was going to happen, the huge, bearded Russian captain fell to his knees and wept uncontrollably, pleading that the ship was all he had in the world. Thierfelder ultimately spared him, revealing a humanitarian streak that was rather at odds with his new profession.

After another leisurely week, during which the liner's crew occupied themselves purging their ship of rats and carrying out the traditional 'Crossing the Line' ceremony, Thierfelder made his first kill, the steamer *Indian Prince*, homeward-bound carrying cocoa and coffee. Look-outs spotted her running lights at 21:00 on 4 September, but *Kronprinz Wilhelm* pursued her for miles through the darkness until her captain finally gave in at dawn. After taking off her crew and passengers, who were assigned accommodation aboard *Kronprinz Wilhelm* appropriate to their class and status (passengers in first class, crew in second), Thierfelder kept her in company for days before finally sending her to the bottom on 9 September by opening her sea cocks:

> In the side of every vessel below the waterline is a large circular manhole ... into which fits a steel plate or plug. The plate is fastened to the reinforced sides of the ship by means of bolts arranged at intervals of a few inches around the circumference of the hole. Into this plate fit large pipes which ... form an intake for salt water. This plug and its manhole are called the ship's sea cocks.[35]

Opening the sea cocks was not without hazard. As Thierfelder's boarders systematically stripped *Indian Prince* of coal and stores, a small party worked deep inside the ship, preparing the sea cocks by carefully unscrewing each rusty bolt and greasing its threads before replacing it, and dismantling pipes and other obstructions. Finally, when the time came, a sailor named Fitzmüller returned below equipped with a sledgehammer and a wrench, and a safety rope tied around his waist. He meticulously removed every other bolt until just two were left and the steel plate was bending inwards with the force of the water pressure. Then Fitzmüller, 'sweating at every pore', called out 'Ready!'

> The men on deck took in the slack of the rope ... Fitzmüller now lifted his sledgehammer, and with a single vigorous blow smashed one of the two protruding bolts through its nut and hole ... with a dull explosion the whole two-foot plate flew loose, and a geyser of sea water gushed upward into the hold. Fitzmüller at once leaped for the ladder and clambered for safety.[36]

It was slow and risky, but this method avoided wasting ammunition or explosives and Thierfelder used it whenever time allowed. Niezychowski found the sight upsetting: 'A ship has always appeared to me like a living being,' he wrote, 'to destroy it seems like murder.'[37] This sentimentality would pass.

It was a full month before *Kronprinz Wilhelm* took another prize, Thierfelder breaking up the monotony with boat races, shark fishing and performances by the ship's band, along with gunnery drill and the relentless work of cleaning ship. There were mid-ocean meetings with an Italian sailing barque, *Macdiarmid* of Genoa, and three more colliers, which as well as coal, provided supplies and naval reservists to join the crew, and took away the prisoners. On 14 September Thierfelder's wireless officer picked up the last despairing signal from the *Cap Trafalgar* and altered course, only reluctantly turning away when the signals abruptly stopped – a sobering reminder that war was not a game.

On 7 October *Kronprinz Wilhelm* took her second prize, a large modern steamer named *La Correntina*. Only two years old, she was carrying a valuable cargo of frozen meat to Liverpool when Thierfelder overhauled her, 320 miles off Montevideo. Captain Murrison recorded what would become a clumsy signature 'style' of boarding for Thierfelder, which contributed to the AMC's careworn appearance:

> The cruiser backed astern and came up on our starboard side, smashing our boats and davits and bridge deck, and her men swarmed on board and took charge of the bridge, engine-room and the ship generally. Then a gangway was put out between the vessels, and passengers and crew and their baggage were transferred to the cruiser, after which the ships parted and steamed away to the eastward in company.[38]

It took a week to strip *La Correntina* of everything useful, including two 4.7-inch guns (without ammunition) before the Germans opened her sea cocks and sped her on her way with explosive charges on 14 October. Shortly afterwards another tender, Heinrich Schaeffer's *Sierra Cordoba*, arrived to bring *Kronprinz Wilhelm* coal and take away the prisoners.

Kronprinz Wilhelm spent 251 days at sea. Thierfelder never took her into the busiest shipping lanes – a wise precaution, perhaps, given the inadequacy of her armament – and the cruise was consequently characterised by extraordinarily long gaps of a month or more between prizes. Thierfelder's determination to strip prizes of anything useful, coupled with the difficulty of transferring booty up the liner's sides, meant that most captures inevitably turned into terribly long-drawn-out affairs. Without doubt the most ridiculous of these epics was the French barque *Union*, which was captured on 28 October and only finally sunk on 22 November. *Union* was carrying over 3,000 tons of coal, which Thierfelder was determined to have, and his unfortunate prize crew spent over three weeks aboard the progressively disintegrating vessel, at one point being entirely abandoned when *Kronprinz Wilhelm* left to seize another French barque, *Anne de Bretagne*, on 21 November. Franz Fehlkamm was part of the long-suffering prize crew:

> Life aboard the *Union* was ... unbearable. The barque was nothing more than a driving wreck upon mountainous seas .... [She] was leaking badly, so that the pumps had to be kept going night and day ... this work went on upon a ship tossing twenty to thirty degrees up on both sides. *Union* was ... thirty-eight years of age and her bottom had seen much repair. As a result of continual rubbing against the sides of the *Kronprinz* she soon began to leak so fast we could not keep her hold free.[39]

Despite the risk, Thierfelder was determined to extract every last ton of coal. By 19 November just a few hundred tons remained, but by now the barque was 'a floating hell':

> We were gambling with death. We bent our backs at the pumps until our muscles gave out. Then we dropped down and rested and got up again to take our turn ... but our labour was lost .... We pumped out a spoonful and a bucketful ran in. The ship was meanwhile beginning to list heavily to starboard. The coal in her hold, wet until it was only a blackened gruel, had shifted to that side, this shifting becoming greater with every lunge of the ship.[40]

By the time *Kronprinz Wilhelm* left to catch *Anne de Bretagne*, Thierfelder's exhausted, terrified boarding party were at the end of their tether. As the AMC drew away, *Leutnant zur See* Hoffman, in command, exhorted them to 'die hard like Germans!' Fehlkamm's vivid account does not include the response to this rousing call; Niezychowski, with spectacular understatement, describes them as 'deeply disappointed'.[41]

Fortunately, by the end of the day *Kronprinz Wilhelm* was back, and the boarding party was safely removed, soaked, battered and frightened, but none the worse for their ordeal beyond a few cuts and bruises. Wisely Thierfelder gave his men Sunday, 22 November off, many of them bizarrely choosing to spend the day catching and releasing albatrosses using complicated tackle manufactured on board.[42]

Anne de Bretagne was carrying timber. Thierfelder decided to sink her by gunfire, but the sturdy barque, only four years old, refused to go down. In an almost farcical sequence of events, which revealed his inexperience, Thierfelder then rammed her four times, buckling *Kronprinz Wilhelm*'s plates and bursting seams in her forward compartments, before setting explosive charges that shattered the barque's bows but still failed to sink her. After ramming her one last time, Thierfelder was forced to leave her, battered but still afloat – an object lesson in the durability of wooden vessels. *Kronprinz Wilhelm* leaked for the rest of the cruise as a result of this poor decision, and eventually her forepeak had to be pumped out and filled with concrete.

Thierfelder caught two ships on 4 December, both steamships: the French *Mont Agel*, in ballast, and *Bellevue*, a rich prize stuffed with coal, gun metal, machine parts, livestock, dyed wool and linen, and a cellarful of wine and whisky, as well as bicycles and a pair of automobiles. One of the latter was brought aboard *Kronprinz Wilhelm* and pushed along the starboard promenade deck in another despairing attempt to create some entertainment during the long, uneventful days at sea. Some sailors amused themselves embroidering tablecloths from the linen. Others, less creative, turned to the alcohol. Thierfelder had planned to send it down with the ship, but despite the best efforts of his officers to keep tabs on it using *Bellevue*'s cargo manifests, case after case was smuggled aboard by the coaling parties: 'Old Smuggler and Black Horse were their favourites,' Niezychowski recalled, 'as we could tell by the empty bottles found in corners ... our men must have had pretty strong heads to guzzle on the sly without showing the effects.'[43]

Mont Agel carried nothing of value, and Thierfelder ordered her sea cocks opened soon after taking her; when she took too long to sink, he once again opted to ram her. It took a week of back-breaking labour to clear out *Bellevue*, interrupted by frustrating bouts of bad weather. Ramming *Mont Agel* and being battered by the *Bellevue* when she was alongside further stressed the raider's weakened plates, and by the time the steamer was scuttled on 20 December *Kronprinz Wilhelm* was leaking badly, defying the efforts of her crew to patch her; in one bunker the water was already 2 metres deep.[44]

And so the cruise went on. On 21 December the prisoners left aboard the collier *Otavi*. The following day Thierfelder gathered his crew and in a sombre address on the AMC's quarterdeck told them about the defeat of the *Kreuzergeschwader*, just under two weeks before. 'The news sank into the hearts of our men,' Niezychowski remembered, 'a premonition of a like fate occurred to their minds ... This undoubted defeat only showed how helpless a ship is when met by an enemy with greater speed and guns of longer range.'[45]

Sturdee had in fact learned of the German raider's presence from *La Correntina*'s prisoners, who had been landed at Montevideo, and had swept for her on his way south from Abrolhos; had *Kronprinz Wilhelm* run into the British battlecruisers that would have been the end of her story, but by this time Thierfelder had returned north.[46] In the event, although the Admiralty were aware of him, Thierfelder took no unnecessary risks and consequently no British ship came close to catching him.

Christmas passed in a strange blur, the men improvising trees from scrap timber and decorating the ship with trinkets and coloured paper scavenged from the prizes, before joining their officers for peaceful and oddly moving celebrations in the mess decks. Thierfelder organised gift boxes for every man, containing fifty cigarettes, ten cigars, two shirts, soap, cake and loose tobacco. Remarkably, although four ships were sighted over the festive season, Thierfelder steadfastly refused to break the festive mood and investigate, reinforcing the otherworldly feel of *Kronprinz Wilhelm*'s cruise. On Boxing Day the unwelcome discovery that the port propeller shaft well had fractured spoiled the mood. By now *Kronprinz Wilhelm* had steamed more than 20,000 miles and burned 20,000 tons of coal, and she was slowly but surely wearing out.

It was 28 December before the raider caught another prize, the old collier *Hemisphere*, and again Thierfelder spent a week clearing her, interrupted by a brief 'holiday' for New Year's Day. Shortly afterwards he overhauled the steamer *Potaro*, which yielded a dozen useful revolvers and a brand-new Marconi wireless set, and on 14 December he caught the big Nelson Steam Navigation Company freighter *Highland Brae*, bound for Buenos Aires carrying silks, hats, furs and a consignment of tennis balls, doubtless urgently required by the British expatriate population of Argentina. Her first mate, 55-year-old Master Mariner Samuel Hitchin, recorded the events in his diary:

He fired a gun across our bow, when we stopped our engines, and he sent an armed boat's crew on board with two officers who hauled down our ensign and took charge and ordered us to steer east (true) cruiser following closely. [They] ordered us to swing out our boat ready for lowering which was commenced but the order was countermanded, the cruiser then left in chase of the three-masted schooner *Wilfred M.* of Barbados.[47]

The owner-operated *Wilfred M.* was carrying cod and potatoes to Bahia. After taking off her crew, Thierfelder again repeatedly rammed her, proving once more that wooden ships were virtually unsinkable. Her wreck stayed afloat for months and was spotted by British warships returning north from the Falklands; she finally drifted ashore at Grenada on 28 April. According to Niezychowski, the horrified watchers aboard *Highland Brae* let out a 'great wail' as the AMC's great bow sliced into the little schooner, and, according to Hitchin's dramatic diary entries, shortly afterwards discipline broke down entirely:

> Some of the crew had broken into the steward's store room and taken some cases of champagne cider, a number of them being under the influence of drink. The officer then placed a sentry at the store-room door and several cases of cider were thrown overboard. [The men] were by this time more or less drunk and engineers had difficulty in keeping the watch at their duties. Quartermaster de Boer, when ordered by the third officer to haul in the log, refused saying he had finished ... and it was with difficulty that the seamen who now showed sign of drink could be got to take up the passengers' and emigrants' baggage. Daley A.B [Able Seaman] was lying on bunker hatch utterly prostrated, crew were now playing accordions and mouth organs and singing, and boatswain collapsed. Nielsen, Quartermaster, kept sober and took the wheel when ordered. Carpenter Books and Stewards kept sober and amenable to discipline. Many of crew and passengers looting. At 5 pm cruiser came alongside and took off passengers, crew and baggage.[48]

Order was only restored when the prisoners were transferred to *Kronprinz Wilhelm*, which by now was carrying 219 mostly British prisoners. Thierfelder kept *Highland Brae* and *Potaro* in company until he had emptied them, but both had been scuttled by early February, along with the unfortunate Norwegian square-rigger *Semantha*, which was intercepted carrying grain for Britain and set ablaze with incendiary shells. Niezychowski, apparently no longer guilt-ridden about 'murdering' ships, waxed lyrical about what he called this 'military funeral', writing that 'it was beautiful to see the shot trail through the night like swift Roman candles'.[49]

By early February Thierfelder had recognised that his cruise could not continue much longer. On the 10th he transferred his prisoners across to the collier *Holger*, which had been steaming in company for several weeks, and offered any sailor over the age of 39 the opportunity to leave. Seventy-three did so, exhausted by the strain of months on the run. They included *Kronprinz Wilhelm*'s former captain, Grahn. Many of those who were left were equally worn out, only pride or youth preventing them from joining their colleagues.

Four more prizes awaited. The first was the British steamer *Chasehill*, caught on 22 February but spared the fate of her predecessors because her cargo of coal and ample passenger accommodation made her an excellent auxiliary. On the following day Thierfelder's birthday, *Kronprinz Wilhelm* caught what Niezychowski called 'the greatest prize of all': the graceful 6,600-ton French passenger liner *Guadeloupe* of Le Havre. The 294 passengers had to be taken off with all their baggage, but the next day Thierfelder's well-practised boarders opened the sea cocks and *Guadeloupe* settled; at 19:20 her boilers blew up in a huge explosion. The prisoners included many women and children and Count Vasco de Orey, a Portuguese nobleman. Among the booty was a leather trunk containing documents addressed to the French Minister of War, and millions of francs' worth of cheques and bankers' drafts.

Thierfelder sent the prisoners away in *Chasehill* on 6 March, once he had taken off most of that ship's coal. By now he had problems with his men as well as his machinery: the constant diet of dried and canned meat with little fresh fruit and vegetables caused an outbreak of beriberi on 22 March. By the end of the month thirty men were down with the virulent nervous system disease. Fresh water was running out, coal supplies were low, the leaky propeller shaft well was worse than ever and the AMC's battered plates were leaking water almost as fast as the crew could pump it out. The *Etappen* despatched the tender *Macedonia* with coal and spares, but by now the vulnerable system was creaking at the seams. Wireless transmissions were intercepted and decoded, and *Macedonia* was captured on 28 March near Atol das Rocas by the erstwhile relentless pursuer of *Goeben*, Captain Howard Kelly, in HMS *Gloucester*.

In the meantime Thierfelder headed north. Knowing that his cruise was ending, he gratuitously used his guns to despatch *Kronprinz Wilhelm*'s last prizes, the Royal Mail Steam Packet Company liner *Tamar* on 24 March, and the steamer *Coleby* on 27 March. By 10 April the AMC was 60 miles off the Virginia coast, and Thierfelder called his officers together. That night he planned to dash through the British blockade into Newport News, Virginia, and internment:

> Our ship shot along at a rate that made her tremble like a locomotive. In the fireroom the stokers were working like slaves ... while we on the bridge were in a cold sweat of suspense watching for enemy lights ... Suddenly, while we were still some 3 miles from the neutral zone, the starboard lights of a cruiser twinkled directly ahead.[50]

This final dash for safety was Thierfelder's finest hour. Keeping his cool and personally taking the helm, he sent his darkened, 15,000-ton ship careering between two British cruisers before anchoring for the last time in Chesapeake

Bay with just 25 tons of coal left. *Kronprinz Wilhelm* had sunk fifteen ships totalling 60,522 tons. Thierfelder and his men stepped ashore into internment; many of them never lost their taste for handicrafts and improvisation, constructing a quaint German 'village' in the heart of Norfolk Navy Yard from scrap timber and other salvage. After the United States entered the First World War, *Kronprinz Wilhelm* was taken into US Navy service as the troopship *General von Steuben*. She was eventually scrapped in 1923.

When *Kronprinz Wilhelm* steamed into Norfolk Navy Yard on the morning of 11 April 1915, she ended her short final journey tied alongside a sister ship, the former Norddeutscher–Lloyd liner *Prinz Eitel Friedrich*, whose cruise had, if anything, been more epic, at least in terms of distance. *Prinz Eitel Friedrich*'s war began on the other side of the world in Tsingtao, where she had been requisitioned, repainted and armed with four 105mm and six 88mm guns, and four 37mm quick-firers, stripped from the obsolete colonial gunboats *Luchs* and *Tiger*. She was placed under the command of the former commanding officer of *Luchs*, *Korvettenkapitän* Max Therichens. Both *Prinz Eitel Friedrich* and the AMC *Cormoran*, formerly *Emden*'s prize, *Ryazan*, joined von Spee at Pagan Island, from where they were detached to operate in Australian waters.

However, the constant, threatening presence of Rear-Admiral George Patey's powerful battlecruiser *Australia*, coupled with the gradual rolling up of Germany's Pacific bases, conspired to make the assignment what one author has called 'a dangerous and impossible task'.[51] Neither ship took any prizes, and they soon separated. *Korvettenkapitän* Adalbert Zuckschwerdt took *Cormoran* to the Caroline Islands, where she was relentlessly pursued by Japanese warships until she eventually entered the US harbour at Apra, on the island of Guam, on 14 December 1914. Zuckschwerdt asked for 1,500 tons of coal; the Americans responded with a counter-offer of 100 tons. After considering his situation overnight, Zuckschwerdt submitted to internment on the following day, ending *Cormoran*'s short and spectacularly unsuccessful career. When the United States entered the First World War on 7 April 1917, the 43-year-old skipper scuttled his ship rather than surrender her; ironically, although no lives were lost during *Cormoran*'s raiding career, nine men died when she capsized and sank in 34 metres of water.

Unlike Zuckschwerdt, Therichens managed to coal before the German bases fell, and thus had bought himself some time. He took *Prinz Eitel Friedrich* back east across the Pacific to South America, where he rejoined von Spee at Isla Más Afuera on 27 October; although so far Therichens had done nothing but burn fuel, four days after returning to the fold he came close to making his first kill, pursuing the British steamer *Colusa* until she found refuge in neutral waters.[52] *Prinz Eitel Friedrich* remained under von Spee's command as part of the *Kreuzergeschwader* for the next month, although she was not present at Coronel. It was not until von Spee decided to round Cape Horn that Therichens was detached, at first to transmit false signals indicating that the *Kreuzergeschwader* was still in the Pacific, and then to cruise independently.

Therichens caught his first prize, the steamer *Charcas*, hugging the Chilean coast in thick fog on 5 December. Therichens sank her with explosive charges and landed her crew in a remote harbour 45 miles north of Valparaiso the following day.[53] His intention was to round the Horn and join von Spee, until he learned of the *Kreuzergeschwader*'s catastrophic defeat at the Falklands and concluded, rightly, that to enter the Atlantic would be suicide. Instead he ran back north to Easter Island, following the eastern Pacific sailing ship route. On the way he sank the British barque *Kildalton* and captured the French barque *Jean*, carrying 3,500 tons of coal.

Therichens was now, in the eloquent words of a contemporary writer, 'like a hungry dog that has found a good meaty bone and desires ... some quiet corner where he can enjoy his discovery without interruption'.[54] Towing *Jean*, he made his way to Easter Island, arriving on 23 December, where the startled islanders watched yet another suspicious ship drop anchor. Therichens did all he could to allay suspicion, offering to purchase as many as forty sheep from the manager of the island's ranch, who was apparently still unaware that there was a war on. The rancher was not, however, entirely naive; when invited aboard to attend some 'theatricals' on Christmas Eve, he politely declined, fearful of becoming a prisoner. Doubtless the signal station Therichens erected at the summit of Rano Aroi, the island's highest peak, did nothing to allay local alarm.[55]

Therichens left after emptying *Jean* and sending her to the bottom with some well-placed shells into the waterline, just outside Easter Island's territorial waters. After landing his prisoners, he went south, creeping around Cape Horn into the Atlantic. By 26 January *Prinz Eitel Friedrich* was operating off Uruguay, where four sailing ships were caught and sunk in three days. The last was a clear violation of international law as the ship, *William P. Frye*, was American, although her cargo of wheat was bound for Great Britain; Therichens did try to have it thrown overboard, but the work took too long. Inspired, he remained in the area for another two weeks, but only caught one more ship, just 30 miles away from where Thierfelder had caught *Semantha* a few days earlier.[56]

Therichens next followed *Kronprinz Wilhelm* north into the area west of Pernambuco, which had been so profitable for *Karlsruhe* months before. Here he snared three steamers by 20 February, but none carried the coal he so desperately needed; unlike Thierfelder, it does not seem to have occurred to him to strip out his prizes' bunker coal to gain a few more miles. By now *Prinz Eitel Friedrich*'s machinery was wearing out and the AMC was packed with prisoners and running out of food; Therichens decided on a neutral port and made his way north, entering Newport News on 11 March 1915. His arrival was a complete surprise to both the British and the American authorities; *Prinz Eitel Friedrich* had landed no prisoners since Easter Island and her prizes had either not yet been logged as overdue, or were assumed to be the work of *Kronprinz Wilhelm* or *Karlsruhe*, as news of the latter's loss had not yet broken. For a month Therichens maintained that he would return to sea once he had carried out vital repairs; in the meantime US President Woodrow Wilson announced ominously that he was planning 'a most searching enquiry' into the sinking of *William P Frye*.[57] The repairs dragged on until 8 April, when two British cruisers appeared outside Newport News, forcing Therichens to admit defeat and inform the Americans that 'I intend to intern SMS *Prinz Eitel Friedrich* ... number and force of enemy cruisers watching the entrance of the bay makes to me impossible the dash for the open sea with any hope of success. I have decided not to deliver the crew and the ship to fruitless and certain destruction.'[58] Therichens was arguably the 'forgotten pirate'; he successfully snatched eleven prizes without anyone really establishing where he was, although most were small sailing vessels and they only totalled 33,423 tons.

Three days later Thierfelder brought *Kronprinz Wilhelm* alongside, ending the long run of the last raider in open water. One pirate remained, marooned on another continent, a prisoner of geography and the Royal Navy for more than five months.

Chapter 10

The Last Raider: Cornering *Königsberg*

'All of us devoutly prayed we would never see the inside of the Rufiji River again.'

Commander R.A. Wilson, HMS *Mersey*

After *Königsberg* burst out from Dar-es-Salaam on 31 July, Max Looff steered north-east. Her lights extinguished, she swept along the African coast, her white tropical paint gleaming in the moonlight like a ghost ship. On 3 August communications with home broke down. Shortly afterwards Looff revealed that they were heading north to find the Norddeutscher–Lloyd liner *Zeiten*, which was in the area carrying coal and reinforcements, part of the crew of the naval survey ship *Planet*.[1]

On 5 August *Königsberg* met the German collier *Goldenfels*, and during the night he was presented with a 'gift horse', the brand-new Ellerman Line steamer *City of Winchester*. As *Königsberg*'s guns trained menacingly on the liner and searchlights played over her bridge and upperworks, a grim-faced boarding party clambered aboard, destroying her wireless set before ordering Captain George Boyck to follow the cruiser.

City of Winchester was carrying tea, but it was her bunker coal Looff wanted. Taking both steamers with him, he successfully collected *Zeiten* and another German steamer, *Ostmark*, before anchoring with his small flotilla at Al-Hallinyah Island, one of a group of notionally British islands off the coast of modern Oman. Here Looff spent most of a week stripping *City of Winchester* of anything useful before sending her to the bottom with three shells below the waterline, Captain Boyck and his disconsolate crew lining the rail of *Goldenfels* to watch her go down. Like most of the pirates, the *Königsberg* men were professional seamen, and sending to the bottom such a 'fine ship', on her maiden voyage and valued by Looff at some 8 million marks, went against their better instincts.[2]

It was a sobering introduction to commerce raiding, but for Looff it was a promising beginning, as he was the first pirate to take a prize: *City of*

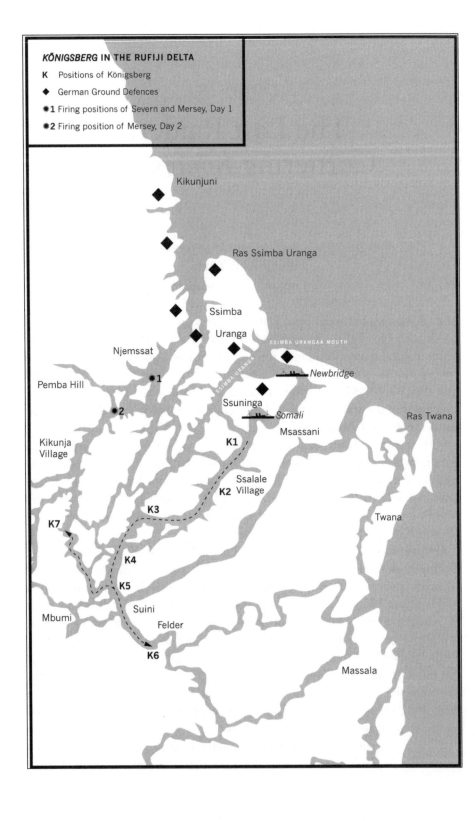

Winchester was only the second British merchant ship lost through enemy action during the First World War.[3] He had successfully rendezvoused with several auxiliaries, and was poised to wreak havoc in the Gulf of Aden, one of the world's busiest shipping channels, where traffic from India, China, Australia and South Africa converged to funnel through the Suez Canal into the Mediterranean. And nobody knew he was there. *Königsberg's* location remained secret until 21 August, when *Goldenfels* landed Captain Boyck and his men at Sabang in West Bengal.[4] With these advantages, Looff might have built a fearsome reputation, but his career would follow a different path. By the time the Admiralty sent forces to search the Gulf of Aden, *Königsberg* had gone. On 13 August he met the ship that was to become his regular tender, Captain Walter Herm's veteran Deutsche–Ostafrika steamer *Somali*, and returned south to the more familiar waters around Dar-es-Salaam.

Local British commanders realised that, without a base, *Königsberg's* life expectancy could be dramatically reduced. As Looff prepared to strip *City of Winchester*, Captain Alfred Sykes's superannuated cruiser *Astraea* arrived at Dar-es-Salaam, where he bombarded the town and destroyed the wireless station. The panicky German authorities added to the devastation by scuttling their expensive floating dock across the harbour mouth; this prevented *Astraea* from entering but destroyed the only local facility in which *Königsberg* could be overhauled, and at the same time trapped several steamers and isolated Looff from his most important supply centre. Admiral King-Hall then lost *Astraea* and *Hyacinth*, which were called away to escort troop convoys in accordance with the Admiralty priority of 'Imperial concentration', leaving only Commander John Ingles' sixteen-year-old cruiser *Pegasus* to protect the East African coast. The Royal Navy was arguably the most powerful armed force in the world in August 1914, but faced with such a monumental workload even this extraordinary service was overstretched. Churchill later wrote of this period that 'the strain upon British naval resources in the outer seas ... was now at its maximum ... we literally could not lay our hands on another vessel of any sort or kind which could be made to play any useful part'.[5] There were simply not enough ships; Churchill and Battenberg had to prioritise, and Looff was the beneficiary, although he failed to capitalise on it.

For a while he vanished, apart from staging an unsuccessful raid on Majunga, in French Madagascar. By early September his men were tired and hungry, and supplies and coal were running low. With Dar-es-Salaam closed, Looff followed the advice of *Somali's* Captain Walter Herm, who knew East Africa well. Before the war Herm had taken his ship far up into the treacherous mangrove swamps of the Rufiji River delta, which disgorged into the Indian Ocean from a remote stretch of jungle-encrusted coastline 100 miles south of Dar-es-Salaam. Looff took *Königsberg* cautiously into the narrow river behind *Somali*, threading his way between the mangroves, every man aware that the river was practically uncharted and their lives were in the hands of an unknown merchant captain. For seven hours the two ships slipped through the muddy brown water, miles of mangroves passing by on either side, the silence broken only by the steady beat of their engines. Sweltering sailors peered over the rail, watching anxiously for the river bed, until finally, at 16:00, Looff ordered 'stop engines' and *Königsberg* tied up alongside *Somali*. For more than two weeks the German sailors got to know and ultimately loathe their swampy bolt-hole, as Looff first stripped *Somali* of her remaining coal, and then took more from the tenders *Gertrude* and *Rovuma*, which arrived on 13 September. It was not until 19 September that he felt ready to rejoin the war. At 13:30 *Königsberg*'s anchor pulled free from the muddy embrace of the river bed, and the cruiser headed back to sea, her objective 'to pay Zanzibar a visit'.[6]

Looff had learned that a British cruiser was at Zanzibar. The weary old engines of John Ingles' *Pegasus* needed urgent repairs. Ingles' orders included a general instruction to protect Zanzibar and, since the island colony was 'inclined to panic' when he was absent, he had decided to carry out the work in full view of the nervous inhabitants.[7] Anchoring his obsolete ship in open water with her fires out and her engines dismantled was hardly ideal, but Ingles was as prepared as he could be: his gun crews slept at their posts, and a captured German tug, *Helmuth*, patrolled the harbour mouth armed with a 3-pounder gun.

At 05:30 on 20 September *Helmuth* sighted a strange warship entering Zanzibar Harbour. The tug fired a warning shot, but the stranger increased speed and broke out the German naval ensign before opening fire on *Pegasus* at a range of about 9,000 metres. *Pegasus*, launched in 1898 and fit only for showing the flag and policing the Empire, would have stood little chance in a fair fight. In these circumstances she was virtually helpless, one eyewitness later recalling that '*Königsberg*'s task was easier than target practice … it wasn't fighting, it was murder'.[8] Looff's gunners straddled *Pegasus* with their first salvo, and then a hail of shells tore through the British cruiser's thin plating.

On board the cruiser 25-year-old Lieutenant Geoffrey Hattersley-Smith was woken by the splash of two shells alongside, and then the shriek of more passing low overhead: 'I was up in my pyjamas and flew forward and up the rigging to my station in the top. Just as I got there the ship was hit, and I could see the *Königsberg* about 4 miles away, firing like mad … the whole thing was so sudden that it seemed a terrible nightmare.'[9]

Meanwhile, 30-year-old Lieutenant Commander Richard Turner, *Pegasus*' first lieutenant, was on watch on the bridge. He was racing aft to report to

Ingles when a shell splinter smashed into his ankle, knocking him to the deck. As two seamen bent to pick him up, another shell exploded nearby, and a huge splinter passed straight through one man, killing him, before tearing away half of Turner's thigh.[10]

Königsberg had fired seven salvoes by the time *Pegasus*' gunners began, sporadically, to reply. But *Königsberg*'s modern guns comfortably outranged the British cruiser's old weapons and there was nothing Ingles could do to get nearer; every British shell dropped at least 1,000 metres short. Within minutes all of *Pegasus*' guns were out of action, their crews dead or wounded. As Hattersley-Smith returned to the deck, an unthinkable word began to pass around the ship: surrender. 'I shouted "No surrender",' Hattersley-Smith remembered, 'but a few seconds later several voices said "Captain's order, Sir" and then I saw the white flag was up ... it was a fearful blow having to lower our colours, and I felt very bitter.'[11]

There was little else Ingles could do. His ship was on fire and sinking, and nearly half of the ship's company had become casualties. The old cruiser was unventilated and many British sailors had slept on deck to escape the heat, which worsened the carnage when the shells began to fall. In total, thirty-four men were killed and fifty-eight wounded, some quite dreadfully. Hattersley-Smith watched his friend Lieutenant John Drake die in front of him:

> Poor old Drake ... was lying with both legs broken and his back shot away. I had seen some awful sights, but it seemed as if I had been used to doing so all my life, and quite natural. Drake recognised me, smiled feebly, and took my hand ... I lifted him on to a hammock, and he whispered he thought he was going; I tried to cheer him up but he was going fast. He asked me to go and see his mother. This was the only thing that upset me ... he died half an hour later.[12]

As Hattersley-Smith made his way along the deck he passed more scenes of appalling horror: a young engine room artificer lying on the deck, his head blown off; a blinded seaman, who seized Hattersley-Smith's hand and begged the young officer to shoot him; Lieutenant Commander Richard Turner, trying to stand with half of his thigh missing and 'the grey look of death on his face'.[13] Below, a terrible tangle of twisted bodies and torn flesh was gradually disappearing under the deluge of water that poured into the stricken ship.

Although it proved impossible to stop the flooding, *Pegasus* took some time to sink. The wounded were safely evacuated, with the help of boats from the big Federal & Shire liner *Banffshire*, whose captain remarked later on the 'wonderful order' that still prevailed on board *Pegasus*.[14] Ingles had time to salvage stores and hammocks for the survivors, before jettisoning everything portable over the side to lighten the ship and bring her damaged plates above the waterline. When this failed, the steamer *Kilwa* towed *Pegasus* into shallow water, but by midday she had rolled over and sunk, only her masts marking the site of the one-sided 'Battle of Zanzibar'.

Looff's gunners fired nine more times at *Pegasus* before spotting the white flag and turning away. On her way out *Königsberg* shelled a disused wireless station and blew a small patrol boat out of the water, before making hurriedly for open water, dropping what appeared to be mines on the way. Had Looff held his nerve and stayed, he could perhaps have rounded up *Banffshire* and the other merchant ships in harbour, and wrecked the town's lighthouse and cable station. Nevertheless, just by sinking one old cruiser, he had struck a significant blow, the echoes of which resounded right back to Whitehall. 'In public opinion, a mistake had been made,' wrote the Official Historian, 'and in Eastern waters the Navy had suffered an appreciable loss of prestige.'[15] For this there would have to be consequences.

Churchill and Battenberg scoured the oceans for ships. Royal Navy assets were stretched to the limit, escorting troop convoys, blockading the Dardanelles and searching for *Emden*, *Karlsruhe* and von Spee, but something had to be done. Far away in the Red Sea Captain Sidney Drury-Lowe received an urgent signal aboard his modern light cruiser *Chatham*: 'Search with all despatch for the German light cruiser *Königsberg*.'[16] The 43-year-old Drury-Lowe, a dapper, good-looking naval officer of the old school, saw opportunity not threat in the *Pegasus* disaster: at least the elusive *Königsberg* had finally been located.

Drury-Lowe left for Mombasa at midnight on 21 September, hoping to find *Königsberg* molesting the Kenyan port, but when he arrived at 07:00 on the 27th the town was quiet, although in a state of some anxiety. German troops had been spotted at Ghazi, just 24 miles away, and Mombasa was almost defenceless, so, before leaving the following day, Drury-Lowe landed two machine guns and helped local volunteers to erect barbed-wire entanglements.

Approaching Zanzibar, *Chatham*'s look-outs sighted several suspicious floating objects, giving credence to the rumour that *Königsberg* had laid mines. Drury-Lowe slowed his ship to a crawl and riflemen lined the rail, but as *Chatham* drew closer it became obvious that the sinister devices were harmless zinc cylinders used by the German navy for storing cordite charges.[17] Zanzibar was a hive of activity. Overcoming the shock of losing his ship and half of his crew, Ingles had mobilised the survivors and the locals:

> Survivors were being employed … as crews of the patrol steam boats, signalmen and look-outs at lighthouse and various other points, W/T operators … artisans in the workshops making field gun carriages etc,

while the remainder formed a much needed reinforcement to the 'Army' of 100 natives, Zanzibar's sole means of defence.[18]

Ingles had also begun to salvage *Pegasus'* guns, most of which had conveniently fallen clear of the ship as she heeled over and sank. With the aid of an anchor chain and a small local steamer with a disproportionately powerful windlass, five 'Peggy Guns' had been retrieved by the end of November, and were taken ashore to supplement the meagre artillery resources available in East Africa.

Drury-Lowe turned his thoughts to the monumental challenge of finding *Königsberg*. Assuming she had not made off into open water, the German cruiser could be hiding anywhere along some 1,700 miles of remote, poorly surveyed and treacherous coastline. The challenge resembled a modern counter-insurgency operation, with *Königsberg* playing the role of guerrilla fighter, and the first task was to deprive her of any useful shore-based infrastructure. The Germans had established a network of coast-watching posts and signal stations, and everywhere *Chatham* went 'signal (or bush) fires sprang up along the hills inland, and they would accompany and precede us along the coast like a veritable *feu de joie*'.[19] Drury-Lowe began the long process of clearing them up on 30 September, when look-outs sighted a suspicious European in bedraggled khaki among the trees on Komo Island opposite the mouth of the Rufiji. Apprehended after a short 3-pounder bombardment and a breathless chase through the forest, he proved to be a local German reservist, *Leutnant* von Neuenstein. The sweating sailors brought him back to *Chatham*, along with three naval ensigns and documents indicating that he had been in contact with *Königsberg*.[20] But where had the cruiser vanished to?

The clues were in the documents, but a combination of poor handwriting, colloquial German and unfamiliar African place-names meant that they might as well have been in code. Von Neuenstein had kept a diary until the day before his capture. In it, he noted that *Königsberg* was at a location, thought by the British to be one of three villages: Salalo, Galalo or Falalo. In fact, Looff's ship was hiding at Ssalale, a remote jungle outpost a few miles up the Rufiji. His look-outs could see *Chatham* as she manoeuvred off Komo, rounding up von Neuenstein and his African staff. An anonymous diarist in *Königsberg* thought the game was up, writing 'Today an English cruiser lay outside the mouth and sent boats ashore twice … on board, all is ready in case we eventually come to grips.'[21]

Looff's men had been busy. *Königsberg*'s immaculate white paint had been covered with an improvised camouflage scheme, her top masts struck and her upperworks draped with foliage. Remarkably, they had also removed one of

Königsberg's worn boilers, sending it overland to Dar-es-Salaam for repair in the capable hands of a local planter and retired naval officer named Werner Schönfeld.[22] While he awaited its return, Looff had made contact with the local military and troops had arrived to defend the cruiser, digging rifle pits on the river bank, supported by batteries improvised from *Königsberg*'s 88mm secondary guns and observation posts, all connected to the ship by field telephone. The Rufiji was a fortress, but it was also a cage. The scale and complexity of Looff's defences indicated that he had abandoned commerce raiding; without reliable coal supplies, and with limited ammunition, he was now a 'fleet in being', tying up as many British assets as possible for as long as he could.

To the relief of the watching Germans, Drury-Lowe failed to decode von Neuenstein's impenetrable diary, and *Chatham* left, missing a priceless opportunity to bring the strange saga of *Königsberg* to an early conclusion. On 6 October the old cruiser *Fox* and the modern light cruisers *Weymouth* and *Dartmouth*, of similar design and age to *Chatham*, arrived and were placed under Drury-Lowe's command. Methodically he divided the coast into sections, and searched every harbour, anchorage and inlet. It was tedious, depressing work, and it took weeks. *Chatham* seaman Robert Fagg recalled 'crossing and recrossing the equator about every 24 hours ... It was so blessed hot we were dished out with tangerines ... to keep our temperature down and cool.'[23]

Drury-Lowe recruited local spies, a two-edged sword since they usually provided nothing but a cacophony of rumours:

> natives ... never had any knowledge of the names of places and ... judged the position and distance solely by the time taken by them to reach the place where the report is made. Their description of a ship's appearance would be equally vague ... with an unlimited number of guns and funnels according to taste.[24]

Painstakingly, the captains narrowed down their search, gathering clues where they could. On 2 October *Chatham* ran aground pursuing a suspicious dhow into shallow waters, much to Robert Fagg's disgust: 'We chased after this blessed light at full pelt', he recollected years later, 'and landed up in a nice little basin of rock ... stranded there in enemy territory ... it was the front that was stuck, the after part of the ship was still ... in the water.'[25] Drury-Lowe tried to free his ship by unloading ammunition into barges to lighten her and mustering his crew aft, where the brute strength of around 500 men was pitted against the immovable African rock. Fagg, unimpressed, recalled how 'we all used to jump up and come down with a bump, but it never moved it'.[26]

It took forty-eight hours to free *Chatham*, which was eventually towed free by *Banffshire*, the second time that ship had aided a British cruiser in distress. The frustrated Drury-Lowe limped to Mombasa, where repairs took nearly two weeks. In the meantime the net closed tighter about *Königsberg*. On 9 October the flamboyantly named Captain Judge D'Arcy of HMS *Dartmouth* captured one of Looff's tenders, the tug *Adjutant*, in the Mozambique Channel. Ten days later Drury-Lowe was back in action, searching the Lindi River for the fourth time. This time he was rewarded with the discovery of the Deutsche–Ostafrika liner *Präsident*, camouflaged and hidden up a creek. Although she was flying a Red Cross flag, Drury-Lowe was in no mood to be charitable: 'her name had not been communicated, her side had not been painted [white], there were no medical stores or preparations of any sort on board, no sick, and no doctors'.[27] Brushing aside the local governor's protests in a bizarre exchange of notes, Drury-Lowe boarded *Präsident*, disabled her engines and removed her compasses, and searched her thoroughly. The papers he discovered finally solved the riddle: on 15 September *Präsident* had sent coal to *Königsberg* at Ssalale on the Rufiji. *Präsident* also gave up a collection of German charts, which proved incontrovertibly that the Rufiji was navigable for a ship of *Königsberg*'s size. Drury-Lowe made for the delta, but was distracted by an odd rumour that *Königsberg* was landing guns at Dar-es-Salaam. Doubtless frustrated at another pointless diversion, he shelled the town and three steamers in the harbour, brushing aside a rather otherworldly truce that had supposedly existed since *Astraea*'s visit in August. 'I cannot say whether the truce … was communicated to the Admiralty,' he bluntly informed the irate Acting Governor of Dar-es-Salaam, 'but I know this: the Admiralty never recognises any terms of truce arranged by the captain of an individual ship … as far as I am concerned, I do not recognise any terms of truce.'[28]And that was that.

By 30 October *Chatham* was outside the Rufiji, arriving just as Looff had retrieved his boiler and was preparing to take his ship out from her hiding place in the Simba Uranga, a minor tributary.[29] The Germans watched from hiding as Drury-Lowe anchored in the channel separating the delta from Mafia Island, and landed armed sailors who began to search the shore; when they discovered that German troops and armed sailors were dug in nearby, they made a hurried departure. Drury-Lowe could not take his big ship, which displaced some 2,000 tons more than *Königsberg*, far up the shallow, poorly charted river. Although local villagers had 'confirmed' that *Königsberg* was there, this kind of intelligence had already proven unreliable, and Drury-Lowe was careful not to get his hopes up too far. But as *Chatham* manoeuvred down the coast, look-outs sighted the masts of two vessels over the tree tops: *Königsberg* and her tender, *Somali*. The next day, perhaps irritated by an unnecessary – and distinctly Churchillian – Admiralty signal reading 'Well done, *Chatham*, hold her and fight without fail', he tried again, following his boats whose crews took careful soundings from the muddy, swirling water. This time he was 4 miles from the entrance to the Simba Uranga when he was forced to stop. Frustrated, he opened fire at extreme range, wounding two men with a lucky hit on *Somali* but not troubling *Königsberg*.[30] At the same time he recalled *Weymouth* from the Comoro Islands and *Dartmouth* from Mozambique. At noon on 2 November one cruiser became three and Drury-Lowe tried again, sending in *Dartmouth*, which had almost empty bunkers and was riding high in the water. Taking advantage of high tide, Captain D'Arcy closed to within 2 miles, giving *Somali* another dose of 6-inch lyddite, before shelling the German trenches on the river bank.

For Looff, defeat and destruction could be only a matter of time. It would, however, be a long time. *Königsberg* was simultaneously protected and imprisoned by the Rufiji's geography: the cruiser could not escape, but the British warships could not reach her. On 3 November Drury-Lowe brought *Chatham* as close as he dared, massing every unoccupied man on the ship's rail and even deliberately flooding *Chatham* to induce a list to port, allowing him to elevate his guns as far as possible. *Chatham*'s spotters had nothing to range on but the dim shadow of *Königsberg*'s camouflaged masts, but Drury-Lowe could not have known how close he came to bringing the campaign to a premature end. The first 6-inch shell screamed over the top of the *Königsberg*, crashing to earth in the mangrove swamps just beyond the cruiser, and badly shaking up the watching Germans: 'we could only sit idle and watch', the diarist recalled. 'The shelling continued for an hour without [our] once receiving one hit, which was an absolute wonder as the shells fell close in front and behind the whole time.'[31]

Drury-Lowe shelled *Königsberg* for two days but on 6 November Looff inched his ship further up the river and no more shells came near him. Moreover, the constant manoeuvring in the shallow, filthy Rufiji had choked *Chatham*'s sensitive condensers, bringing her to a standstill while they were cleaned. The British needed something different to break the deadlock, and Drury-Lowe opted for a boat attack, arming the cruisers' steam cutters, a local steamer named *Duplex* and the picket boat from the old battleship *Goliath*, which was refitting at Mombasa. The attack went in at 05:00 on 7 November, the cutters and *Duplex* providing covering fire while *Goliath*'s picket boat tried to get within torpedo range. The plan was always optimistic, and it went wrong almost as soon as it began. Raked by heavy fire from concealed defences among the mangroves, the boats were forced to turn and race back out, one German shell smashing the picket boat's torpedo-dropping gear and sending a live torpedo running wildly towards the mangrove swamps. Round one had gone to Looff, although one fortunate success made the operation worthwhile; while giving covering fire, *Chatham* scored a lucky hit on *Somali*, starting a fire. The supply ship was a tinderbox, packed with grain and timber and coated with layers of old paint, and she burned for nearly two days until she was a gutted hulk.

The improvised flotilla returned three days later, Drury-Lowe having decided that he would at least ensure *Königsberg* could never leave. At Mombasa he requisitioned the collier *Newbridge* and fitted her with rudimentary armour to protect a volunteer crew commanded by his first lieutenant, Commander Raymond Fitzmaurice. Explosive charges were wedged into the bilges, and tied under the hull. *Newbridge* was about to embark on a new, if short, career as a blockship.

At 05:15 on 10 November *Chatham* and *Weymouth* bombarded the German defences and fifteen minutes later, just before sunrise, *Newbridge* entered the Simba Uranga, surrounded by the armed boats. The blockship immediately came under heavy fire: 'There was a regular hail of Maxim [machine-gun] and rifle bullets on the temporary protective plating on the bridge and other exposed positions [and] the ship and superstructure were repeatedly hit by 3-pounder shells.'[32]

The German defenders concentrated on *Newbridge*, probably because she was simply the biggest vessel taking part. *Duplex* and the other boats steamed as close to the shore as possible, laying down covering fire, but the enemy were almost invisible, and only the occasional shadowy figure could be seen moving carefully between the trees. Nevertheless, Fitzmaurice held his nerve, expertly anchoring the collier in the middle of the deep water channel and blowing the charges; the watching Germans heard a sharp detonation and watched glumly as a thick black cloud issued from the collier's hull.[33] As the shot-riddled raiding flotilla turned away, *Newbridge* slowly settled into the muddy bottom, her squat silhouette a visible symbol of the stalemate that characterised the next eight months.

Despite the extraordinary volume of fire, only nine men were wounded on the British side, with two fatalities: Leading Seaman Walter Fitzjohn of *Weymouth*'s cutter, and a 26-year-old Irishman from *Goliath*'s picket boat, Leading Seaman Timothy McCarthy, who was shot through the head while tending a wounded comrade and died later in Kenya. Ronald Murray, a young officer in *Goliath*, remembered the bullet-scarred boat returning on 12 November 'amidst great enthusiasm', the battle and McCarthy's death under fire seemingly marking a rite of passage for the old battleship's crew, whose war had been uneventful until now.[34] Four Germans were wounded; the number of African troops who became casualties was not recorded.[35]

Round two was a close call, but Looff was unlikely to be bringing *Königsberg* out of the Simba Uranga unless the war ended.

The subsequent frustrating, sweltering deadlock lasted for months and was hard on men and machinery alike. Looff could do little but improve his defences, while the British tightened the noose. On 14 November, as *Newbridge* settled into the river bed and *Weymouth*, the duty guard-ship, prowled back and forth like a frustrated tigress, accompanied by her unruly cubs, the armed steamers *Helmuth* and *Adjutant*, the AMC *Kinfauns Castle* arrived, bringing a Curtiss seaplane and its pilot. Lieutenant Denis Cutler of the Royal Marines was an adventurer and entrepreneur who just days before had been a civilian giving flying displays to the awestruck citizens of Durban. Drury-Lowe described Cutler as 'absolutely without fear', but he was short of mechanics and spares and had no training in observation work, and the heat and humidity of the delta were hardly ideal conditions in which to operate a flimsy flying machine made from wood, canvas and animal glue.[36] Cutler disappeared on his first flight and, although both pilot and aircraft were recovered from a nearby island, where Cutler was calmly enjoying a swim, the aircraft's radiator was wrecked. Further operations had to wait until a replacement could be salvaged from a car and sent from Mombasa.[37] On his second flight Cutler pinpointed *Königsberg* in her new lair but again crashed on landing, this time smashing the Curtiss beyond repair. When a replacement aircraft arrived from Durban, Cutler resumed his flights, aided by an enthusiastic midshipman named Gallehawke, until he crash-landed and was finally taken prisoner on 10 December. Gallehawke eventually reached the crash site by boat and retrieved the battered aircraft under heavy fire.[38] Aerial observation would be the key to destroying *Königsberg*, but it would be some time before suitable aircraft were available.

The British also rounded up the remaining German observation posts. Mafia Island was cleared after a vicious little firefight, and *Chatham*'s Albert Wright recalled how the bored sailors found some small amusement in returning to von Neuenstein's home on Komo Island and bayoneting a portrait of the Kaiser before blowing up the house.[39] On 28 November a landing party under Commander Henry Ritchie of *Goliath* entered Dar-es-Salaam to neutralise the remaining German ships in the harbour. The port was quiet, baking in the brilliant sunshine with a few white flags hanging listlessly in the heat, when Ritchie chugged into the harbour in the ex-German tug *Helmuth*, supported by *Goliath*'s long-suffering picket boat. He boarded the hospital ship *Tabora*, at the same time sending demolition parties to lay explosives in the steamers *König* and *Feldmarschall*. Apparently the Germans were not prepared to put up with another British violation of the supposed *Astraea* truce and, as Ritchie prepared to leave, he was subjected to a withering storm of small-arms fire from the shore. Ritchie, at the wheel of the picket boat, was wounded eight times but safely extracted most of his men, apart from *Goliath*'s Surgeon E.C. Holtom, three other officers and eight men, who were stranded aboard *Tabora* and taken prisoner. He was later awarded the Victoria Cross for his actions.[40] Furious in turn at the German violation of the white flag, the British returned and bombarded the town, reducing much of Dar-es-Salaam's waterfront to matchwood.

Christmas was grim, although Looff organised gifts provided by grateful settlers, along with an extra ration of cigarettes and beer. *Königsberg*'s anonymous diarist lamented that 'every good German should have a Xmas tree, as we have no such thing here we had to be content with a small mango'.[41] On New Year's Day *Weymouth*'s Captain William Church sent a signal wishing Looff 'Happy New Year' and hoping he would have the pleasure of meeting him soon; 'Same to you,' replied the irrepressible pirate, 'I am always at home when you want to see me.'[42] And so the weary protagonists entered 1915.

In January Drury-Lowe left for Aden, leaving Church in command. Back in Europe both sides were trying to break the deadlock. In Germany the *Admiralstab* was fitting out a relief ship, the ex-British prize *Rubens*, a strikingly ugly three-island freighter with a ridiculous smokestack rising from her amidships like a remonstrating finger. Packed with coal, ammunition, stores and spares, along with rifles for the German military, the blockade-runner left Hamburg on 18 February disguised as the Danish *Kronborg*, with a Danish-speaking crew commanded by *Oberleutnant zur See* Carl Christiansen. In Whitehall the Admiralty had found the solution to the *Königsberg* problem in three river monitors, originally ordered by the Brazilian government. Flat-bottomed, shallow-draught ships armed with two 6-inch guns and two 4.7-inch howitzers, along with smaller weapons, they were ugly, unseaworthy and capable of only 4 knots in open water, and as a type had been broadly despised by the Royal Navy before the war as irrelevant to the needs of a global superpower. But Churchill had swept them up in his harvest of foreign vessels completing in British yards, and the service commissioned them as HM ships *Humber*, *Severn* and *Mersey* soon afterwards. They were ideal for the Rufiji, but months of bombardment work on the Belgian coast had left them badly in need of a refit before they could leave for East Africa.

In the meantime other steps could be taken. The first involved good old-fashioned 'human intelligence'. In March 1915 the British recruited the famous South African big-game hunter and adventurer Pieter Pretorius, a British loyalist who had recently been waging a one-man war against the German colonial administration in East Africa after they had confiscated his farm and briefly imprisoned him for hunting without a permit. 'I wrote a letter', he recalled, 'informing the Germans that from then onward I should be hunting elephants in the district, and I challenged them to catch me.'[43] Pretorius agreed to help and travelled to join *Goliath* at Durban, via Pretoria and Simonstown: 'at no place did anyone say a word about what they wanted me for.'[44] The tired and frustrated adventurer was assigned a 'splendid cabin' aboard the battleship and went to bed none the wiser; as he gratefully collapsed into his bunk, he saw the shore slip past his porthole as *Goliath* made for sea.[45]

The next day Admiral King-Hall bluntly asked Pretorius whether he could find *Königsberg* and identify a suitable approach route for the monitors. Pretorius replied equally bluntly that 'the only way is to go onshore as near the German as possible, catch some natives, and make them tell'.[46] And in the event this was exactly what he did, landing and hiding up until dark, then making his way carefully by canoe and on foot deep into the mangroves, drawing on every ounce of his considerable fieldcraft skills to remain undetected. Finding two unfortunate locals walking along a bush road near Ssalale, he had them beaten with bamboo canes until they talked, then paid them afterwards to ensure their silence; according to Pretorius they went away 'quite happy', and even returned to find him the next night:

> They took me through the bush and up a hill and, sure enough, when day broke I found I was looking down on the *Königsberg*. Her topmasts were down and there were machine guns in the tops. She was also lost in the trees which, with the high land, hid her from the sea. The Germans were living ashore; I could see all their tents.[47]

Pretorius had taken just a week to get closer to *Königsberg* than King-Hall's squadron had been in months. Rewarded with the rank and pay of a lieutenant, he returned to the bush and spent the next four months surveying the maze of creeks and waterways, noting the location of mines, torpedoes, rifle pits and gun batteries, and creeping out on the water after dark to take soundings with a marked pole. The lean, hard-bitten Boer was a regular visitor to *Goliath*, arriving at night to deliver his reports before being delivered back ashore before daybreak. His background was carefully concealed: Midshipman Ronald Murray believed he was a local Rufiji farmer.[48]

While Pretorius toiled among the mangroves, the 'Rufiji Air Service' was being reinforced. Back in Britain two brand-new Sopwith seaplanes and a small detachment of personnel had been assembled, including two pilots, Royal Naval Air Service Flight Lieutenants John Tulloch Cull, in command, and Harold Watkins. Leaving Tilbury on SS *Persia*, they travelled to Bombay, where they worked all night to transfer aircraft, stores and equipment across to the *Kinfauns Castle*, which was fast establishing a reputation as an aviation support ship. From there they made their way to remote Nyororo Island, south of Zanzibar, where they assembled the aircraft and carried out the first trial flight at the end of February, the duty pilot and an assistant climbing over the great folded beast as it lay at rest on the water and spreading the huge wings before a watching circle of solemn, fascinated islanders. Once this ritual was complete, and the aircraft was clear of the ship, the passenger swung the propeller, started the engine and dived dramatically into the water, swimming for his life to a nearby whaler, trying his best to beat the sharks, while the pilot took off.[49]

The first weeks were a catalogue of disaster. The Sopwiths could not take off carrying more than one of the small bombs which the detachment had brought. Aircraft No. 921 was hopelessly wrecked within a week, and the fuel supply system for the temperamental new Monosoupape engines proved unreliable in the tropical conditions. A problem with the floats meant that the surviving machine, No. 920, partially sank every time it landed on water. And all of the detachment suffered terribly from sunburn.[50] Nevertheless, training continued, interrupted only by excursions to Mombasa or Zanzibar to collect stores, until the end of the month, when it became clear that better aircraft would be necessary before Cull and Watkins could contribute to the campaign. In the meantime the detachment decamped to Shimamzi Point, Mombasa, where 'everyone settled down as comfortably as possible ... and experiments continued in place of anything better to do'.[51]

Back at the Rufiji Looff had scored a minor success by seizing the steamboat *Adjutant* on 6 February, when her British crew ran her aground, but the *Admiralstab*'s efforts to help had ended in disaster. After a tortuous six-week journey, during which she had broken through the British blockade, avoided patrolling cruisers in the Atlantic and rounded the Cape of Good Hope, the *Kronborg* had hugged the treacherous, jungle-lined East African coast and arrived within wireless range of *Königsberg*. Looff, rightly surmising that the freighter would never get through the tight blockade outside the river, ordered *Kronborg* to make for the German port of Tanga, but it was too late. King-Hall, now flying his flag in the old cruiser *Hyacinth* as *Goliath* had left for the Dardanelles, intercepted Looff's wireless traffic and caught *Kronborg* north of Tanga on 13 April. *Hyacinth*'s starboard engine broke down but, before *Kronborg* could run, the cruiser's gunners hit her repeatedly below the waterline, set her on fire and drove her ashore, fierce flames reaching halfway up her mainmast and her holds filling with water.[52] *Hyacinth* sent away boarding parties, but their efforts were hindered by the fire and constant sniping, so King-Hall departed, leaving most of the munitions intact inside the freighter's flooded holds. Although the small arms were later retrieved by the German military, this was small comfort to Looff; *Kronborg*'s heroic effort deserved a greater reward, but Round three definitely went to the British.[53]

For the British most of the key building blocks for an assault were now in place. The RNAS detachment had returned, re-equipped with three more modern Short Folder seaplanes; these had seen hard service in the North Sea and were definitely 'used' rather than 'showroom fresh' but they were 'an improvement on the previous machines', according to Watkins.[54] On 25 April, while thousands of miles to the north history was being made at Gallipoli on what would become known as 'Anzac Day', Cull made his first reconnaissance flight over *Königsberg*. He took several photographs, recording that she looked 'very spick and span', apparently newly painted, with her sidescreens and awnings spread and smoke issuing from her funnels.[55] Cull was greeted with accurate anti-aircraft fire from the cruiser's big guns and a fusillade of rifle shots: 'the German officers and Askaris [African soldiers] being easily distinguished from the height of 600 feet, firing for all they were worth'.[56] As Cull's aircraft was, in his own laconic words, 'not flying very well', he turned for home, crash-landing in the sea 7 miles short of the anchorage. When the aircraft was towed back and the fault investigated, Cull discovered that a rifle bullet had wrecked the main oil feed, narrowly missing his observer on the way in.[57] A few days later Watkins' rudder was smashed by rifle fire and he was forced to crash-land dangerously near the beach. Cull went out to find him with his observer, Leading Mechanic Boggis. Discovering the two airmen sitting disconsolately in their rapidly disintegrating aircraft, Cull landed alongside and took them aboard, only to discover that his own aircraft was now too overloaded to fly. Instead he taxied for miles out to sea until he ran into a convenient patrol boat.

At the beginning of June the flight relocated to a new airfield on Mafia Island, which even boasted a hangar, constructed from wood and corrugated iron by the Zanzibar Public Works Department and shipped up in sections. Here they were joined by three more pilots, extra mechanics and four more aircraft. The detachment had now reached squadron strength, and also acquired a squadron commander, Robert Gordon, a dapper, moustachioed ex-Royal Marine and pioneer aviator, ending Cull's enjoyable semi-piratical independent command.[58] Round the clock reconnaissance flights over *Königsberg* now began, prompting cynical matelots in *Chatham*, which had returned in May, to compose a ditty mocking the doubtless irritatingly glamorous flyers:

From Aeroplane Island to Königsberg *Bay,*
We do a trip just three times a day,
But what we are doing no one can say,
From Aeroplane Island to Königsberg *Bay.*[59]

The monitors arrived on 3 June, after a long voyage through the Mediterranean, where they were delayed for much of April when their tugs were commandeered for the Gallipoli operation, along with HMS *Humber*, which never came back. The low-freeboard monitors were in constant danger of being swamped and made much of the journey under tow, the crews wedged into the accompanying troopship *Trent* and suffering terribly from the heat.

The force spent over a month preparing. Shoring and breakwaters fitted to the monitors at Chatham dockyard to ensure that their flimsy hulls survived the long sea passage had to be stripped out, and additional armour plates installed to provide extra protection around the exposed upper decks. Hundreds of sandbags had to be filled to protect the bridge, and below decks compartments were filled with empty kerosene tins for extra buoyancy. The two ships were painted a murky and decidedly un-naval green to provide concealment against the mangroves, and every non-essential fitting was stripped out. *Severn* and *Mersey* were ready for war.[60]

Thanks to their shallow draught and the efforts of Pretorius and his African scouts, the monitors would be able to pass further up the Rufiji than any British warship had before, but the dense mangroves and undulating landscape meant they would still not be able to see *Königsberg*. Instead, they would pioneer a new technique: spotting by aircraft. Cull, Captain Eric Fullerton of *Severn* and Lieutenant Commander Allan Wilson of *Mersey* prepared a complex system of two-letter codes, the most important being 'HT', or 'Harry Tommy', signifying a hit.[61] Then the ships and aircraft carried out endless practice shoots over the top of Mafia Island, its tranquillity disturbed from dawn to dusk by the sewing-machine buzz of aero engines and the steady boom of 6-inch guns.

The Germans knew what was going on. *Königsberg*'s diarist reported the arrival of the monitors on 2 June, and on the 16th he noted 'English cruisers practising indirect fire'.[62] Visits by the RNAS aircraft became more frequent, and on 2 July one of the flyers dropped four bombs a few hundred metres from the ship. Finally, on 6 July the long-expected attack began, timed to coincide with an exceptionally high tide and a break in the monsoon. Further north, an Indian expeditionary force made a diversionary assault on Tanga, to ensure Looff's land defences could not be reinforced.

At 03:45 the monitors made their way carefully into the river; officers and men were tense at their action stations and shivering in the pre-dawn chill, indistinguishable in the gloom and their home-dyed khaki uniforms.[63] Just after 04:00 they slipped quietly between a pair of whalers, each flying a hooded lamp to indicate the perimeter of the deep water channel. 'It was a weird feeling entering an unknown river in the dark,' recalled one officer in *Mersey*, 'not knowing what was in store for us.'[64] One of *Severn*'s officers was more upbeat, writing that 'I feel extraordinarily cheerful about it; I don't know why, as I am as big a coward, or as little brave as anyone.'[65]

At 05:00 Harold Watkins bombed *Königsberg* as a diversion. Looff's men took it for yet another day of wearying skirmishing, until the boom of heavy-calibre gunfire from the river mouth made them realise that 'this time it was in real bloody earnest'.[66] Shortly afterwards an urgent signal informed Looff that the enemy had entered the Rufiji in force. As the monitors manoeuvred steadily through the confined, mangrove-flanked waters, they were shot at by the riflemen and field guns entrenched along the banks, but the fire was inaccurate; the enemy had been caught unawares and were stunned by a covering bombardment from King-Hall's cruisers. The monitors passed unscathed, sweeping the banks with a hail of machine-gun and 3-pounder fire as they went. By 06:25 they were anchored in their bombardment positions behind a small island, but before they could open fire Looff's well-drilled gunners got in the first blow:

> *Königsberg* started firing at us five minutes before we were ready ... The first shot fell on the island, the next was on the edge of it, and very soon she was straddling us. Where they were spotting from I don't know but they must have been in a good position and their spotting was excellent ... she was firing salvoes of four with great regularity, about three times a minute and every one of them close.[67]

Severn's gunners prepared their weapons, trying to ignore the high-explosive shells which raised plumes of filthy river water just metres away, and spattered their ship with wickedly jagged shell splinters. Around the monitors floated hundreds of fish, stunned or killed by the explosions. But *Königsberg*'s free shoot did not last for long; soon the German cruiser was also surrounded by high-explosive fire, plunging into the river alongside, or tearing apart the sheltering mangroves.

It was an hour before either side scored a hit, and the first blow went to Looff; at 07:40 a shell exploded on *Mersey*'s forward 6-inch gun, igniting a lyddite charge, which sent a dramatic column of flame shooting 50 feet into the air. The flash passed down into the monitor's magazine, starting another fire which badly burned a petty officer and could have destroyed the ship if a quick-witted sailor had not put it out. On deck the scenes were horrific:

> Only one man remained standing and after swaying about he fell dead. One had his head completely blown off, another was lying with his arm torn out at the shoulder, and his body covered with yellow flames from the lyddite charge which caught fire. The RNR lieutenant in charge was

knocked senseless and covered with blood ... the gunlayer had an extraordinary escape and only lost three fingers.[68]

A second shell burst alongside, smashing *Mersey's* motor boat; had this impacted a few metres to either side, it would have penetrated the monitor's thin side and probably sunk her. Wilson got his ship under way to throw off the German gunners' aim; he was only just in time – circling overhead, Harold Watkins watched a salvo plunge down on the spot the monitor had left, deluging her quarterdeck with river water.

The monitors struck next. At 07:55 a howitzer shell plunged into *Königsberg's* galley, killing one man. Minutes later a second shell smashed a 105mm gun mount, killing another man and tearing the foot off *Leutnant zur See* Richard Wenig, the gunnery officer. Unable to bring her port guns to bear, as they faced the shore, *Königsberg's* salvoes dropped from four to three guns. Shortly afterwards, a sharp-eyed observer aboard *Severn* spotted a figure perched on a platform halfway up a mangrove tree, a few hundred metres away. A devastating barrage of 3-pounder shells swept him from his eyrie, and the quality of the German gunnery visibly deteriorated thereafter, Looff's gunners being forced to switch to a secondary spotting position much further away.

As the long day wore on, the monitors' superior firepower began to tell. *Königsberg* was hit repeatedly, the killer blow arriving early in the afternoon when a 6-inch shell ripped open the cruiser's side and river water began to pour into one of her bunkers. Morale deteriorated and one officer, his reserves of courage exhausted, shot himself in his cabin.[69] But none of this was apparent to the watching British. At 16:00 a disconsolate Fullerton pulled the monitors from the river, his men exhausted and his guns low on ammunition, counting his blessings that he had not lost a ship. 'From all points the day had been disappointing,' Harold Watkins recalled, 'considerable damage had been done to the monitors with grave loss of life ... above everything, the fact that the *Königsberg* had not been destroyed was patent to everyone.'[70] In the monitors the mood was sombre, one officer writing, 'Feeling very tired ... I don't believe we can do any more than we did yesterday ... The ships are falling to pieces and the bulkheads [have] started to burst.'[71]

Five days later they returned to do it again, the grim-faced men knowing exactly what faced them: 'How well we seemed to know the place! I knew exactly where the beastly field guns in the mouth would open fire and exactly when they would cease ... I knew each creek, almost each tree.'[72] The cruisers again provided covering fire but this time the German gunners were ready, and hit *Mersey* twice, one shell passing through her after bulkhead and wounding three sailors.

Mersey began firing from the old location behind the small island, but Fullerton opted to push further upstream in *Severn*, hoping that his sister ship would draw *Königsberg*'s fire. It was a forlorn hope: as the monitor's crew secured the stern anchor, two shells exploded on either side, scattering fragments across her deck. But despite this worrying beginning, it soon became clear that *Königsberg* was badly damaged, and running short of ammunition. *Severn* and *Mersey* were plentifully supplied, and overhead the experienced Cull was spotting, flying as low as he dared to report back corrections. Every salvo hit and the British gunners began to work their way along *Königsberg*'s hull, perforating her entire length. The German cruiser's fire became steadily more ragged.

At 12:50 Cull, flying ever lower in an effort to spot the fall of shot, signalled laconically 'Am hit. Send boat', and his wounded bird fluttered to earth. His observer, Boggis, still found time to send one last spotting report, an act that *Mersey*'s Commander Wilson later recalled as 'one of the most gallant episodes of the war', before the aircraft touched gently down on the river and promptly turned over.[73] Cull faced a desperate underwater struggle to free himself from his seatbelt, and the tangle of wood and wires which his aircraft had become, but both airmen survived to watch the remainder of the action from *Mersey*.[74]

There was not much left to watch. The shell that had hit Cull's aircraft was one of the last four left aboard *Königsberg*. A few minutes after the dripping airmen were hauled aboard the monitor, a huge explosion shook the stricken cruiser and she ceased fire altogether. Determined to finish the job, the British ships continued firing for almost another two hours, at the end of which, according to Wilson, '*Königsberg* was burning everywhere, one funnel fallen out of her, and eight separate explosions had taken place in her, so I should think there was precious little left of her. The poor wretches on board must have had a terrible time.'[75]

They had indeed. At 13:30 the severely wounded Looff ordered his men to abandon ship, after detonating torpedo warheads below decks to ensure *Königsberg* could never be captured. Many of his crew were wounded, and it took nearly two hours to carry them ashore. They included *Königsberg*'s anonymous diarist. As well as several minor wounds, a shell splinter had torn through his lung, and he had to swim ashore in terrible pain, wearing only his boots and underclothes: 'After that, I was wrapped up in a sack … I naturally froze as the cold was unendurable … and I had lost much blood.'[76]

The following day Looff's surviving men buried the thirty-three German sailors who had been killed, erecting a simple memorial over their grave. The Germans still held the Rufiji banks and it was weeks before the British reached the wreck, giving Looff's men time to salvage *Königsberg*'s guns, which were taken ashore and changed the balance of power in the poorly resourced East African theatre of operations. Afterwards the 188 survivors marched inland to join *Oberstleutnant* Paul von Lettow-Vorbeck's army. A handful of men from what became the *Königsberg-Abteilung* survived disease, hardship and later capture to march triumphantly through the Brandenburg Gate behind Max Looff in 1919. *Königsberg* remained in the remote, inaccessible Rufiji. Her remains were still visible until the 1950s, when she eventually vanished into the mud: the very last of the Kaiser's Pirates.

Conclusion

'Nearly every one of these German cruisers took its prey before being
caught, not only of merchant ships but of ships of war'

Winston Churchill

The pirates' war was violent and tragic, sometimes oddly quixotic and occasionally humorous. It has often been described as 'honourable', an arguably anachronistic word sitting more comfortably in the age of sail than in the age of steam and steel. It was fought in some of the world's most inaccessible regions, far from the epicentre of the war, and it was never repeated. As well as unleashing her far more effective U-boats, Germany sent raiders to sea again, in fact *Meteor*, the first, left before the battered hulk of *Königsberg* settled into the Rufiji mud, but the later pirates were very different: small, anonymous freighters with low fuel consumption and carefully disguised armament. Cruisers and armed liners made poor raiders: their complex, fragile machinery required regular maintenance by a skilled, well-equipped workforce; they consumed far too much coal far too quickly; and they were very hard to hide.

But was the pirates' war worth it? The pirates were doomed from the outset. They could not 'win', and their eventual sinking or internment was almost inevitable. Germany did not have the overwhelming naval strength required to hold her bases, with their dockyards, wireless stations and coal stocks. Without bases, the pirates were just maritime vagrants with only two choices: they could roam the oceans, living off what they could capture until their ships fell apart or the enemy tracked them down, a *modus operandi* at which von Müller, Köhler and Thierfelder proved rather adept. Or they could rely on the *Admiralstab* and the *Etappen* to mobilise the colliers they needed to keep going. But this complex, undeniably efficient structure also carried the seeds of its own destruction. The *Etappen* system relied on heavy wireless traffic, but every time a raider used his wireless he gave himself away, as Fritz Lüdecke discovered to his cost. As the Allies rolled up German colonies and warships, neutral powers became less keen to defy the global superpower that was Great Britain by playing host to the infrastructure that sustained her enemies. Furthermore, every time the pirates contributed to the war effort by sinking ships or raiding harbours, they drew attention to themselves, and made their destruction a higher priority for Churchill and the Admiralty in London; after Coronel, battlecruisers were sent to catch von Spee, and after Looff despatched *Pegasus*, three modern cruisers arrived off the Rufiji.

The only pirate who had a direct, long-term and strategic impact on the subsequent course of the war was Souchon, who brought Turkey into the war almost single-handed. The rest of the pirates captured some seventy merchant ships, totalling some 282,000 gross registered tons.[1] They also accounted for four elderly cruisers, a torpedo boat destroyer and a decommissioned gunboat, as well as dislocating trade to an extent that is hard to quantify. Most of the damage was done by *Emden*, *Karlsruhe*, *Prinz Eitel Friedrich* and *Kronprinz Wilhelm*, the four most successful commerce raiders, and in cold economic terms these were probably the only four which inflicted losses justifying their original build costs. To put their achievements in perspective, three times as much tonnage was destroyed by the Kaiser's U-boats in April 1917, the deadliest month of Germany's second unrestricted submarine warfare campaign.[2] However, whether these ships would have been better employed alternately making futile sorties and swinging at anchor in Wilhelmshaven with the rest of the High Seas Fleet is debatable; the Germans were short of modern light cruisers, but the possibility that another seven might have made the difference at Jutland seems unlikely.

Yet the pirates' worth cannot be measured solely in pounds sterling, Reichsmarks, or tons of cargo. This book began with the birth of the Imperial German Navy. It came of age during that first year of the First World War, when the Kaiser's pirates sank ships, won the occasional battle and stole more than their fair share of headlines. Navies need more than just ships and men, they need legends and heroes, which are in many ways harder to acquire. No service knew this better than the Royal Navy, its own institutional culture forged in the fires of centuries of warfare.

The pirates inspired those who followed them, an achievement that cannot easily be valued or measured. It is surely no surprise that the first new ship of Germany's postwar navy was a graceful cruiser named *Emden*. By 1939 she had been joined by the pocket battleship *Admiral Graf Spee*, the battlecruisers *Scharnhorst* and *Gneisenau*, and the cruisers *Leipzig*, *Nürnberg*, *Karlsruhe* and *Königsberg*. Thus are traditions built.

Ship Data

German ships

Ship	Class	Armament	Propulsion/Speed	Armour
Goeben	Battlecruiser	10 × 280mm (11-inch) 12 × 150mm (5.9-inch) 12 × 88mm (3.5-inch) 4 × torpedo tubes	Turbines 4 × screws 29 knots (53km/h)	Belt 10½ inch (266mm) Turrets 9¼ inch (235mm)
Breslau	Light Cruiser	12 × 105mm (4.1-inch) 2 × torpedo tubes	4 × Turbines 2 × screws 30 knots (55km/h)	Belt 2¾ inch (70mm) Deck ½ inch (12.7mm)
Karlsruhe	Light Cruiser	12 × 105mm (4.1-inch) 2 × torpedo tubes	Turbines 2 × screws 27¼ knots (50km/h)	Belt 2½ inch (63.5mm) Deck ¾ inch (19mm)
Emden	Light Cruiser	10 × 105mm (4.1-inch) 2 × torpedo tubes	Triple Expansion 2 × screws 24½ knots (45km/h)	Deck 2 inch (51mm)
Scharnhorst *Gneisenau*	Armoured Cruiser	8 × 208mm (8.2-inch) 6 × 150mm (5.9-inch) 20 × 88mm (3.4-inch)	Triple Expansion 3 × screws 22½ knots (42km/h)	Belt 6 inch (152mm) Deck 2 inch (51mm)
Leipzig	Light Cruiser	10 × 105mm (4.1-inch) 2 × torpedo tubes	Triple Expansion 2 × screws 23 knots (42½km/h)	Deck 2 inch (51mm)
Nürnberg	Light Cruiser	10 × 105mm (4.1-inch) 2 × torpedo tubes	Triple Expansion 2 × screws 25½ knots (47km/h)	Deck 2 inch (51mm)
Dresden	Light Cruiser	10 × 105mm (4.1-inch) 2 × torpedo tubes	Turbines 4 × screws 25 knots (46km/h)	Deck 2 inch (51mm)
Cap Trafalgar	Armed Merchant Cruiser	2 × 105mm (4.1-inch) 6 × 37mm (1.5-inch)	Triple Expansion 2 × screws 17 knots (31½km/h)	n/a
Prinz Eitel Friedrich	Armed Merchant Cruiser	4 × 105mm (4.1-inch) 6 × 88mm (3.5-inch) 4 × 37mm (1.5-inch)	Triple Expansion 2 × screws 15 knots (28km/h)	n/a

Ship		Armament	Propulsion/Speed	Armour
Kronprinz Wilhelm	Armed Merchant Cruiser	2 × 120mm (4.7-inch) 2 × 88mm (3.5-inch) 1 Maxim MG	Triple Expansion 2 × screws 23 knots (42½km/h)	n/a
Kaiser Wilhelm der Grosse	Armed Merchant Cruiser	6 × 105mm (4.1-inch) 2 × 37mm (1.5-inch)	Triple Expansion 2 × screws 22½ knots (42km/h)	n/a
Cormoran (ex-Russian Ryazan)	Armed Merchant Cruiser	8 × 105mm (4.1-inch)	Triple Expansion 1 × screw 17 knots (31½km/h)	n/a
Königsberg	Light Cruiser	10 × 105mm (4.1-inch) 2 × torpedo tubes	Triple Expansion 2 × screws 23 knots (42½km/h)	Deck 2 inches (51mm)

British ships

Ship	Class	Armament	Propulsion/Speed	Armour
Invincible Inflexible Indomitable	Battlecruiser	8 × 12-inch (305mm) 16 × 4-inch (100mm) 4 × torpedo tubes	Turbines 4 × screws 26 knots (48km/h)	Belt 6 inch (152mm) Turrets 7 inch (178mm) Deck 2½ inch (63.5mm) max
Indefatigable	Battlecruiser	8 × 12-inch (305mm) 16 × 4-inch (100mm) 3 × torpedo tubes	Turbines 4 × screws 27 knots (50km/h)	Belt 6 inch (152mm) Turrets 7 inch (178mm) Deck 2½ inch (63.5mm) max
Goliath Canopus	Battleship	4 × 12-inch (305mm) 12 × 6-inch (152mm) Up to 16 × 12-pdr (76mm) 4 × torpedo tubes	Triple Expansion 2 × screws 18 knots (33km/h)	Belt 6 inches (152mm) Turrets 8 inches (203mm) Deck 2 inches (51mm)
Warrior	Armoured Cruiser	6 × 9.2-inch (233mm) 4 × 7.5-inch (190mm) 3 × torpedo tubes	Triple Expansion 2 × screws 23 knots (42½km/h)	Belt 6 inch (152mm) Turrets 8 inch (203mm) Deck 1½ inch (38mm) max
Black Prince Duke of Edinburgh	Armoured Cruiser	6 × 9.2-inch (233mm) 10 × 6-inch (152mm) 3 × torpedo tubes	Triple Expansion 2 × screws 23 knots (42½km/h)	Belt 6 inch (152mm) Turrets 8 inch (203mm) Deck 1½ inch (38mm) max
Defence	Armoured Cruiser	4 × 9.2-inch (233mm) 10 × 7.5-inch (190mm) 16 × 12-pdr (76mm) 5 × torpedo tubes	Triple Expansion 2 × screws 23 knots (42½km/h)	Belt 6 inch (152mm) Turrets 8 inch (203mm) Deck 1½ inch (38mm) max
Cornwall Kent Monmouth Berwick Suffolk Hampshire	Armoured Cruiser	14 × 6-inch (152mm) 13 × 12-pdr (76mm) 2 × torpedo tubes	Triple Expansion 2 × screws 23 knots (42½km/h)	Belt 4 inch (101mm) Deck 2 inch (51mm)

Carnarvon	Armoured Cruiser	4 × 7.5-inch (190mm) 6 × 6-inch (152mm) 2 × 12-pdr (76mm) 2 × torpedo tubes	Triple Expansion 2 × screws 22 ¼ knots (41km/h)	Belt 6 inch (152mm) Deck 2 inch (51mm)
Good Hope	Armoured Cruiser	2 × 9.2-inch (233mm) 16 × 6-inch (152mm) 12 × 12-pdr (76mm) 2 × torpedo tubes	Triple Expansion 2 × screws 24 knots (44½km/h)	Belt 6 inch (152mm) Deck 3 inch (76mm)
Highflyer *Hyacinth*	Protected Cruiser	11 × 6-inch (152mm) 9 × 12-pdr (76mm) 2 × torpedo tubes	Triple Expansion 2 × screws 20 knots (37km/h)	Deck 3 inch (76mm)
Pegasus	Protected Cruiser	8 × 4-inch (100mm) 2 × torpedo tubes	Triple Expansion 2 × screws 20½ knots (38km/h)	Deck 2 inch (51mm)
Astraea	Protected Cruiser	2 × 6-inch (152mm) 8 × 4.7-inch (120mm) 4 × torpedo tubes	Triple Expansion 2 × screws 19½ knots (36km/h)	Deck 2 inch (51mm)
Bristol *Glasgow* *Gloucester*	Light Cruiser	2 × 6-inch (152mm) 10 × 4-inch (100mm) 2 × torpedo tubes	Turbines 4 × screws 26 knots (48km/h)	Deck 2 inch (51mm) max
Dartmouth *Weymouth*	Light Cruiser	8 × 6-inch (152mm) 2 × torpedo tubes	Turbines 4 × screws 25½ knots (47km/h)	Deck 2 inch (51mm) max
Chatham *Dublin* *Sydney*	Light Cruiser	8 × 6-inch (152mm) 2 × torpedo tubes	Turbines 4 × screws 25½ knots (47km/h)	Belt 3 inch (76mm) Deck 2 inch (51mm) max
Goliath *Canopus*	Battleship	4 × 12-inch (305mm) 12 × 6-inch (152mm) Up to 16 × 12-pdr (76mm) 4 × torpedo tubes	Triple Expansion 2 × screws 18 knots (33km/h)	Belt 6 inches (152mm) Turrets 8 inches (203mm) Deck 2 inches (51mm)
Mersey *Severn*	Monitor	3 × 6-inch (152mm) 2 × 4.7-inch (120mm) Howitzer	Triple Expansion 2 × screws 12 knots (22km/h)	Belt 2 inch (51mm)
Carmania	Armed Merchant Cruiser	8 × 4.7-inch (120mm)	Turbines 3 × screws 18 knots (33km/h)	n/a
Otranto	Armed Merchant Cruiser	4 × 4.7-inch (120mm)	Triple Expansion 2 × screws 18 knots (33km/h)	n/a
Macedonia	Armed Merchant Cruiser	8 × 4.7-inch (120mm)	Triple Expansion 2 × screws 18 knots (33km/h)	n/a
Zhemchug (Russian)	Light Cruiser	8 × 120mm (5-inch) 4 × 47mm (2-inch) 6 × Maxim MG	Triple Expansion 4 × screws 24½ knots (45km/h)	Deck 1 inch (25.5mm) Belt 1 inch (25.5mm)

Principal source: Le Fleming, H.M., *Warships of World War 1* (Ian Allan, London, 1967).

Anatomy of Piracy

Raider	Captured Ships	Gross Registered Tonnage
Karlsruhe	17	76,609
Emden	15	66,023
Kronprinz Wilhelm	15	60,522
Prinz Eitel Friedrich	11	33,423
Leipzig	4	15,279
Dresden	4	12,960
Kaiser Wilhelm der Grosse	3	10,685
Königsberg	1	6,601
Total	70	282,102

Sources: *British Vessels Lost at Sea* (HMSO, London, 1919), and www.naval-history.net.

Comparative Table of Naval Ranks (Officers)

Great Britain	Imperial Germany	United States
Admiral of the Fleet	*Großadmiral*	Admiral of the Navy
Admiral	*Admiral*	Admiral
Vice Admiral	*Vizeadmiral*	Vice Admiral
Rear Admiral	*Konteradmiral*	Rear Admiral
Commodore	–	Commodore
Captain	*Kapitän zur See*	Captain
Commander	*Fregattenkapitän*	Commander
Lieutenant Commander	*Korvettenkapitän*	Lieutenant Commander
Lieutenant	*Kapitänleutnant*	Lieutenant
Sub Lieutenant	*Oberleutnant zur See*	Lieutenant (Junior Grade)
–	*Leutnant zur See*	Ensign
Midshipman	*Fähnrich zur See*	Midshipman

Glossary

Action stations – positions in a ship taken up by sailors in preparation for battle.

Admiralstab – the German Imperial Admiralty Staff, the body responsible for naval affairs, under the direct authority of the Kaiser, from 1899 to 1918.

Admiralty, Board of – the British government department responsible for naval affairs from 1628 until 1964, when it became part of the Ministry of Defence.

AMC – Armed Merchant Cruiser, a merchant vessel converted into a warship.

Beam – the maximum width of a ship.

Boxer Rebellion – nationalist rebellion by the Righteous Harmony Society against foreign influence in China, 1898–1901.

Bridge – elevated, transverse platform from which, in 1914, a warship was navigated and fought.

Bunkers – compartments in which coal is stored in a steam ship.

Calibre – the diameter of a shell or bullet.

Capital ship – during the First World War battleships and battlecruisers.

Condenser head – an apparatus for cooling steam and turning it into water.

Cutter – a ship's boat with double-banked oars and one or two sails.

Derrick – a jib crane with a boom hinged near the base of the mast, so as to rotate about the mast and move a load towards or away from the mast by raising or lowering the boom.

Die Wacht am Rhein – Literally 'The Watch on the Rhine', German nineteenth-century patriotic anthem inspired by Franco-German conflict.

Discharge valve – device which made it possible to monitor and control the flow of water, sewage or other substances out of a ship.

Elevation – the angle formed between the muzzle of a gun and the horizontal.

Executive Officer – the second-in-command of a warship. His rank varied depending on the size of the ship.

Fire control – technical and sometimes automatic supervision of gunfire onto a target, using a range-finder.

Fire main – red-painted pipes running through a ship and carrying water for fire-fighting.

Flag officer – a senior officer, usually an admiral, entitled to fly his own command flag.

Fleet – the largest formation of warships in a navy, usually commanded by an admiral and subdivided into subordinate squadrons.

Fo'c'sle or **forecastle** – originally the castle-like structure built in the bows of a medieval warship as a platform for archers; more recently the foremost part of the upper deck.

Galley – a ship's kitchen.

Half pay – the allowance given to an officer who was retired or temporarily unemployed.

Heads – a ship's toilet.

In ballast – a merchant ship steaming empty, without cargo.

Knots – nautical miles per hour.

Kreuzerkrieg – Literally 'cruiser war', commerce raiding.

Lighter – a type of flat-bottomed barge used to transport stores, ammunition, etc., to and from moored ships.

Lyddite – high explosive first manufactured in Lydd, Kent, from picric acid and guncotton.

Magazine – a compartment in a warship used to store ammunition.

Matelot – colloquial term for a British sailor, probably French or Dutch in origin.

Navalism – championing the interests of a navy, by 'navalists'.

Paid off – originally a sailing term, later used to mean the end of a commission when a ship went into dockyard hands and the crew left.

Pilot – a local official qualified to steer a ship in and out of a harbour, river mouth, etc.

Port – the left-hand side of a ship, looking forwards.

Porthole – round opening in the side of a ship with a hinged, watertight glass cover.

Pre-dreadnought – armoured battleship with multiple types of heavy guns and reciprocating engines, rendered obsolete by the arrival of HMS *Dreadnought* in 1906, with her standardised all-big-gun armament and turbines.

Range-finder – instrument for determining the distance from a ship to its target.

Rate operator – rating responsible for operating a warship's range-finder.

Reciprocating engine – an engine in which pistons move backwards and forwards inside cylinders.

Reichstag – the German parliament.

Rifling – spiral grooves cut inside a gun barrel to spin the shell and make it more accurate.

Rig – a sailing term meaning to fit sails, etc., to the mast. Later used to describe naval uniform, as in 'rig of the day'.

Russian Volunteer Fleet Association – The *Dobrovolny Flot* was created by Tsar Alexander III in 1878. Funded by public subscription, its ships operated commercially but were taken into state service in wartime.

Russo-Japanese War – sparked by colonial rivalry in Manchuria and Korea, and fought between the Japanese and Russian empires between February 1904 and September 1905.

Sea cocks – valves in the hull of a ship for controlled admission of water.

Sea Lords – the four (after 1917, five) senior admirals who managed the Royal Navy during the First World War. The civilian, administrative head was the First Lord of the Admiralty.

Shadow – to follow an enemy ship without bringing it to action.

SMS – *Seine Majestät Schiff*, His Majesty's Ship.

Squadron – formation of three or four warships, usually commanded by a commodore or senior captain.

Staff – specialist officers intended to provide support and advice to the Sea Lords.

Starboard – the right-hand side of a ship, looking forwards.

Tiddly – naval slang for neat or tidy.

Torpedo boat destroyer – small, fast, gun-armed ships designed to protect the battle fleet from 'torpedo boats', which were considered a threat in the 1880s. Eventually the two types morphed into one, the 'destroyer'.

Torpedo flat – the compartment of a ship where the torpedo tubes were located.

Turbine – engine powered by a rotor, the vanes or blades of which are driven by steam pressure.

Turret – rotating, armoured gun platform.

Victoria Cross – Great Britain's highest award for gallantry 'in the face of the enemy'.

Weltmacht – literally 'world power'.

Notes

Prologue

1. Franz Joseph, Prinz von Hohenzollern-Emden, *Emden: The Last Cruise of the Chivalrous Raider – 1914* (Lyon Press, London, 1989), p. 83.
2. Meager, W.M., Imperial War Museum Department of Documents Record (henceforth IWM Docs) P451, p. 1.
3. Van der Vat, Dan, *The Last Corsair: the Story of the Emden* (Granada, London, 1985), p. 127.
4. Meager, IWM Docs P451, p. 1.
5. Franz Joseph, *Emden*, p. 84.
6. *New York Times*, 20 December 1914, www.nytimes.com.
7. *Poverty Bay Herald*, 10 December 1914.
8. Van der Vat, *The Last Corsair*, p. 32 and p. 38.
9. Duckworth, I.H., 'Echoes of the *Emden*', *The Naval Review* (henceforth NR), 1973, p. 251.
10. Franz Joseph, *Emden*, p. 87.

Chapter 1: *Kreuzerkrieg*

1. Principal sources for this very brief canter through pre-war German naval policy have been Massie, Robert K., *Dreadnought: Britain, Germany and the coming of the Great War* (Random House, New York, 1991); Marder, Professor Arthur J., *From the Dreadnought to Scapa Flow: The Royal Navy in the Fisher Era 1904–1919* (London: Oxford University Press, 1961–1965); and Corbett, Sir Julian, *Naval Operations Volume 1: To the Battle of the Falklands* (Longmans, Green & Co., London, 1920).
2. Gauss, C., *The German Kaiser as Shown in his Public Utterances* (Charles Scribner & Sons, New York, 1915), pp. 181–3.
3. Ibid.
4. Bülow, Prince Bernhard von, *Memoirs Volume 2* (Boston, Little, Brown, 1931–32), p. 36, quoted in Massie, *Dreadnought*, p. 151.
5. Massie, *Dreadnought*, pp. 167–8.
6. Tirpitz, Grand Admiral Alfred von, *My Memoirs Volume I* (Dodd, Mead, New York, 1919), p. 60, quoted in Massie, *Dreadnought*, p. 168.
7. Ibid, p. 76, quoted in Massie, *Dreadnought*, p. 169.
8. Ibid, p. 85, quoted in Massie, *Dreadnought*, p. 169.
9. Mahan, Alfred Thayer, *The Influence of Sea Power upon History* (Sampson Low, Marston, Searle & Rivington, London, 1889), p. 539 (footnote).
10. Ibid, pp. 539–40.
11. Massie, *Dreadnought*, pp. 178–9.
12. Marder, *From the Dreadnought to Scapa Flow: Volume 1*, p. 4.
13. Churchill, The Rt Hon. Winston S., CH, MP, *The World Crisis 1911–1918: Volume 1* (Odhams Press, London, 1938), p. 11.

14. Maffeo, Steven E., *Seize, Burn or Sink: The Thoughts and Words of Admiral Lord Horatio Nelson* (Scarecrow Press, Lanham, Maryland, 2007), pp. 147–56.
15. Three British battlecruisers were sunk at Jutland in 1916, but this tragedy owed more to poor deployment and inadequate procedures than it did to bad design.
16. Massie, *Dreadnought*, p. 464.
17. Marder, *From the Dreadnought to Scapa Flow: Volume 1*, p. 38.
18. Le Fleming, H.M., *Warships of World War 1* (Ian Allan, London, 1967).
19. The Royal Navy's new 65,000-ton *Queen Elizabeth* class aircraft carriers, under construction at the time of writing, will have a complement of just 686, exclusive of air crew. www.royalnavy.mod.uk.
20. Bennett, Geoffrey, *Coronel and the Falklands* (Pan, London, 1967), p. 22.
21. Bryant, Lieutenant (JG) S.F., USN, '*Goeben* and *Breslau*' (NR, 1917), p. 231.
22. Massie, Robert K., *Castles of Steel: Britain, Germany and the Winning of the Great War at Sea* (Pimlico, London, 2005), p. 27.
23. Souchon, Admiral Wilhelm, 'The Breakthrough of the *Goeben* and *Breslau* from Messina to the Dardanelles' (NR, 1922), Issue 3, p. 480.
24. Ibid, p. 481.
25. Ibid, p. 483.
26. Aust, *Kapitänleutnant*, 'The War Cruises of H.I.M.S. *Karlsruhe*: Extracts from my War Diary' (NR, 1917), p. 181.
27. Ibid, p. 183.
28. Ibid, p. 184.
29. De Bassi, Maria Teresa Parker, *Tras La Estela Del Dresden* (Ediciones Tusitala, Santiago, 1987), p. 34, and Hoyt, Edwin P., *Kreuzerkrieg* (World Publishing Company, New York, 1968), p. 143, both quoted in Jannings, Dr Christopher M., 'SMS Dresden's War: The Benefits of Protracted Evasion over Spirit of Enterprise' http://www.militaryhistoryonline.com/wwi/articles/smsdresden.aspx.
30. Aust, 'War Cruises of H.I.M.S. *Karlsruhe*' (NR, 1917), pp. 185–6.
31. Chatterton, E. Keble, *The Königsberg Adventure* (Hurst & Blackett, London, n/d), p. 15.
32. Scheer, Admiral Reinhard, *Germany's High Seas Fleet in the World War* (Cassell, London, 1920), p. 15.
33. Bennett, *Coronel and the Falklands*, p. 46.
34. Ibid, p. 47.
35. Hurd, Sir Archibald, *History of the Great War: The Merchant Navy, Volume 1, 1914 to Spring 1915* (John Murray, London, 1921), pp. 137–85 (reproduced on www.naval-history.net).
36. Ibid.
37. The London Declaration is reproduced on the web site of the International Committee of the Red Cross http://www.icrc.org/ihl.nsf/FULL/255?OpenDocument. All quotations come from this source.
38. Hurd, *The Merchant Navy: Volume 1*, pp. 137–85 (reproduced on www.naval-history.net).
39. Terraine, John, *Business in Great Waters: The U-boat Wars 1916–1945* (Wordsworth Editions Ltd, Ware, 1999), p. 5.
40. Mücke, Hellmuth von, *The Emden* (Ritter & Company, Boston, 1917), p. 11.
41. Chatterton, E. Keble, *The Sea Raiders* (Hutchinson & Co., London, n/d), p. 24.
42. Walter, John, *The Kaiser's Pirates: German Surface Raiders in World War 1* (Arms & Armour Press, London, 1994), p. 35.
43. Hurd, *The Merchant Navy: Volume 1*, pp. 137–85 (reproduced on www.naval-history.net).

44. Admiral Sir Herbert Richmond, quoted in Gretton, Vice Admiral Sir Peter, KCB, DSO, OBE, DSC, *Former Naval Person: Winston Churchill and the Royal Navy* (Cassell, London, 1968), p. 162.
45. Strachan, Hew, *The First World War, Volume I: To Arms* (Oxford University Press, 2001), p. 380.
46. Churchill, *The World Crisis: Volume 1*, Appendix C, p. 703.

Chapter 2: Fate of Nations: the Pursuit of *Goeben*
1. Souchon, 'The Breakthrough of the *Goeben* and *Breslau*' (NR, 1922), p. 483.
2. Ibid, pp. 483–4, and Massie, *Castles of Steel*, p. 29.
3. Souchon, 'The Breakthrough of the *Goeben* and *Breslau*' (NR, 1922), p. 484.
4. Ibid.
5. Dewar, Vice-Admiral K.G.B., 'The Escape of the *Goeben* and *Breslau*' (NR, 1956), p. 34.
6. Ibid.
7. Anonymous, 'The Escape of the *Goeben*: Narrative from the *Indomitable*' (NR, 1919), p. 120.
8. Marder, *From the Dreadnought to Scapa Flow: Volume 2*, p. 181.
9. Massie, *Castles of Steel*, p. 32.
10. Imperial War Museum Sound Archive Record (henceforth IWM Sound) 720 Masters, Albert.
11. Souchon, 'The Breakthrough of the *Goeben* and *Breslau*' (NR, 1922), p. 484.
12. Carlyon, L.A., *Gallipoli* (Doubleday, London, 2002), p. 42.
13. Churchill, *The World Crisis: Volume 1*, p. 169.
14. IWM Docs Misc 254 (3484).
15. Souchon, 'The Breakthrough of the *Goeben* and *Breslau*' (NR, 1922), p. 485.
16. Ibid, p. 485.
17. Anonymous, 'The Escape of the *Goeben*: Narrative from the *Indomitable*' (NR, 1919), p. 113.
18. Ibid, p. 114.
19. Ibid.
20. Dewar, 'The Escape of the *Goeben* and *Breslau*' (NR, 1956), p. 37.
21. Churchill, *The World Crisis:* Volume 1, p. 183.
22. Anonymous, 'The Escape of the *Goeben*: Narrative from the *Indomitable*' (NR, 1919), p. 117.
23. Souchon, 'The Breakthrough of the *Goeben* and *Breslau*' (NR, 1922), pp. 485–6.
24. Ibid, p. 486.
25. Ibid, p. 488.
26. Ibid, p. 487.
27. Ibid, p. 489.
28. Dewar, 'The Escape of the *Goeben* and *Breslau*' (NR, 1956), p. 39.
29. Massie, *Castles of Steel*, p. 42.
30. IWM Docs PP/MCR/46 Horniman, Fleet Paymaster Henry.
31. IWM Docs 76/191/1 Fitch, Lieutenant H.M.
32. IWM Docs Misc 64/1009 Signal Log of HMS *Defence*.
33. At the Battle of Jutland three of the four ships in the 1st Cruiser Squadron were rapidly sunk by accurate heavy gunfire.
34. IWM Docs Misc 64/1009 Signal Log of HMS *Defence*.
35. IWM Docs P389, Warner, Captain G.H.
36. IWM Docs Misc 64/1009 Signal Log of HMS *Defence*.
37. Ibid.
38. IWM Docs 05/63/1 Baker, A.E.

39. Ibid.
40. IWM Docs Misc 64/1009 Signal Log of HMS *Defence*.
41. Ibid.
42. Ibid.
43. IWM Docs P160 Acheson, Lieutenant Commander the Honourable P.G.E.C.
44. Arthur, Max, *The True Glory: The Royal Navy 1914–1919: A Narrative History* (Hodder & Stoughton, London, 1996), p. 22.
45. Anonymous, 'The Escape of the *Goeben*: Narrative from the *Indomitable*' (NR, 1919), p. 123.
46. Corbett, *Naval Operations*, p. 67.
47. Massie, *Castles of Steel*, p. 44.
48. Souchon, 'The Breakthrough of the *Goeben* and *Breslau*' (NR, 1922), p. 490.
49. Ibid, pp. 490–1, and Miller, Geoffrey, 'Superior Force: The Conspiracy behind the Escape of the Goeben and *Breslau*', www.flamboroughmanor.co.uk/superiorforce.
50. Souchon, 'The Breakthrough of the *Goeben* and *Breslau*' (NR, 1922), p. 491.
51. Churchill, *The World Crisis: Volume 1*, p. 209.
52. Souchon, 'The Breakthrough of the *Goeben* and *Breslau*' (NR, 1922), p. 491.
53. Ibid.
54. Ibid.
55. IWM Sound 4256 Whittle, T.M.
56. Ibid.
57. Ibid.
58. Churchill, *The World Crisis: Volume 1*, p. 206.
59. Marder, *From the Dreadnought to Scapa Flow: Volume 2*, p. 27.
60. Ibid, footnote.
61. Dewar, 'The Escape of the *Goeben* and *Breslau*' (NR, 1956), pp. 42–3. For a masterful analysis of the rigid command structure that paralysed the Royal Navy at the start of the First World War, see Gordon, Andrew, *The Rules of the Game: Jutland and British Naval Command* (John Murray, London, 1996).
62. Dewar, 'The Escape of the *Goeben* and *Breslau*' (NR, 1956), p. 44.

Chapter 3: Phantom Raider: the Cruise of *Karlsruhe*

1. 'Lead and Line: The Journal of the Naval Officers' Association of Vancouver Island' (Volume 24, Issue 3, November 2009), p. 6. Brodeur's story seems unlikely but was too good to leave out! http://ml.islandnet.com/pipermail/noavi_ll/attachments/20090228/f705b20c/attachment-0001.
2. Hoyt, Edwin P., *The Karlsruhe Affair* (Arthur Barker Ltd, London, 1976), p. 32.
3. Aust, 'War Cruises of H.I.M.S. *Karlsruhe*' (NR, 1917), p. 186.
4. Hoyt, *The Karlsruhe Affair*, p. 37.
5. Aust, 'War Cruises of H.I.M.S. *Karlsruhe*' (NR, 1917), p. 188.
6. *New York Times*, 14 August 1914, www.nytimes.com.
7. Ibid.
8. IWM Docs 14964 King, H.
9. Ibid.
10. Corbett, *Naval Operations*, pp. 48–9.
11. *New York Times*, 12 August 1914, www.nytimes.com, and *New York Tribune*, 12 August 1914, http://fultonhistory.com/Newspapers.
12. *New York Times*, 14 August 1914, www.nytimes.com.
13. Aust, 'War Cruises of H.I.M.S. *Karlsruhe*' (NR, 1917), p. 191.

14. Corbett, *Naval Operations*, p. 49.
15. Aust, 'War Cruises of H.I.M.S. *Karlsruhe*' (NR, 1917), p. 191.
16. Corbett, *Naval Operations*, p. 49.
17. Bennett, *Coronel and the Falklands*, p. 78.
18. Aust, 'War Cruises of H.I.M.S. *Karlsruhe*' (NR, 1917), p. 192.
19. *New York Times*, 10 August 1914, www.nytimes.com.
20. Hoyt, *The Karlsruhe Affair*, p. 55.
21. Chatterton, *The Sea Raiders*, p. 106.
22. Aust, 'War Cruises of H.I.M.S. *Karlsruhe*' (NR, 1917), p. 194.
23. Ibid, p. 195.
24. Ibid, p. 194.
25. Chatterton, *The Sea Raiders*, p. 106.
26. Corbett, *Naval Operations*, p. 52.
27. Aust, 'War Cruises of H.I.M.S. *Karlsruhe*' (NR, 1917), p. 196.
28. Ibid, p. 197.
29. Ibid.
30. Ibid, p. 198.
31. Ibid, p. 199.
32. *Patagonia* never returned; after coaling at Pernambuco she went to support von Spee.
33. Aust, 'War Cruises of H.I.M.S. *Karlsruhe*' (NR, 1917), p. 203.
34. IWM Docs 17542 Forbes, F.W.
35. Aust, 'War Cruises of H.I.M.S. *Karlsruhe*' (NR, 1917), p. 204.
36. Corbett, *Naval Operations*, pp. 322–3.
37. Aust, 'War Cruises of H.I.M.S. *Karlsruhe*' (NR, 1917), p. 206.
38. Hurd, *The Merchant Navy: Volume 1*, pp. 137–85 (reproduced on www.naval-history.net).
39. Hoyt, *The Karlsruhe Affair*, p. 99.
40. *Asuncion* left on 6 September. Once she was empty, her crew took the coal from *Strathroy* and sank her.
41. Aust, 'War Cruises of H.I.M.S. *Karlsruhe*' (NR, 1917), p. 208.
42. Corbett, *Naval Operations*, p. 323.
43. Ibid, p. 324. According to Corbett, *Indrani* was renamed *Hoffnung*.
44. Aust, 'War Cruises of H.I.M.S. *Karlsruhe*' (NR, 1917), p. 209.
45. Hurd, *The Merchant Navy: Volume 1*, pp. 137–85 (reproduced on www.naval-history.net).
46. Aust, 'War Cruises of H.I.M.S. *Karlsruhe*' (NR, 1917), pp. 212–13.
47. Ibid, p. 213.
48. Ibid, p. 214.
49. Corbett, *Naval Operations*, p. 325.
50. IWM Docs 17542 Forbes, F.W.
51. Aust, 'War Cruises of H.I.M.S. *Karlsruhe*' (NR, 1917), p. 216.
52. Hurd, *The Merchant Navy: Volume 1*, pp. 137–85 (reproduced on www.naval-history.net).
53. IWM Docs 17542 Forbes, F.W.
54. Aust, 'War Cruises of H.I.M.S. *Karlsruhe*' (NR, 1917), p. 217.
55. IWM Docs 17542 Forbes, F.W.
56. Corbett, *Naval Operations*, p. 327.
57. Aust, 'War Cruises of H.I.M.S. *Karlsruhe*' (NR, 1917), p. 221.
58. Ibid.
59. *New York Times*, 20 November 1914, www.nytimes.com.
60. Ibid.

61. *New York Times*, 29 November 1914, www.nytimes.com.
62. Hurd, *The Merchant Navy: Volume 1*, pp. 137–85 (reproduced on www.naval-history.net).
63. Aust, 'War Cruises of H.I.M.S. *Karlsruhe*' (NR, 1917), p. 225.
64. The British battleships *Bulwark* and *Vanguard* and the cruiser *Natal* were lost in similar circumstances.
65. Aust, 'War Cruises of H.I.M.S. *Karlsruhe*' (NR, 1917), p. 226.
66. *New York Times*, 22 January 1915, www.nytimes.com.
67. *New York Times*, 13 January 1915, www.nytimes.com.

Chapter 4. *Emden*: Swan of the East

1. Franz Joseph, *Emden*, p. 30.
2. Ibid, p. 31.
3. Anonymous, 'Escape of the *Emden* from Tsingtao' (NR, 1919), p. 243.
4. Churchill, *The World Crisis: Volume 1*, p. 248.
5. *Elsbeth* was scuttled by her own crew when Jerram's China Squadron arrived at Yap on 12 August.
6. Franz Joseph, *Emden*, p. 32.
7. Von Mücke, *The* Emden, p. 7.
8. Ibid, p. 21.
9. Ibid.
10. Franz Joseph, *Emden*, p. 34.
11. Tsingtao fell to an Anglo-Japanese assault in November.
12. Von Spee's options are summarised in translation in Naval Intelligence Department report 1173 of July 1918, entitled *Graf Von Spee's Squadron: Compiled from a German Semi-Official Account*, p. 7 (henceforth NID 1173). A copy can be found in IWM Docs 96/33/1–4 Phillimore, Admiral Sir Richard.
13. Van der Vat, *The Last Corsair*, p. 58.
14. Corbett, *Naval Operations*, p. 288.
15. Churchill, *The World Crisis: Volume 1*, p. 239.
16. Technically a '4th Class Cruiser', *Geier* was launched in 1895. Part-rigged for sail, poorly protected and slow, she was eventually interned in Honolulu.
17. Franz Joseph, *Emden*, p. 46.
18. Ibid, p. 51.
19. Ibid.
20. Von Mücke, *The Emden*, pp. 64–5.
21. Ibid, p. 55.
22. IWM Docs 96/21/1 Bray, A.G.
23. Quoted in Bennett, Geoffrey, *Naval Battles of the First World War* (Pan, London, 1983), p. 5.
24. Franz Joseph, *Emden*, p. 57.
25. Corbett, *Naval Operations*, p. 289.
26. Franz Joseph, *Emden*, p. 57.
27. Van der Vat, *The Last Corsair*, p. 87.
28. Franz Joseph, *Emden*, p. 60.
29. Ibid.
30. Von Mücke, *The Emden*, p. 81.
31. 'Ceylon Times', subsequently reported in the *Launceston Examiner* (Tasmania), on 2 November 1914, p. 6. http://trove.nla.gov.au.
32. Ibid.

33. Ibid.
34. Churchill, *The World Crisis: Volume 1*, pp. 255–6.
35. http://www.hindu.com, 22 August 2007.
36. Spencer-Cooper, Commander H., *The Battle of the Falkland Islands* (Cassell & Co. Ltd, London, 1919), p. 15.
37. Franz Joseph, *Emden*, p. 64. Both ships were run to earth three weeks later by the British cruiser *Yarmouth*, just outside Dutch territorial waters near Sumatra.
38. Ibid, p. 68.
39. Von Mücke, *The Emden*, p. 129.
40. IWM Docs 97/31/1 Mole, Edgar Horace.
41. Ibid.
42. Franz Joseph, *Emden*, p. 73.
43. Von Mücke, *The Emden*, p. 138.
44. Franz Joseph, *Emden*, p. 77.
45. Ibid, p. 79.
46. Churchill, *The World Crisis: Volume 1*, pp. 250–1.
47. Ibid, p. 257.
48. IWM Docs 86/19/1 Billings, Hubert.
49. Franz Joseph, *Emden*, p. 91.
50. Van der Vat, *The Last Corsair*, p. 18.
51. IWM Docs 97/31/1 Mole, E.H.
52. IWM Docs 86/19/1 Billings, Hubert.
53. Glossop, Captain John, 'Narrative of the Proceedings of HMAS *Sydney* Part I' (NR, 1915), pp. 9–10.
54. Darby, Surgeon Lieutenant Leonard, 'The Wounded in the Action between the *Sydney* and the *Emden*', originally anonymous (NR, 1917), p. 243.
55. Franz Joseph, *Emden*, p. 94.
56. Glossop, 'Narrative of the Proceedings of HMAS *Sydney* Part II' (NR, 1915), p. 453.
57. Glossop, 'Narrative of Proceedings Part I' (NR, 1915), pp. 15–16.
58. Bennett, *Naval Battles of the First World War*, p. 51.
59. Franz Joseph, *Emden*, p. 96.
60. IWM Docs 76/232/1 Broome, Richard Henry.
61. Franz Joseph, *Emden*, p. 104.
62. Glossop, Captain John C.T., 'Official Report of Action with the *Emden*' (NR, 1915), p. 162.
63. Von Mücke wrote an account of this experience, entitled *Ayesha*. Details also appear in van der Vat, *The Last Corsair*, pp. 173–247.
64. Franz Joseph, *Emden*, p. 105.
65. Darby, 'The Wounded' (NR, 1917), p. 247.
66. IWM Sound 9038 Kiel, Bertram.

Chapter 5. Coronel: to the Bitter End
1. NID 1173, p. 7, in IWM Docs 96/33/1–4 Phillimore, Admiral Sir Richard.
2. Lockyer, H.C., 'Coronel and the Falklands' (NR, 1963), p. 301.
3. Churchill, *The World Crisis: Volume 1*, p. 253.
4. NID 1173, p. 8, in IWM Docs 96/33/1–4 Phillimore, Admiral Sir Richard.
5. Anonymous letter entitled 'German Pacific Squadron' (NR, 1915), p. 164.
6. *The Straits Times*, 10 November 1914, p. 10, from http://newspapers.nl.sg.
7. Ibid.

8. Ibid.
9. 'German Pacific Squadron' (NR, 1915), p. 165.
10. See Corbett, *Naval Operations*, p. 310, and Churchill, *The World Crisis: Volume 1*, p. 366.
11. Massie, *Castles of Steel*, p. 218.
12. *Sporting Notes in the Far East* (1889), *Wrinkles in Seamanship* (1894) and *Whispers from the Fleet* (1907).
13. Bennett, *Coronel and the Falklands*, p. 26.
14. Churchill, *The World Crisis: Volume 1*, p. 369.
15. 'The Work of the *Glasgow* and the Action off Coronel: Part 1' (NR, 1915), p. 380. Originally anonymous.
16. Bennett, *Coronel and the Falklands*, p. 81.
17. Ibid, pp. 82–3.
18. Hirst, Lloyd, *Coronel and After* (Peter Davies, London, 1934), p. 15, quoted in Massie, *Castles of Steel*, p. 204.
19. IWM Docs P327 Cardew, Basil.
20. Churchill, *The World Crisis: Volume 1*, p. 370.
21. Bennett, *Coronel and the Falklands*, p. 83.
22. NID 1173, p. 8, in IWM Docs 96/33/1–4 Phillimore, Admiral Sir Richard.
23. 'German Pacific Squadron' (NR, 1915), p. 166.
24. *Sydney Morning Herald*, 21 October 1914 (from http://news.google.com).
25. 'German Pacific Squadron' (NR, 1915), p. 166.
26. 'Work of the *Glasgow*: Part 1' (NR, 1915), p. 383.
27. Churchill, *The World Crisis: Volume 1*, p. 368.
28. Marder, *From the Dreadnought to Scapa Flow: Volume 2*, p. 85.
29. Massie, *Castles of Steel*, p. 287, and Marder, *From the Dreadnought to Scapa Flow: Volume 1*, p. 21.
30. Massie, *Castles of Steel*, p. 360.
31. Marder, *From the Dreadnought to Scapa Flow: Volume 1*, p. 21.
32. Bennett, *Coronel and the Falklands*, p. 23, and IWM Docs P103 Young, Commander T., pp. 23–4.
33. Dewar, Vice Admiral Kenneth, 'The Coronel Campaign' (NR, 1955), p. 172.
34. Churchill, *The World Crisis: Volume 1*, p. 372.
35. Ibid, p. 372.
36. Dewar, 'The Coronel Campaign', p. 171.
37. IWM Docs 01/2/1 Cartwright, L.V.
38. IWM Docs 76/191/1 Fitch, Lieutenant H.M.
39. IWM Docs 76/141/2 Roe, Acting Mate R.C.T.
40. Churchill, *The World Crisis: Volume 1*, p. 373.
41. 'Work of the *Glasgow*: Part 1' (NR, 1915), p. 385.
42. IWM Docs 76/141/2 Roe, Acting Mate R.C.T.
43. 'Narrative of the Action off the Coast of Chile', by an anonymous officer of the *Glasgow* (NR, 1915), p. 159.
44. Selkirk was marooned on the island for four years and probably inspired Defoe's *Robinson Crusoe*.
45. NID 1173, p. 15, in IWM Docs 96/33/1–4 Phillimore, Admiral Sir Richard.
46. Ibid, p. 16.
47. IWM Docs 96/47/1 Morris, A.
48. IWM Sound 4047 Bushkin, A.A.

49. Ibid.
50. IWM Docs 90/41/1 Woodcock, Captain H.W.
51. Originally anonymous account in IWM Docs Misc 12/260.
52. 'Work of the *Glasgow*: Part 1' (NR, 1915), p. 390.
53. 'Narrative of the Action off the Coast of Chile', by an anonymous officer of the *Glasgow* (NR, 1915), p. 161.
54. 'Translations of extracts from letters by Vice-Admiral Count von Spee and his son, Lieutenant Count Otto Spee' (NR, 1915), p. 403.
55. IWM Docs 85/25/1 Hawkes, Able Seaman W.T.C.
56. Ibid.
57. 'Work of the *Glasgow*: Part 1' (NR, 1915), p. 390.
58. IWM Docs 96/47/1 Morris, A.
59. NID 1173, p. 20, in IWM Docs 96/33/1–4 Phillimore, Admiral Sir Richard.
60. IWM Sound 692 Pullen, Edward.
61. 'Work of the *Glasgow*: Part 1' (NR, 1915), p. 391.
62. IWM Docs 76/235/1 Rooke, P.
63. IWM Docs P103 Young, Commander T., p. 32.
64. Luce's despatch in Spencer-Cooper, *The Battle of the Falkland Islands*, pp. 172–3.
65. IWM Docs 85/25/1 Hawkes, Able Seaman W.T.C.
66. NID 1173, p. 20, in IWM Docs 96/33/1–4 Phillimore, Admiral Sir Richard.
67. Ibid, p. 20.
68. Ibid, p. 21.
69. Santa Maria was a nearby island.

Chapter 6: 'Instruments of Nemesis': the Combination against von Spee

1. Churchill, *The World Crisis: Volume 1*, p. 251.
2. 'Translation of a Pocket Diary found on an Officer Survivor from the *Gneisenau*' (NR, 1915), p. 409.
3. Pitt, Barrie, *Coronel and Falkland* (Cassell, London, 1960), p. 56.
4. Ibid, p. 67.
5. NID 1173, p. 11, in IWM Docs 96/33/1–4 Phillimore, Admiral Sir Richard.
6. *Hizen* was formerly the Russian battleship *Retvizan*, which was captured during the Russo-Japanese War. To add to her mongrel antecedents, she had been built by William Cramp & Sons of Philadelphia, USA!
7. Pitt, *Coronel and Falkland*, p. 58.
8. Churchill, *The World Crisis: Volume 1*, p. 375.
9. Ibid, p. 375.
10. Dewar, 'The Coronel Campaign', p. 176.
11. Churchill, *The World Crisis: Volume 1*, pp. 378–82.
12. Ibid, p. 382.
13. IWM Docs P103 Young, Commander T., p. 30.
14. Massie, *Castles of Steel*, p. 219.
15. IWM Docs P103 Young, Commander T., p. 34.
16. IWM Sound 692 Pullen, Edward.
17. IWM Docs P103 Young, Commander T., pp. 35–6.
18. Ibid, p. 41.
19. Ibid.

20. 'Translation of a Pocket Diary found on an Officer Survivor from the *Gneisenau*' (NR, 1915), p. 410.
21. Pitt, *Coronel and Falkland*, p. 70.
22. NID 1173, p. 12, in IWM Docs 96/33/1–4 Phillimore, Admiral Sir Richard.
23. Pitt, *Coronel and Falkland*, pp. 73–4.
24. Ibid, p. 411.
25. Ibid.
26. NID 1173, p. 12, in IWM Docs 96/33/1–4 Phillimore, Admiral Sir Richard.
27. http://trove.nla.gov.au/ndp/del/.
28. NID 1173, p. 23, in IWM Docs 96/33/1–4 Phillimore, Admiral Sir Richard.
29. IWM Sound 8201 Murray, Joseph.
30. Corbett, *Naval Operations*, p. 364.
31. Churchill, *The World Crisis: Volume 1*, p. 384.
32. Ibid, p. 284.
33. Ibid, p. 390.
34. Patterson, A. Temple (ed.), *The Jellicoe Papers Volume 1: 1893–1916* (Spottiswoode, Ballantyne & Co. Ltd, London, for the Navy Records Society, 1966), p. 82.
35. Massie, *Castles of Steel*, pp. 247–8.
36. Massie, *Castles of* Steel, p. 247, and Ranft, B. Mcl. (ed.), *The Beatty Papers Volume 1: 1902–1918* (Scholar Press, Aldershot, for the Navy Records Society, 1989), p. 164.
37. IWM Sound 9063 Stewart, Ross.
38. IWM Docs 76/207/3 Duckworth, Captain A.D.
39. Ibid.
40. IWM Docs 78/25/1 Stewart, Captain R.R.
41. IWM Sound 10882 Miller, George.
42. IWM Sound 9011 Stevens, Bert.
43. IWM Sound 10882, Miller, George.
44. Bingham, Commander the Honourable Barry, *Falklands, Jutland and the Bight* (John Murray, London, 1919), p. 50. Bingham was awarded the Victoria Cross at Jutland in 1916.
45. IWM Docs P400 Shaw, Engineer Captain J. Fraser, p. 8.
46. Ibid.
47. Ibid, p. 9
48. Ibid, p. 11.
49. Ibid.
50. Ibid, p. 12.
51. Ibid.
52. IWM Docs 76/207/3 Duckworth, Captain A.D.
53. Corbett, *Naval Operations*, p. 409.
54. IWM Docs 76/191/1 Fitch, Lieutenant H.M.
55. Portman, Maurice, 'The Work of the *Glasgow* and the Action off Coronel: Part 2' (NR, 1916), p. 61. Originally anonymous.
56. Bingham, *Falklands, Jutland and the Bight*, p. 51.
57. Hickling, Vice Admiral Harold, *Sailor at Sea* (William Kimber, London, 1965), p. 66, quoted in Massie, *Castles of Steel*, p. 250.
58. IWM Docs 82/39/1 Townsend, Commander R.H.D.
59. Ibid.
60. Ibid.
61. IWM Docs 76/207/3 Duckworth, Captain A.D.

62. IWM Docs 82/39/1 Townsend, Commander R.H.D.
63. Bingham, *Falklands, Jutland and the Bight*, p. 62.
64. Spencer-Cooper, *The Battle of the Falkland Islands*, pp. 81–2.
65. Ibid, p. 88. The Admiralty rewarded Mrs Felton with a silver salver, and her maid with a silver teapot. Admiral Sturdee gave the Sapper Hill lookout £5.
66. Bingham, *Falklands, Jutland and the Bight*, p. 66.

Chapter 7: In the Old Style: the Battle of the Falklands
1. NID 1173, p. 27, in IWM Docs 96/33/1–4 Phillimore, Admiral Sir Richard.
2. Corbett, *Naval Operations*, p. 411.
3. Dannreuther, Admiral H., transcript of speech in IWM Docs 76/207/3 Duckworth, Captain A.D.
4. Anonymous, 'The Action off the Falkland Islands: The Chase of the German Squadron and the *Kent*'s Action with the *Nürnberg*' (NR, 1915), p. 143.
5. IWM Docs Misc 68/1045, p. 2.
6. IWM Docs P103 Young, Commander T., p. 44.
7. Ibid, p. 45.
8. Dannreuther, Admiral H., transcript of speech in IWM Docs 76/207/3 Duckworth, Captain A.D.
9. IWM Docs P400 Shaw, Engineer Captain J. Fraser, letter dated 10 December 1914.
10. Anonymous, 'The Action off the Falkland Islands: The *Cornwall*'s Share' (NR, 1915), p. 244.
11. Anonymous letter in IWM Docs 76/202/1 Vernon, Major W.F.
12. Spencer-Cooper, *The Battle of the Falkland Islands*, p. 95.
13. IWM Docs 96/33/1 Phillimore, Admiral Sir Richard.
14. IWM Docs PP/MCR/84 Gardner, Midshipman L.
15. IWM Docs 92/18/1 Sinclair, Captain R.
16. Naval Intelligence Department Report NID 1015, 'The Falkland Islands Action 8 December 1914: Account Supplied by Sub-Lieutenant Richarz of the *Dresden*, August 1915', in IWM Docs 96/33/1–4 Phillimore, Admiral Sir Richard
17. Marder, *From the Dreadnought to Scapa Flow: Volume 2*, p. 122.
18. IWM Docs 76/86/1 James, Vice Admiral T.N.
19. Verner, Commander Rudolph H.C., 'Action off the Falkland Islands: 8 December 1914' (NR, 1916), p. 73.
20. IWM Docs P400 Shaw, Engineer Captain J. Fraser.
21. IWM Sound 10882 Miller, G.
22. Verner, 'Action off the Falkland Islands: 8 December 1914' (NR, 1916), p. 74.
23. IWM Docs 78/25/1 Stewart, Captain R.R.
24. IWM Docs 96/20/1 Montagu, Midshipman R.S.
25. NID 1173, p. 32, in IWM Docs 96/33/1–4 Phillimore, Admiral Sir Richard.
26. Spencer-Cooper, *The Battle of the Falkland Islands*, p. 98.
27. IWM Docs 76/207/3 Duckworth, Captain A.D.
28. IWM Docs 82/39/1 Townsend, Commander R.H.D.
29. Dannreuther, Admiral H., transcript of speech in IWM Docs 76/207/3 Duckworth, Captain A.D.
30. NID 1173, p. 32, in IWM Docs 96/33/1–4 Phillimore, Admiral Sir Richard.
31. Quoted in Corbett, *Naval Operations*, p. 422.
32. Bennett, *Coronel and the Falklands*, pp. 149–50.

33. NID 1173, p. 33, in IWM Docs 96/33/1–4 Phillimore, Admiral Sir Richard.
34. Ibid.
35. Ibid.
36. Verner, 'Action off the Falkland Islands: 8 December 1914' (NR, 1916), p. 75.
37. IWM Docs 96/33/1–4 Phillimore, Admiral Sir Richard.
38. IWM Docs 76/207/3 Duckworth, Captain A.D.
39. IWM Docs P327 Laborde, Commander C.F.
40. IWM Docs P447 Leslie, Commander A.G.
41. IWM Sound 9063 Stewart, R.
42. Spencer-Cooper, *The Battle of the Falkland Islands*, p. 98.
43. IWM Docs 82/39/1 Townsend, Commander R.H.D.
44. Quoted in Marder, *From the Dreadnought to Scapa Flow: Volume 2*, p. 124.
45. IWM Docs 06/49/1 King, H., p. 2.
46. IWM Sound 8835 Bourne, C.A.
47. IWM Docs 96/20/1 Millar, Captain K.B.
48. IWM Docs P400, Shrubsole, Rear Admiral P.J.
49. Anonymous, 'The Action off the Falkland Islands: The *Cornwall*'s Share' (NR, 1915), p. 246.
50. NID 1173, p. 47, in IWM Docs 96/33/1–4 Phillimore, Admiral Sir Richard.
51. Ibid, p. 45.
52. Anonymous, 'The Action off the Falkland Islands: The *Cornwall*'s Share' (NR, 1915), p. 247.
53. IWM Docs DS/Misc/62 Ellerton, Captain J.
54. Anonymous, 'The Action off the Falkland Islands: The *Cornwall*'s Share' (NR, 1915), p. 248.
55. NID 1173, p. 49, in IWM Docs 96/33/1–4 Phillimore, Admiral Sir Richard, p. 48.
56. Ibid, p. 49.
57. Massie, *Castles of Steel*, p. 276.
58. NID 1173, p. 51, in IWM Docs 96/33/1–4 Phillimore, Admiral Sir Richard.
59. 'The Action off the Falkland Islands: Sidelights on the Battle from HMS *Cornwall*' (NR, 1915), p. 277.
60. IWM Docs PP/MCR/84 Gardner, Midshipman L.
61. Portman, 'The Work of the *Glasgow* and the Action off the Falkland Islands: Part 2' (NR, 1916), p. 66.
62. IWM Docs DS/Misc/62 Ellerton, Captain J.
63. 'Action off the Falkland Islands: The Chase of the German Squadron, and the *Kent*'s action with the *Nürnberg*' (NR, 1915), p. 143.
64. Ibid, p. 153.
65. IWM Docs 90/41/1 Danckwerts, Vice Admiral V.H.
66. IWM Docs Misc 68/1045.
67. Ibid.
68. IWM Docs 09/54/1 Austin, W.
69. IWM Docs Misc 68/1045.
70. 'The Action off the Falkland Islands: The Chase of the German Squadron, and the *Kent*'s action with the *Nürnberg*' (NR, 1915), p. 151.
71. IWM Docs 09/54/1 Austin, W.
72. NID 1173, p. 38, in IWM Docs 96/33/1–4 Phillimore, Admiral Sir Richard.
73. IWM Docs 09/54/1 Austin, W.

74. Ibid.
75. Marder, *From the Dreadnought to Scapa Flow: Volume 2*, p. 124.

Chapter 8: Fugitive: the Pursuit of *Dresden*
 1. Hurd, *The Merchant Navy: Volume 1*, pp. 137–85 (reproduced on www.naval-history.net).
 2. Ibid.
 3. Ibid.
 4. 'Extracts from the Log of the *Dresden*, with Comments on Her Career' (NR, 1915), p. 421.
 5. NID 1173, p. 36, in IWM Docs 96/33/1–4 Phillimore, Admiral Sir Richard.
 6. Marder, *From the Dreadnought to Scapa Flow: Volume 2*, p. 125.
 7. Transcripts of signals in IWM Docs 76/207/3 Duckworth, Captain A.D.
 8. Churchill, *The World Crisis: Volume 1*, pp. 406–7.
 9. Transcripts of signals in IWM Docs 76/207/3 Duckworth, Captain A.D.
10. Marder, *From the Dreadnought to Scapa Flow: Volume 2*, p. 126. A debate also erupted in the Royal Navy over ammunition expenditure during the *Leipzig* pursuit, when *Glasgow*, in commission for two years, fired off almost all her ammunition. *Cornwall* used far less, despite only recommissioning in 1914 after grounding in Canada and years in a drydock. I am grateful to Rod Suddaby for bringing this point to my attention.
11. IWM Docs 82/39/1 Townsend, Commander R.H.D.
12. IWM Docs DS/Misc/52 Hickling, Vice Admiral H.
13. NID 1173, p. 39, in IWM Docs 96/33/1–4 Phillimore, Admiral Sir Richard.
14. Corbett, *Naval Operations*, pp. 434–5.
15. 'Calafate' (Robert Riddell), 'Concealing the *Dresden*' (*Blackwoods Magazine*, January 1935, Volume 237, No. 1431), via http://patlibros.org/ctd/. The writer was a British farmer in the region in 1914, who assisted in the hunt for *Dresden*. He interviewed Pagels in 1934.
16. Ibid.
17. Ibid.
18. Chatterton, *The Sea Raiders*, p. 69.
19. 'Calafate', 'Concealing the *Dresden*'.
20. Ibid.
21. Ibid.
22. Ibid.
23. Ibid.
24. Ibid.
25. Ibid.
26. Massie, *Castles of Steel*, pp. 282–3.
27. IWM Docs P400 Shrubsole, Rear Admiral P.
28. IWM Docs 09/54/1 Austin, W.
29. Portman, 'The Work of the *Glasgow* and the Action off the Falkland Islands: Part 2' (NR, 1916), p. 69.
30. IWM Docs 06/49/1 King, H.
31. IWM Docs 83/51/1, Barker, Lieutenant Commander G.W., and IWM Docs Con Shelf Welch, H.S.
32. 'Calafate', 'Concealing the *Dresden*'.
33. IWM Docs 06/49/1 King, H.
34. Ibid.
35. Bennett, *Coronel and the Falklands*, p. 179.
36. Chatterton, *The Sea Raiders*, p. 67.

37. Ibid, p. 71.
38. 'Calafate', 'Concealing the *Dresden*'.
39. IWM Docs 06/49/1 King, H.
40. 'Extracts from the Log of the *Dresden*, with Comments on Her Career' (NR, 1915), p. 426.
41. 'An Account of the Search for and Ultimate Destruction of the German Cruiser *Dresden*' (NR, 1916), p. 81.
42. Chatterton, *The Sea Raiders*, p. 85.
43. IWM Docs Con Shelf Welch, H.S.
44. 'An Account of the Search for and Ultimate Destruction of the German Cruiser *Dresden*' (NR, 1916), p. 82.
45. Chatterton, *The Sea Raiders*, p. 87.
46. IWM Docs 09/54/1 Austin, W.
47. Chatterton, *The Sea Raiders*, p. 91.
48. Ibid, p. 90.
49. Bennett, *Coronel and the Falklands*, p. 183.
50. NID 1173, p. 40, in IWM Docs 96/33/1–4 Phillimore, Admiral Sir Richard.
51. Ibid.
52. IWM Docs 83/51/1 Barker, Lieutenant Commander G.W.
53. Canaris escaped and returned to Germany in 1917, commanding several U-boats before the war ended. As head of the *Abwehr*, German military intelligence, he conspired to depose Hitler and was executed in April 1945 for his role in the so-called 'July Plot'.
54. IWM Docs 85/25/1 Hawkes, Able Seaman W.T.C.
55. IWM Docs Con Shelf Welch, H.S.
56. IWM Docs P149 Welham, S.
57. IWM Docs 83/51/1 Barker, Lieutenant Commander G.W., and IWM Docs Con Shelf Welch, H.S.
58. IWM Docs P400 Shrubsole, Rear Admiral P. Tirpitz was brought back to the RN Gunnery School at Whale Island, Portsmouth. In 1919 he was auctioned in aid of the British Red Cross. His (rather magnificent) head survives, stuffed, in the Imperial War Museum.
59. Hoyt, *Kreuzerkrieg*, p. 143, quoted in Jannings, 'SMS *Dresden*'s War'.
60. Pitt, *Coronel and Falkland*, p. 168.
61. Jannings, 'SMS *Dresden*'s War'.

Chapter 9: Part-time Pirates: the Armed Liners

1. Hurd, *The Merchant Navy: Volume 1*, pp. 117–36 (reproduced on www.naval-history.net).
2. *New York Times*, 7 August 1914, www.nytimes.com.
3. Simpson, Colin, *The Ship that Hunted Itself* (Penguin, Harmondsworth, Middlesex, 1977), p. 29.
4. Putnam, William Lowell, *The Kaiser's Merchant Ships in World War 1* (MacFarland & Company, North Carolina, 2001), p. 53.
5. Ibid, p. 49.
6. Hurd, *The Merchant Navy: Volume 1* (reproduced on www.naval-history.net).
7. *New York Times*, 27 August 1914, www.nytimes.com.
8. Hurd, *The Merchant Navy: Volume 1*, pp. 137–85 (reproduced on www.naval-history.net).
9. Corbett, *Naval Operations*, p. 134.
10. *New York Times*, 30 August 1914, www.nytimes.com.
11. Putnam, *The Kaiser's Merchant Ships in World War 1*, p. 54.
12. Corbett, *Naval Operations*, p. 135.

13. *New York Times*, 18 September 1914, www.nytimes.com.
14. *New York Times*, 28 August 1914, www.nytimes.com.
15. Simpson, *The Ship that Hunted Itself*, p. 17.
16. Ibid, p. 18.
17. Corbett, *Naval Operations*, p. 260.
18. Simpson, *The Ship that Hunted Itself*, p. 16.
19. IWM Docs 17495 Kendall, Engineer Lieutenant H., letter from Steffan, Admiral O.
20. Simpson, *The Ship that Hunted Itself*, pp. 134–9.
21. IWM Docs 17495 Kendall, Steffan letter.
22. Ibid.
23. Ibid.
24. Simpson, *The Ship that Hunted Itself*, p. 21.
25. IWM Docs 17495 Kendall, *Carmania* Souvenir Book Extracts.
26. Ibid, Steffan letter.
27. Ibid, Kendall letter.
28. Ibid, *Carmania* Souvenir Book Extracts.
29. *New York Times*, 4 August 1914, www.nytimes.com.
30. See Chapter 3.
31. Niezychowski, Count Alfred von, *The Cruise of the* Kronprinz Wilhelm (Selwyn & Blount, London, 1928).
32. Ibid, p. 40.
33. Ibid, p. 44.
34. Ibid, p. 55.
35. Ibid, p. 89.
36. Ibid, p. 91.
37. Ibid, p. 83.
38. Hurd, *The Merchant Navy, Volume 1*, pp. 137–85 (reproduced on www.naval-history.net).
39. Niezychowski, *Cruise of the* Kronprinz Wilhelm, pp. 147–8.
40. Ibid, pp. 148–9.
41. Ibid, p. 156.
42. Ibid, pp. 162–3.
43. Ibid, p. 193.
44. Ibid, p. 192.
45. Ibid, p. 199.
46. Corbett, *Naval Operations*, p. 410.
47. http://www.naval-history.net.
48. Ibid.
49. Niezychowski, *Cruise of the* Kronprinz Wilhelm, p. 237.
50. Ibid, p. 277.
51. Chatterton, *The Sea Raiders*, p. 170.
52. Ibid, p. 171.
53. *New York Times*, 8 December 1914, www.nytimes.com.
54. Chatterton, *The Sea Raiders*, p. 173.
55. Ibid, p. 174.
56. Ibid, p. 177.
57. *New York Call*, 12 March 1914.
58. Hurd, *The Merchant Navy, Volume 1*, pp. 137–85 (reproduced on www.naval-history.net).

Chapter 10: The Last Raider: Cornering *Königsberg*

1. *Planet* scuttled at Yap in the Caroline Islands in September 1914 and her crew joined the raider *Cormoran*. *Zeiten* was on her way back to Germany carrying the crew from her previous commission, who had been relieved before the war.
2. IWM Docs Ger Misc 113.
3. The first was the oil tanker *San Wilfrido*, mined and sunk off Cuxhaven on 3 August. www.naval-history.net.
4. Corbett, *Naval Operations*, p. 156.
5. Churchill, *The World Crisis: Volume 1*, pp. 388–9.
6. Ibid.
7. Corbett, *Naval Operations*, p. 295.
8. *Wanganui Chronicle*, 23 December 1914, http://paperspast.natlib.govt.nz.
9. 'Incident at Zanzibar, 1914' (NR, 1967), p. 139.
10. Ibid, p. 139.
11. Ibid, p. 140.
12. Ibid. Hattersley-Smith went on to serve ashore in the East African campaign, contracting the dysentery that would eventually kill him at the age of 26.
13. Ibid.
14. *Wanganui Chronicle*, 23 December 1914, http://paperspast.natlib.govt.nz.
15. Corbett, *Naval Operations*, p. 296.
16. Drury-Lowe, Captain S., 'Narrative of Proceedings of HMS *Chatham*: Off East Coast of Africa in Search of German Light Cruiser *Königsberg*' (NR, 1915), p. 472.
17. Ibid, p. 474.
18. Ibid.
19. Ibid, p. 475.
20. Chatterton, *The* Königsberg *Adventure*, pp. 39–42.
21. IWM Docs Ger Misc 113.
22. Walter, *The Kaiser's Pirates*, pp. 119–20.
23. IWM Sound 9019 Fagg, R.
24. Drury-Lowe, 'Narrative of Proceedings', p. 478.
25. IWM Sound 9019 Fagg, R.
26. Ibid.
27. Drury-Lowe, 'Narrative of Proceedings', p. 480.
28. Ibid, pp. 63–5.
29. IWM Docs Ger Misc 113.
30. IWM Docs 85/25/1 Denby, V.E., and IWM Docs Ger Misc 113.
31. IWM Docs Ger Misc 113.
32. Drury-Lowe, 'Narrative of Proceedings', pp. 485–6.
33. IWM Docs Ger Misc 113.
34. IWM Docs P281 Murray, Rear Admiral R.G.
35. IWM Docs Ger Misc 113.
36. Chatterton, *The* Königsberg *Adventure*, p. 111.
37. Ibid, pp. 112–13.
38. The Curtiss was eventually taken to Durban and placed in a museum.
39. Chatterton, *The* Königsberg *Adventure*, pp. 112–13.
40. Ibid, pp. 260–3.
41. IWM Docs Ger Misc 113.
42. IWM Docs Misc 164/2541 log from HMS *Weymouth*.

43. http://frontierpartisans.com/142/cruiser-killer.
44. 'Pretorius and the *Königsberg*', by 'Walrus' (NR, 1915), p. 37.
45. Ibid, pp. 37–8.
46. Ibid, p. 38.
47. Ibid.
48. IWM Docs P281 Murray, Rear Admiral R.G.
49. IWM Docs 74/88/1 Watkins, Wing Commander H.
50. Ibid.
51. Ibid.
52. IWM Docs P281 Murray, Rear Admiral R.G.
53. Anderson, Ross, *The Forgotten Front 1914–1918: The East African Campaign* (Tempus, Stroud, 2007), pp. 74–5.
54. Layman, R.D., *Naval Aviation in the First World War: Its Impact and Influence* (Caxton Editions, 1996), pp. 134–5, and IWM Docs 74/88/1 Watkins, Wing Commander H.
55. IWM Docs 74/88/1 Watkins, Wing Commander H.
56. Ibid.
57. Ibid.
58. Ibid.
59. IWM Docs 96/47/1 Wright, A.J.
60. 'Narrative of Events During Attacks on the German Cruiser *Königsberg:* July 6th and 11th, 1915' (NR, 1916), pp. 335–6.
61. 'The Attacks on the *Königsberg*' (NR, 1915), p. 697.
62. IWM Docs Ger Misc 113.
63. 'The Attacks on the *Königsberg*' (NR, 1915), p. 685.
64. 'Narrative of Events During Attacks on the German Cruiser *Königsberg*' (NR, 1916), p. 336.
65. 'The Attacks on the *Königsberg*' (NR, 1915), p. 683.
66. IWM Docs Ger Misc 113.
67. 'The Attacks on the *Königsberg*' (NR, 1915), p. 688.
68. Ibid, pp. 688–9.
69. IWM Docs Ger Misc 113.
70. IWM Docs 74/88/1 Watkins, Wing Commander H.
71. 'The Attacks on the *Königsberg*' (NR, 1915), p. 691.
72. Ibid, p. 693.
73. IWM Docs P190, Acheson, Lieutenant Commander the Honourable P.G.E.C.
74. Ibid.
75. Ibid.
76. IWM Docs Ger Misc 113.

Conclusion

1. *British Vessels Lost at Sea* (HMSO, London, 1919).
2. Terraine, John, *Business in Great Waters: The U-boat Wars 1916–1945* (Wordsworth Editions Ltd, Ware, 1999), Appendix C, p. 766.

Select Bibliography

Imperial War Museum Documents
IWM London, Lambeth Road, London, SE1 6HZ, United Kingdom
(www.iwm.org.uk/collections-research)

Acheson, Lieutenant Commander the Honourable P.G.E.C., IWM Docs P160.
Austin, W., IWM Docs 09/54/1.
Baker, A.E., IWM Docs 05/63/1.
Barker, Lieutenant Commander G.W., IWM Docs 83/51/1.
Billings, H., IWM Docs 86/19/1.
Bray, A.G., IWM Docs 96/21/1.
Broome, R.H., IWM Docs 76/232/1.
Cardew, B, IWM Docs P327.
Cartwright, L.V., IWM Docs 01/2/1.
Danckwerts, Vice-Admiral V.H., IWM Docs 90/41/1.
Defence, HMS, signal log, IWM Docs Misc 64/1009.
Denby, V.E., IWM Docs 85/25/1.
Duckworth, Captain A.D., IWM Docs 76/207/3.
Ellerton, Captain J., IWM Docs DS/Misc/62.
Fitch, Lieutenant H.M., IWM Docs 76/191/1.
Forbes, F.W., IWM Docs 10/19/1.
Gardner, Midshipman L., IWM Docs PP/MCR/84.
Hawkes, W.T.C., IWM Docs 85/25/1.
Hickling, Vice-Admiral H., IWM Docs DS/Misc/52 Hickling.
Horniman, Fleet Paymaster H., WM Docs PP/MCR/46.
IWM Docs Ger Misc 113.
IWM Docs Misc 12/260.
IWM Docs Misc 254 (3484).
IWM Docs Misc 68/1045.
James, Vice-Admiral T.N., IWM Docs 76/86/1.
Kendall, Engineer Lieutenant H., IWM Docs 10/7/1.
King, H., IWM Docs 06/49/1.
Laborde, Commander C.F., IWM Docs P327.
Leslie, Commander A.G., IWM Docs P447.
Meager, W.M., IWM Docs P451.
Millar, Captain K.B., IWM Docs 96/20/1.
Mole, E.H., IWM Docs 97/31/1.
Montagu, Midshipman R.S., IWM Docs 96/20/1.
Morris, A., IWM Docs 96/47/1.
Murray, Rear-Admiral R.G., IWM Docs P281.

Phillimore, Admiral Sir Richard, IWM Docs 96/33/1–4.
Roe, Acting Mate R.C.T., IWM Docs 76/141/2.
Rooke, P., IWM Docs 76/235/1.
Shaw, Engineer Captain J.F., IWM Docs P400.
Shrubsole, Rear Admiral P.J., IWM Docs P400.
Sinclair, Captain R., IWM Docs 92/18/1.
Stewart, Captain R.R., IWM Docs 78/25/1.
Townsend, Commander R.H.D., IWM Docs 82/39/1.
Vernon, Major W.F., IWM Docs 76/202/1.
Warner, Captain G.H., IWM Docs P389.
Watkins, Wing Commander H., IWM Docs 74/88/1.
Welch, H.S., IWM Docs Con Shelf.
Welham, S., IWM Docs P149.
Weymouth, HMS, log, IWM Docs Misc 164/2541.
Woodcock, Captain H.W., IWM Docs 90/41/1.
Wright, A.J., IWM Docs 96/47/1.
Young, Commander T., IWM Docs P103.

Imperial War Museum Sound Archive
IWM London, Lambeth Road, London, SE1 6HZ, United Kingdom
(www.iwm.org.uk/collections-research)

Bourne, C.A., IWM Sound 8835
Bushkin, A.A., IWM Sound 4047
Fagg, R., IWM Sound 9019
Kiel, B., IWM Sound 9038
Masters, A., IWM Sound 720
Miller, G., IWM Sound 10882
Murray, J., IWM Sound 8201
Pullen, E., IWM Sound 692
Stevens, B., IWM Sound 9011
Stewart, R., IWM Sound 9063
Whittle, T.M., IWM Sound 4256

The Naval Review
(www.naval-review.org/archive)

'Action off the Falkland Islands: 8 December 1914', by Commander R.H.C. Verner, 1916.
'Action off the Falkland Islands: The Chase of the German Squadron and Kent's Action with the Nürnberg', 1915.
'An Account of the Search for and Ultimate Destruction of the German Cruiser *Dresden*', 1916.
'Coronel and the Falklands', by H.C. Lockyer, 1963.
'Echoes of the *Emden*', by I.H. Duckworth, 1973.
'Escape of the *Emden* from Tsingtao', 1919.
'Extracts from the Log of the *Dresden*, with Comments on Her Career', 1915.
'German Pacific Squadron', 1915.
'*Goeben* and *Breslau*', by Lieutenant (JG) S.F. Bryant, USN, 1917.
'Incident at Zanzibar, 1914', 1967.
'Narrative from the *Indomitable:* The Escape of the *Goeben*', 1919.

'Narrative of Events during Attacks on the German Cruiser *Königsberg*: July 6th and 11th 1915', 1916.

'Narrative of Proceedings of HMS *Chatham:* Off East Coast of Africa in Search of German Light Cruiser *Königsberg*', by Captain S. Drury-Lowe, 1915.

'Narrative of the Action off the Coast of Chile', by an anonymous officer of the *Glasgow*, 1915.

'Narrative of the Proceedings of HMAS *Sydney* Parts 1 & 2', by Captain J.C.T. Glossop, 1915.

'Official Report of Action with the *Emden*', by Captain John J.C.T. Glossop, 1915.

'Operation Boomerang', by 'Seagee' (Lieutenant Commander C.B.), 1956.

'Pretorius and the *Königsberg*', by 'Walrus', 1952.

'The Action off the Falkland Islands: Sidelights on the Battle from HMS *Cornwall*', 1915.

'The Action off the Falkland Islands: The *Cornwall's Share*', 1915.

'The Attacks on the *Königsberg*', 1915.

'The Attacks on the *Königsberg*; various authors', 1915.

'The Breakthrough of the *Goeben* and *Breslau* from Messina to the Dardanelles', by Admiral W. Souchon, 1922.

'The Coronel Campaign', by Vice Admiral K.G.B. Dewar, 1955.

'The Escape of the *Goeben* and *Breslau*', by Vice Admiral K.G.B. Dewar, 1956.

'The War Cruises of H.I.M.S *Karlsruhe*: Extracts from my War Diary', by Kapitänleutnant Aust, 1917.

'The Work of the *Glasgow* and the Action off Coronel: Parts 1 & 2', by M. Portman (originally anonymous), 1916.

'The Wounded in the Action between the *Sydney* and the *Emden*', by Surgeon Lieutenant L. Darby (originally anonymous), 1917.

'Translation of a Pocket Diary found on an Officer Survivor from the *Gneisenau*', 1915.

'Translations of Extracts from letters by Vice Admiral Count von Spee and his son, Lieutenant Count Otto Spee', 1915.

Published Works

Anderson, Ross, *The Forgotten Front 1914–1918: The East African Campaign* (Tempus, Stroud, 2007).

Arthur, Max, *The True Glory: The Royal Navy 1914–1919: A Narrative History* (Hodder & Stoughton, London, 1996).

Bennett, Geoffrey, *Coronel and the Falklands* (Pan, London, 1967).

Bennett, Geoffrey, *Naval Battles of the First World War* (Pan, London, 1983).

Bingham, Commander the Honourable Barry, VC, RN, *Falklands, Jutland and the Bight* (John Murray, London, 1919).

Bülow, Prince Bernhard von, *Memoirs Volume 2* (Boston, Little & Brown, 1931–1932).

Carlyon, L.A., *Gallipoli* (Doubleday, London, 2002).

Carver, Field-Marshal Lord, *The National Army Museum Book of the Boer War* (Pan, London, 1999).

Chatterton, E. Keble, *The* Königsberg *Adventure* (Hurst & Blackett, London, n/d).

Chatterton, E. Keble, *The Sea Raiders* (Hutchinson & Company, London, n/d).

Churchill, The Rt Hon. Winston S., *The World Crisis 1911–1918*, two volumes (Odhams Press, London, 1938).

Corbett, Sir Julian S., *Naval Operations Volume 1: To the Battle of the Falklands* (Longmans, Green & Co., London, 1920).

Dixon, Surgeon T.B., RNVR, *The Enemy Fought Splendidly: Being the 1914–1915 Diary of the Battle of the Falklands and its Aftermath* (Blandford Press, Poole, 1983).

Gauss, C., *The German Kaiser as Shown in his Public Utterances* (Charles Scribner & Sons, New York, 1915).

Gordon, Andrew, *The Rules of the Game: Jutland and British Naval Command* (John Murray, London, 1996).

Gottschall, Terrell D., *By Order of the Kaiser: Otto von Diederichs and the Rise of the Imperial German Navy 1865–1902* (Naval Institute Press, Annapolis, 2003).

Gretton, Vice Admiral Sir Peter, KCB, DSO, OBE, DSC, *Former Naval Person: Winston Churchill and the Royal Navy* (Cassell, London, 1968).

Hickling, Vice Admiral Harold, *Sailor at Sea* (William Kimber, London, 1965).

Hirst, Lloyd, *Coronel and After* (Peter Davies, London, 1934).

Hoehling, A.A., *The Great War at Sea: The Dramatic Story of Naval Warfare 1914–1918* (Corgi, London, 1967).

Hough, Richard, *Fighting Ships* (Michael Joseph, London, 1969).

Hoyt, Edwin P., *Kreuzerkrieg* (World Publishing Company, New York, 1968).

Hoyt, Edwin P., *The Karlsruhe Affair* (Arthur Barker Ltd, London, 1976).

Hurd, Sir Archibald, *History of the Great War: The Merchant Navy Volume 1, 1914 to Spring 1915* (John Murray, London, 1921), pp. 137–85 (reproduced on www.naval-history.net).

Layman, R.D., *Naval Aviation in the First World War: Its Impact and Influence* (Caxton Editions, London, 1996).

Le Fleming, H.M., *Warships of World War 1* (Ian Allan, London, 1967).

Lenton, H.T., *Warships from 1860 to the Present Day* (Hamlyn, London, 1970).

Lochner, R.K., *Last Gentleman of War: The Raider Exploits of the Cruiser* Emden (Naval Institute Press, Annapolis, 1988).

Maffeo, Steven E., *Seize, Burn or Sink: The Thoughts and Words of Admiral Lord Horatio Nelson* (Scarecrow Press, Lanham, Maryland, 2007).

Mahan, Alfred Thayer, *The Influence of Sea Power upon History* (Sampson Low, Marston, Searle & Rivington, London, 1889).

Marder, Arthur J., *From the Dreadnought to Scapa Flow: The Royal Navy in the Fisher Era 1904–1919*, five volumes (Oxford University Press, London, 1961–).

Massie, Robert K., *Dreadnought: Britain, Germany and the coming of the Great War* (Random House, New York, 1991).

Massie, Robert K., *Castles of Steel: Britain, Germany and the Winning of the Great War at Sea* (Pimlico, London, 2005).

Niezychowski, Count Alfred von, *The Cruise of the* Kronprinz Wilhelm (Selwyn & Blount, London, 1928).

Patterson, A. Temple (ed.), *The Jellicoe Papers Volume 1: 1893–1916* (Spottiswoode, Ballantyne & Co. Ltd, London, for the Navy Records Society, 1966).

Pitt, Barrie, *Coronel and Falkland* (Cassell, London, 1960).

Putnam, William Lowell, *The Kaiser's Merchant Ships in World War 1* (MacFarland & Company, North Carolina, 2001).

Raeder, Erich, and von Mantey, Eberard, *Der Kreuzerkrieg in den Ausländischen Gewässern*, three volumes (Ernst, Mittler und Sohn, Berlin, 1922–1937).

Ranft, B. Mcl. (ed.), *The Beatty Papers Volume 1: 1902–1918* (Scholar Press, Aldershot, for the Navy Records Society, 1989).

Roskill, Stephen, *Churchill and the Admirals* (Pen & Sword Books, Barnsley, 2004).

Scheer, Admiral Reinhard, *Germany's High Seas Fleet in the World War* (Cassell, London, 1920).

Simpson, Colin, *The Ship that Hunted Itself* (Penguin, Harmondsworth, Middlesex, 1977).

Spencer-Cooper, Commander H., *The Battle of the Falkland Islands* (Cassell & Co. Ltd, London, 1919).

Strachan, Hew, *The First World War* (Pocket Books, London, 2006).

Terraine, John, *Business in Great Waters: The U-boat Wars 1916–1945* (Wordsworth, Ware, 1999).

Tirpitz, Grand Admiral Alfred von, *My Memoirs Volume I* (Dodd, Mead, New York, 1919).

Van der Vat, Dan, *The Last Corsair: the Story of the* Emden (Panther, London, 1985).

Von Hohenzollern-Emden, Prinz Franz Joseph, *Emden: The Last Cruise of the Chivalrous Raider – 1914* (Lyon Press, London, 1989).

Von Mücke, Hellmuth, *The* Emden (Ritter & Company, Norwood, Mass., 1917).

Walter, John, *The Kaiser's Pirates: German Surface Raiders in World War 1* (Arms & Armour Press, London, 1994).

Online Sources

Jannings, Dr Christopher M., 'SMS Dresden's War: The Benefits of Protracted Evasion over Spirit of Enterprise' (www.militaryhistoryonline.com/wwi/articles/smsdresden.aspx).

http://frontierpartisans.com/142/cruiser-killer

http://trove.nla.gov.au/ndp/del/

www.hindu.com

www.naval-history.net

Miller, Geoffrey, 'Superior Force: The Conspiracy behind the Escape of the *Goeben* and *Breslau*' (www.flamboroughmanor.co.uk/superiorforce).

'Calafate' (Robert Riddell), 'Concealing the *Dresden*' (*Blackwoods Magazine*, January 1935, volume 237, no. 1431) (via http://patlibros.org/ctd/).

'Ceylon Times', subsequently reported in the *Launceston Examiner* (Tasmania), on 2 November 1914 (http://trove.nla.gov.au).

'Lead and Line: The Journal of the Naval Officers' Association of Vancouver Island', Volume 24, Issue 3, November 2009 (http://ml.islandnet.com/pipermail/noavi_ll/attachments/20090228/f705b20c/attachment-0001).

Poverty Bay Herald, 10 December 1914 (http://trove.nla.gov.au).

Sydney Morning Herald, 21 October 1914 (http://news.google.com).

The Straits Times, 10 November 1914, from the National Library of Singapore, (http://newspapers.nl.sg).

Wanganui Chronicle, 23 December 1914 (http://paperspast.natlib.govt.nz).

New York Tribune, 12 August 1914 (http://fultonhistory.com/Newspapers).

Finally, I am also indebted to the excellent, free, archive of the incomparable *New York Times*, notably for information relating to the depredations of the *Karlsruhe* and the armed liners in the Atlantic (www.nytimes.com).

Index